Autobiography of a Theory

of related interest

Circular Reflections
Selected Papers on Group Analysis and Psychoanalysis
Malcolm Pines
ISBN 1 85302 492 9 pb
ISBN 1 85302 493 7 hb
International Library of Group Analysis 1

Group Psychotherapy of the Psychoses
Edited by Victor L. Schermer and Malcolm Pines
ISBN 1 85302 584 4 pb
ISBN 1 85302 583 6 hb
International Library of Group Analysis 2

Attachment and Interaction
Mario Marrone
ISBN 1 85302 586 0 pb
ISBN 1 85302 587 9 hb
International Library of Group Analysis 3

Self Experiences in Groups
Intersubjective and Self Psychological Pathways to Human Understanding
Edited by Irene N.H. Harwood and Malcolm Pines
ISBN 1 85302 597 6 pb
ISBN 1 85302 596 8 hb
International Library of Group Analysis 4

Taking the Group Seriously
Towards a Post-Foulkesian Group Analytic Theory
Farhad Dalal
ISBN 1 85302 642 5 pb
International Library of Group Analysis 5

Active Analytic Group Therapy for Adolescents
John Evans
ISBN 1 85302 586 0 pb
ISBN 1 85302 587 9 hb
International Library of Group Analysis 6

The Group Context
Sheila Thompson
ISBN 1 85302 657 3
International Library of Group Analysis 7

Group
Claudio Neri
ISBN 1 85302 416 3
International Library of Group Analysis 8

Autobiography of a Theory

Developing the Theory of Living Human Systems and its Systems-Centered Practice

Yvonne M. Agazarian and Susan P. Gantt

Jessica Kingsley Publishers
London and Philadelphia

First published in the United Kingdom in 2000 by
Jessica Kingsley Publishers Ltd
116 Pentonville Road
London N1 9JB, England
and
325 Chestnut Street,
Philadelphia, PA19106, USA

www.jkp.com

Copyright ©2000 Yvonne M. Agazarian and Susan P. Gantt

Library of Congress Cataloging in Publication Data
Agazarian, Yvonne.
    Autobiography of a theory : developing systems-centered theory / Yvonne M. Agazarian and Susan P. Gantt.
        p.   cm. -- (International library of group analysis ; 11)
    Includes index.
    ISBN 1 85302 847 9 (pbk. : alk paper)
    1. Group psychotherapy--Philosophy. 2. Group psychoanalysis--Philosophy. 3. social systems. I. Gantt, Susan Porter, 1951-II. Title. III. Series.

RC488. A6224 2000
616.89'152'01-dc21   99--056717

British Library Cataloguing in Publication Data
Agazarian, Yvonne
    Autobiography of a theory : developing systems-centered theory
    1. Agazarian, Yvonne 2. Social psychology - Philosophy
    3. Group psychotherapy 4. Group psychoanalysis
    I. Title II. Gantt, Susan P.
    616.8'9152
ISBN 1 85302 847 9

Printed and Bound in Great Britain by
Athenaeum Press, Gateshead, Tyne and Wear

Contents

Acknowledgements

For my son Jack for his appreciation of theory.

For my mentors David Jenkins, Jay Fidler, Len Horwitz; for the members of the theory seminars who have lived through many versions of the theory chart; for Ken Eisold for understanding; for my friends Anita, Claudia and Fran; and particularly for Berj.

From me, Susan, enormous gratitude for all the support I received, most especially from Kirk.
Much thanks to my mother in her generosity, especially in using Lake Burton as our writing site; and for the support from my family (Betsy, Marty, Joel, Jessica, Julian), and from Jan, Vicki, Carol, Robin; and for all the training and mentoring from Fran. Thank you all.

Two more important dedications – to all our systems-centered colleagues, and to Jessica Kingsley and Helen Parry with our gratitude and affection for their warmth, the quite wonderful experience of working with them, and for their support that helped us bring this book into reality.

Introduction
Curiosity and Early Musings

Curiosity Killed the Cat – Information Brought it Back!

When Nanny answered my 'whys' with 'because the sky is so high', I'd ask, 'How high is the sky?' When she cautioned me that 'Curiosity killed the cat', I would say, 'Information brought it back', and sometimes, when I was feeling very uppity, 'Well, I must have nine lives then.' It was not that I asked different questions from the questions that every child asks, it was that I asked them all the time whenever I could. When Nanny would say that I must not ask any more questions for ten minutes, I would explain that they filled me up inside and I'd burst if I couldn't let them out. And that indeed, was how I felt.

As I was a child of the early 1930s (I was born in 1929), I was brought up to be seen and not heard. All the questions that built up inside me would burst out as soon as I was with Nanny. Nanny, somewhat understandably, often took refuge in the kitchen with Cook and Edith and Maisy (why was I not allowed in the kitchen?) bringing me up my meals and going back down again, while I made mountains and rivers and forests out of my food. It never seemed strange to me that, although I had a Nanny, I often played alone.

When the weather was good enough I was let out to play in the garden, watching the shadow of the house travel slowly back over the lawn (why do shadows move when nobody is moving them?). When the weather was bad, I would play in the nursery. There was a gate at the nursery door and I spent much time leaning over the gate listening to the house. I became very good at knowing what was going on by the noises and voices that drifted up the stairwell.

There was a difference in the voice tone of the servants when 'we' were in and when 'we' were out. Later I was to recognize what a difference the environment makes in who one is. Then I simply knew that if I called out when the servants had their 'out' voices, they would come to visit me, and sometimes to play with me for a while. When I asked about the different voices they used, Nanny said 'Little pitchers have long ears.'

Recognizing people by their voices was easy. I also knew who was who by their footsteps. In the winter, my father came home after the lamplighter had walked down the street, lighting the lamps with his long pole. In summer, the lamplighter didn't come until long after I heard my father come home. (Why does it get dark before teatime in winter?)

I could never guess when my mother would come and go. Sometimes she would come up to the nursery to blow me a kiss before she went out, sometimes I didn't know she was going until I heard Whitney (our chauffeur) banging the door of the Daimler. When I asked Nanny where my Mother went, she would tell me it was none of my business. When I asked her why Mummy told Grey (our butler) to tell people she was out when she was in, Nanny said, 'When you grow up, you'll understand.'

As for the 'boys' (my brothers, who were respectively 12, 13, 14 and 15 years older than me) – they came clattering in anytime – calling out 'hello darling' as they ran up to the floor above the nursery. When I asked Nanny why I was never allowed to go up to my brothers' rooms, she would say 'just because!'

My sister (10 years older) was nearly always away at boarding school. When she was home on holidays, we would share my nursery and she would sing me songs when she came to bed, sit up with me when there was a thunderstorm, and dry my bottom sheet by the fire when I wet my bed. When I asked my sister questions, she always tried to answer, but the answers often didn't make much sense: 'Why do you go to boarding school?' 'Because everybody does.'

In the nursery I had a mix of toys – 'mine' that came at Christmas and my birthday and 'theirs' that came from my brothers. My toys consisted of dolls and doll's clothes and a doll's house (clearly girls' toys). My 'real' toys were an elephant on wheels and a horse on a rocker that I could ride. My constant companion was my teddy bear, called Teddy. (It is clear that I was a literal child.) 'Theirs' were an enormous set of building blocks that would not fit in the box, a large farm of animals, buildings and fences (my brother Buddy's) and armies of different generations of soldiers. The oldest soldiers were missing arms and muskets and paint and sometimes heads (they were my brother Levon's (who was the eldest). The newer ones were divided into the guards, splendid in paint and plumes and horses, and the infantry in drab khaki with cannons and rifles and officers to lead them over the ridge.

At home I played a lot with my soldiers. They came together in different formations, climbed the ridges of the carpet and slipped quietly through the valleys. It was by organizing my soldiers that I first acquired an understanding of the group-as-a-whole – in which the fate of the individual depended not so much on their own heroism (of which my individual soldiers had plenty) but on being part of a successful group. I always put my favorite soldiers into the successful group. On red-letter days one or other of 'the boys' would climb over my nursery gate and give me lessons on strategy, 'Look – send a small army of soldiers over there to distract the enemy while your main army is creeping up behind them where they can't see.' I was caught between the mixture of excitement that one of my brothers would be teaching me how to play, and distress at how unfair it was to pretend one thing and to do another. Asking about it did not help – the answer was either, 'That's the way life is' or 'That's because you're a girl!'

I kept my dolls for playing with girls. We undressed them, put them to bed, got them up and then dressed them again. Sometimes we had a tea party. Later, I understood that my dolls had helped me 'fit into the norms' and behave like the other little girls in the group. Then, I only knew that I had a better time when I climbed trees with the boys, where I learned that the little boys would let me play with them until the bigger boys came out, and then they told me to go away because I was only a girl. I wondered what made the difference – whether, if I cut my hair and wore shorts, I would not be sent away. Girls and boys were a great mystery to me. If girls were meant to stay clean and neat and pretty, it was quite clear that I should have been a boy who could run and be rowdy and get dirty. I thought it was a compliment when my brothers said I was a tomboy.

I looked forward to Sundays all week. Sunday was Nanny's half-day off, and I had lunch with my family. On Sundays I was a good little girl who was seen and not heard. Indeed, I dared not speak unless I was spoken to in case I was sent back to the nursery to wait and wait and wait until the next Sunday, but I could watch. It was at Sunday lunches that I learned all about the non-verbal communication which goes on between people, and how often it does not match the verbal. Later I was to understand how often people's words don't match their music. Then, Nanny simply said that I had 'an overactive imagination'.

In the garden I was a different person. Rather than watching and listening, Teddy and I ran to the back garden away from the house where we could whoop and holler as much as we liked. I was a leader of a band that had its headquarters underground; I was a Red Indian brave who sped silently through the bluebell wood. I gathered pods and flowers for Teddy and me to eat, and both of us spent a lot of time helping Richards with his gardening. It was Richards who comforted me one day when I was crying because one of my favorite pansies had withered. He pointed out to me how new small buds took its place, grew into sunny-faced flowers and then withered back to make room for more small buds. Later I was to understand how to frame, for others, painful events in the context of a larger picture that made universal sense.

My early life was a mixture of the nursery, the silence of watching and listening and waiting and playing by myself, and the noise of the summer days on the lawn with all my family, or the excitement of summer holidays in France where I had breakfast, lunch and tea with everyone every day, and sometimes played with them on the beach. Once we all went to Italy in the Daimler. My brothers always stuck up for me. Even when I got car sick all over my brother Noel, all he said was, 'It's not her fault, she told us she was feeling sick!' Another time, when we went skiing in Font Remeu, I got lost in a snowstorm and found my way back only to discover that my whole family, and almost everybody else in the hotel, were out looking for me! I felt so important that I didn't mind the scolding.

I started school at 3 years old, not today's baby school, but a proper sit-at-your-desk-and-work school with recreation in which one played games like 'Simon says', 'Mother-may-I?' and 'Grandmother's footsteps'. My desk was in a large room with many other classes in it. I would imitate the bigger girls by sucking my pencil and frowning and sighing on a worried note. I found it hard to sit still (teacher called me Fidgety Phil – and my name wasn't Phil!). I hated Dick and Jane and Spot. They didn't play the kind of games I played. Most of the time I was very, very bored.

Sometime when I was about 4 years old, Nanny left and Teddy disappeared. I went for my walk one day and when I came back the wicker chair in which Teddy sat was empty. My mother said that Teddy must have been

stolen. Even at the age of 4 my common sense told me that was nonsense –
who and how would someone come up the long drive, into the house, up the
stairs and into my nursery to take Teddy away? But on the other hand there
was no better explanation. Perhaps he went for a walk and got lost – well? …
maybe! Perhaps he drank a magic drink and disappeared – unlikely! I
became a difficult child. Through a succession of replacement nannies, I
refused to go on my walk – tugging and pulling and screaming and
tantrumming and breaking free and running back to the nursery to see if
Teddy had come home. Later my analyst would suggest that this was a
displacement from losing my Nanny. No way! It was Teddy who was my
constant companion, Teddy I cradled at night, lying still so as not to wake
him up. It was Teddy who listened to all my questions, and Teddy whose
tummy I hugged to my face, on the window box, behind my nursery
curtains, when I had to cry.

The next year I went to boarding school for a while when my parents
went to America, where I went on being a difficult child. At 7 years old I was
sent to the Convent of the Sacred Heart where I remained as a boarder until I
left school at 17. Catholic children make their first communion at the age of
7. It was summer, the grounds were full of rhododendrons, azaleas and roses,
the birds sang, and we first communicants had the privilege of meeting every
day with the priest in the nuns' garden while we learned our catechism and
prepared to confess our sins at confession and receive the holy sacrament. I
loved the specialness and the ceremony but at the same time had to struggle
with my common sense. I found it hard to believe that God really minded if I
didn't do as I was told or answered back, but by then I was becoming wise
enough not to say so. Communion, however, was another matter. I truly
believed that God would come into my heart and that something very
important, that I had been waiting for all my life, would happen. The day
came. We first communicants wore long white dresses, with veils and a
wreath of roses, we carried a bouquet and we knelt on a special white satin
'prie-dieu' between the altar and the school. We went up for communion
before anybody else. Kneeling there waiting for the priest, I was almost
suffocated with excitement. The priest put the host on my tongue. Nothing
happened! I went reverently back to my prie-dieu and waited. Still nothing
happened. Looking back, I know that I was looking for a communion that
happens in communicating – and that what I questioned that day was

answered some fifty years later when functional subgrouping had become established and people worked together in attunement and resonance. Then I was bewildered – I could not understand. The rest of the day went by in a dream. My parents, my brothers and my sister were all there to celebrate the day, but it was as if they did not really exist. I went through the motions of being with them. I didn't cry when they left. I think I was both depersonalized and depressed for a while afterwards, and when I came fully back into myself I found I was wondering about God.

The Sacred Heart nuns are Jesuits and interested in questions. They encouraged me to speak out. I could say out loud, 'If God made us so that we could know him and love him and serve him in this world and be happy with him in the next, why did he invent hell? So that we could exercise free will? But if God knew everything and was everywhere, and was powerful enough to do anything, why did He let us commit sins that sent us to hell?' I struggled with the idea of free will from the age of 7 until 9, when I decided that God 'could' stop us if He wanted to, but He didn't because by letting us go free it was even to His greater glory when we chose heaven over hell. At 9, I wasn't entirely happy with this explanation. I wasn't so certain how free my will was. I knew that I was often not allowed to do what I wanted to do – like run in the corridors or talk in class. What worried me more was that I often did things that I didn't want to – like lose my apron and keep the whole school silent in the refectory until I found it.

The whole business of free will came to a head for me in December of 1938. Before important feast days we would have what is called a 'practice' in which we practiced being 'obedient' or 'tidy' or 'polite'. In the senior school, there was a big chart on which were marked the little black infraction marks beside each name. In the junior school we had instead nine steps (for the nine days of practice) leading up to the crib with baby Jesus in it. We started the practice with our little white lamb at the bottom. Each night, at prayers, we would find out if our lamb had climbed up a step or not – or (horrors) been placed on a step further down. I did not get very far up the steps when I was 6, 7 or 8. This year I was 9 and determined. Each day I was as good as I could possibly be. Each day I did something that cost me a step. On the ninth day I was still at the bottom, while all the other little white lambs were spread out near the top. I don't remember exactly what I did that last day, but I know it was bad. I prayed and prayed and prayed every spare minute before night prayers, reminded baby Jesus that I was a little lamb that had gone astray – that there is much joy in heaven when a sinner repents – and to have mercy on the prodigal son (even though it was a story I never liked because it seemed so unfair). At last, the day came to a close and we filed in for night prayers. I looked at the bottom of the steps – no lamb! In great hope, I looked to the top of the steps. Was my lamb forgiven and placed right up next to baby Jesus? No! With my heart rattling around in my chest I searched for my lamb. Then I caught a glimpse of a little black thing, a black lamb – mine – standing in a corner, with its back to baby Jesus.

I remember thinking that my life would always be like that –that I would try and try and try and never get it right, and that God would not help. And then, in a flash, I intuited my first heresy – predestination. Believing God has damned you whether you did anything or not was not really a good solution for a 9-year-old. I struggled to find a way out and introduced the problem of free will into every doctrine class. Finally, I asked, 'If God is all good, where does evil come from?' 'Write an essay,' said the nuns. I did.

I wrote about Lucifer, the best and most chosen of all God's angels – adoring God as hard as he possibly could. I wrote about how Lucifer was never satisfied that he was adoring God enough, so he decided to turn his face away – deprive himself of God's light, so that when he turned back towards God his return would be to God's greater glory. And God was pleased. Then, in one instant of time as Lucifer turned his head away, he glimpsed his own shadow – and became curious and asked 'How can the darkness behind me be a reflection of God's light?' And God struck with a terrible rage – cast him out of His light and into the shadow. And that was how hell was created. For a while I was quite satisfied with this explanation, until predestination surfaced again in my mind. Was Lucifer predestined to become the devil? Had God given him the fatal flaw of curiosity? Worse still, was the fatal flaw God's because he didn't answer questions?

Much as I hated what seemed like every minute of the ten years I was at school in the convent, looking back I can see that the nuns were very good with me. They encouraged me to think through all the different heresies that I intuited.

War was declared when I was 10. The school was evacuated from London into the country to an old manor house near Rugby. My brothers all joined the air force, except for Buddy, who was called to remain farming the land.

My sister became a pilot in the Air Transport Auxiliary and ferried planes between the factory and the airfields, and my father went to America to establish a home for his sons when they returned from the war. My mother stayed in London, refusing to let 'the Boche put us out of our beds' and I joined her in my school holidays. Winifred, our cook, joined up, and the windows were blown out so often in our St James's Square flat that we moved to Knightsbridge into a tiny service flat that overlooked the park (and the guns and the searchlights). 'Service' stopped almost immediately after we moved in and Mummy and I learned how to cook on a hot plate and do the washing up in the bathroom sink!

It seemed that overnight the world changed from a large flat full of family noise to just Mummy and me. Noel was shot down in 1941 in the Middle East after getting through the Battle of Britain; my father died in America in 1944; and in 1945 Jack was shot as a political prisoner just hours before the concentration camp he had survived for two years was liberated.

I became an atheist after my brother Jack was killed. The nuns arranged for three Hail Marys to be said after mass for the reconversion of Yvonne (it seemed unfair that there should be three Hail Marys for Russia and three Hail Marys for my reconversion). They gave me a prayer to say: 'Oh God, if there is a God, save my soul, if I have a soul!'

I left school at 17, gave up Oxford to help my mother, who was learning how to be poor, and at 18 (after I discovered that I hated being a secretary even more than I hated school) went to Vancouver to stay with a school friend and discovered that I could work my way through the University of British Columbia. I read English and Philosophy, and in Philosophy found that there were many other people who had spent their lives asking and trying to answer questions. It was like coming home. Canada was good for me. My whooping and hollering side had the best time since I had run free in the back garden. I spent the first two summer vacations working, one in a mental hospital as a nurse and one cooking in a logging camp. The third summer I spent riding freight trains across Canada with my about-to-be husband, working in factories and picking tobacco to pay our way. After I graduated, and five months pregnant with my son, I left my husband and came back to England.

All through university I had taken it for granted that I would write, and in fact I did win the one-act playwriting competition in British Columbia and had my play produced. With a son (born blind for no good reason that anyone could suggest), I took my author-playwright-poet self into advertising as a copywriter. By the time I was 30, I had made enough money to go to Philadelphia: for my son the special schooling for the blind that is better in the USA than in England, and for myself I could again work my way through school while I studied to be an analyst and get an advanced degree.

I had first become interested in becoming a therapist when I took a summer job as a nurse at Essondale mental hospital on the suicidal and homicidal women's chronic ward. The experience was a profound one, in that it was the first time in my life that I felt that I knew what I was doing. This was clearly odd as I had no training in psychiatry and no training as a nurse. Looking back, strangely enough I can see how my convent education had actually prepared me for the job. The nuns managed difficult students by giving them responsibility, and I had been 'in charge' of the junior school dormitories and study halls since I was 10 and I had the manners taught to British children: 'Always be polite to people less fortunate than yourself.' Also, I had no preconceived ideas about mental patients and I liked the people I met on the ward very much indeed, admiring the way they managed the frustrations of their lives and the generosity with which they supported each other, even if their support often came in surprising ways.

As the junior nurse I had no privileges. I did not take the women walking, dancing, to church, or to the cinema. I was the 'day-room nurse' from 7.30 in the morning until 7.30 every evening for a four-day shift with one day off in between. As day-room nurse, I was in charge of two large rooms and two large porches as well as two corridors of dormitories. I was alone quite often when the other nurses went to meals or when we were short staffed. There were many patients on the ward who could do little but manage themselves; others were so agitated that they roamed the day room in a stream of noise and activity. But there were also many patients who could manage themselves quite well. It was they whom I asked to join me to organize 'our' ward. (Clearly, I was already working with groups!) We managed fights on the ward and arranged bridge games, knitting and needlework groups. We set up a suicide detail that could spring into action and reach both porches simultaneously if necessary. In the bathrooms at night, often the place of most chaos, I stood a trustworthy patient by each plug, ready to pull it out. Every night I pushed three or four of the catatonics into the bathroom, raised their arms so that they formed towel racks and turned their palms up so that they could hold the soap.

Then one day a new resident came into the bathroom, took one look, turned a withering blast of disapproval and disgust toward me and said, 'Nurse, how can you use human beings this way?' Suddenly seeing the world through his eyes, my stomach filled with iced water and horror. For a long, disoriented moment I thought I was going to faint. Then, a metallic, machine-like voice, rusty from long disuse, came from one of the 'towel racks'. It said: 'On Nurse Agazarian's ward, everyone works.'

During my four months at Essondale as an untrained but commonsensical and practical 19-year-old, intermittently responsible for 150 unmedicated psychotic patients, side room admissions dropped, fewer fights occurred and there was less violence. One patient was even discharged – at that time an unusual event. Looking back, how can I understand this? What were the key variables behind this improvement? I had no training and I certainly could not make interpretations as I did not know any psychodynamics. So what did I have? From the convent education I knew how to provide structure and how to delegate responsibility. I was clear about goals and could give clear guidelines for work. I also had a genuine fellow feeling for the patients.

I returned to university determined to enter medical school and become a psychiatrist. However, students were not allowed to work their way through medical school, so I gave up the idea and continued with English and Philosophy.

It was not until I went into therapy myself after my mother died that I connected again with my earlier interest in being a therapist. My therapist was interested in training his patients as well as treating them. He introduced his students not only to the psychoanalytic literature, but also to the more interesting innovations in the field, like the new science of ethology, the science fiction that grew up around the 'nul A' hypothesis developed from Korzybski's non-Aristotelian thinking and Schrodinger's *What Is Life*. In our seminars, the ideas of entropy and negative entropy gave me a sense of the principles of the universe that seemed to fit better than any of the religion or philosophy that I had studied up until then.

By 1960 I had saved enough money from my (unbelievably successful) career in advertising to emigrate to the USA with my son and to formally join the Psychoanalytic Studies Institute. There, history began to repeat itself.

Studying Freud I had 'intuited' his second theory of instincts before I had finished reading his first, and questioned analytic theory much as I had once questioned Catholicism. In the first paper I wrote for the Psychoanalytic Studies Institute in the early 1960s, I attempted to reconcile psychoanalysis and the idea that maturation came as a function of the discrimination and integration of differences: foreshadowing the conflict resolution technique of functional subgrouping which I was to develop 30 years later.

The rest of this book picks up at this point, organized around key aspects as I trace the autobiography of the theory of living humans systems and its systems-centered practice.

Chapter 1 Trying to Make it Make Sense

The first chapter highlights important threads early in my work, beginning with my initial struggles with psychoanalysis, as I began to work explicitly to integrate the 'other' influences on my thinking, specifically the information theory of Shannon and Weaver, Korzybski, Lewin, Tinbergen on intention movements, and the work of the ethnologists on maturation as a function of discrimination/integration. I illustrate this with excerpts from an early paper I wrote applying discrimination/integration to Sechehaye's case of Renee. The transition from university life to working at Pennsylvania Hospital in the community mental health center meant confronting new realities necessitating much clinical innovation. I detail this in a case presentation of my work with Sarah, a psychotic patient, where I am working clinically to apply the principle of maturation as a function of discrimination and integration. The chapter ends with my first attempts to apply Lewinian thinking to clinical work, looking at the driving and restraining forces in the process of change.

Chapter 2 First Try at Theory

In the second chapter I 'find' group dynamics and consolidate the direction of my first serious efforts at theorizing. This chapter highlights my bewilderment and excitement in my first T-group experiences and introduction to Bennis and Shepard which stimulated me to begin working with the definition of group as a function of the interdependence of parts and role or parts as clusters of behavior. Soon I was collaborating with Anita Simon to develop SAVI, which enabled me to begin defining my first theory by looking at the parts of a group in terms of communication bits. SAVI has proved invaluable in understanding isomorphy, in discriminating individual and group dynamics, in operationally defining and researching group process as a research tool, as a consultation tool and eventually in operationally defining the methods of the theory of living human systems.

Chapter 3 Second Theory: Theory of the Invisible Group

I begin Chapter 3 by describing my work at Devereux Schools for Children and what I knew at the time and did not yet know. I knew the importance of group norms in influencing individual behavior and I was beginning to conceptualize the different systems of the individual and the group. I did not yet know how to use what I was beginning to understand or how to take the next step in putting my understandings together. My work here builds on Bion and my Tavistock experiences, both invaluable, frustrating and important experiences toward my next steps in theorizing. My frustration over not finding a coherent group theory spurred me to develop the theory of the invisible group and its component systems of person, member, group role, group-as-a-whole. Seeing the component systems for the individual and the group gave me a way to think multi-dimensionally and at different levels of abstraction and to develop the concept of role as a bridge construct between group and individual systems, and group role as a function of group dynamics. In this process, I worked extensively with the role of scapegoat and the group dynamics related to deviance. I end this chapter with the image that enabled me to pull together the theory of the invisible group.

Chapter 4 Theory of the Group-As-A-Whole

Focusing on my group-as-a-whole theory leads me straight to my work with Dave Jenkins at Temple and the enormously important influences that Dave and through Dave, Kurt Lewin, had on my work. Working with the Lewinian concept of the life space, applying this to the two different hierarchical levels of the individual and the group, and integrating this with Howard and Scott's formulation that all behavior moves toward or away from problem solving, I trace the path I followed to build my theory of the group-as-a-whole. Using implicit and explicit goals and the modifications I made in Lewin's force field (so that the restraining forces relate to behavior moving away from the explicit goal) enabled me to develop a way to diagnose system goal and laid the groundwork for the major method in systems-centered practice. Understanding role (as a bridge construct between the individual and group system levels) in its function of equilibrating a group system was also important in seeing the group-as-a-whole. I use a transcript to illustrate how learning to see group roles facilitated hearing the group-as-a-whole and the voices of the group and its subsystems: in the first illustration, the voices of group isolation and loneliness, and the second, the structuring subgroup and the intimacy subgroup. I then use a transcript of my work with a group to illustrate the theory of the group-as-a-whole, highlighting the group voices and discussing how I think about the goals of my interventions.

Chapter 5 Thinking Systems

In Chapter 5 I start with my early work on systems thinking (1960s) when I tried to find a way to contribute to the field of blindness. I ended up frustrated and with more experience of the gap between what I knew and what I could actually do with what I knew. It was not until I joined the General Systems Theory (GST) Committee of the American Group Psychotherapy Association with Helen Durkin that I began to fully work with systems theory. Both exciting and stimulating, the GST Committee left us all with the charge of how to develop a systems theory that could be put into practice, a charge I took to heart. My systems theorizing continued to develop as I did more work in integrating Lewin's life space and systems theory. Equally important was the influence of Davanloo and his Short-term Dynamic Psychotherapy which permanently changed how I intervened and re-awakened my interest in defenses and nonverbal communication.

During all of this, I was continuing to work with two training groups in a group-as-a-whole approach, one of which participated on stage with me as a demonstration group where we were able to work together to integrate a 'shameful' experience and I began to understand how much difference I was introducing in my way of working. Later, Anne Alonso and I did a videotape about the group. Still later, due to Anne's invitation, I presented as a discussant with Sampson and Weiss, where my theoretical integrity was challenged in that it almost seemed too much to follow my conclusions which at the time seemed to lead to a break with psychoanalysis. This did lead to my fully understanding that it is the narcissistic individualism in our culture (and in psychoanalysis) that is at the root of taking things personally;

that it is this same narcissism that group-centered approaches reduce, and that taking things personally is the source of the anguish which takes people into therapy more often than the life events that trouble them. I end the chapter with a description of the process of my guest editorship for *Group* on group-as-a-whole where I present the premises of a systems framework and compare this to other therapies.

Chapter 6 Systems-Centered Therapy

Starting the weekend workshop series gave me the forum to begin applying systems theory and developing system-centered practice. I describe the first workshop and the ingenuity (mine and the group's) as we moved through our development (including a whopping authority issue) and the tremendous learnings that occurred for me. My major focus as I began was on deliberately introducing functional subgrouping, requiring members to come together around similarities instead of stereotyping differences, which operationalized the principle that systems develop and transform through discrimination/integration.

As my confidence in using subgrouping grew, I also began to introduce my defense modification and to develop the methods and techniques of systems-centered training (SCT) and practice. I describe the four methods in SCT (subgrouping, boundarying, vectoring, contextualizing) and discuss how SCT is put into practice. I then summarize the SCT hierarchy of defense modification which I developed and integrated with the stages of group development. I end this chapter with my final impetus for developing SCT as a protocol for therapy, the current health-care climate and need for short-term treatments, and outline the usefulness of SCT as a short-term psychotherapy.

Chapter 7 Theory of Living Human Systems

In the final chapter I present the theory of living human systems. My explicit transition from a group-as-a-whole to system-centered was marked by my article in the *International Journal of Group Psychotherapy* (1992a) where I summarized the influences on my work. I then integrate the theoretical building blocks and present the constructs of the theory. (The theory of living human systems defines a hierarchy of isomorphic systems that are energy organizing, goal directed and self-correcting.) I define each construct in relation to its methods and techniques. I also present the research hypothesis for each construct and for each of the four methods. Each SCT intervention then serves as a research hypothesis for the constructs and methods of systems-centered practice.

I end by discriminating the theory of living human systems as a potential meta-theory from the specific practice of systems-centered therapy, and consider the contribution that understanding context makes for reducing human anguish.

CHAPTER 1

Trying to Make it Make Sense

Change as a Function of
Discrimination and Integration

The Psychoanalytic Studies Institute

Having studied with a small psychoanalytic group in England, I joined the second year in the Psychoanalytic Studies Institute soon after moving to Philadelphia and became immersed in Ferenzi, Jones and, of course, Freud (the Brill translation – Strachey had not yet finished his!). I attended seminars every Saturday and during the week began my clinical internship with the patients at the Philadelphia Mental Health Clinic.

I was happy and broke. I was tempted to go back into advertising to tide me over, but although I was offered a full-time job (the incredible 'American' salary of $9,000 to start and $12,000 in three months), 'they' would not offer me any freelance. However, three of the osteopathic interns generously took me into their office in return for doing the housework and referred patients to me. I was launched.

It became clear to me very soon that, although in England having a degree made little difference to one's status as an analyst, this was not true in the USA. So in early summer I used my 'security money' and registered at Temple University in the Group Dynamics Center where I was introduced both to experiential learning and research. Inevitably, I was also introduced to conflict between two disciplines, psychoanalysis and group dynamics.

Psychoanalysis in the early 1960s was far simpler and far more pro-scribed than it is now. I studied Freud with the same doubts and questions as I had studied the catechism at the convent. Also, like in the convent, there was an opportunity to question and speculate in the seminars, and no opportunity to do anything but follow the rules in the classes. And nowhere in the institute was there room to apply the objectivity that was required in my courses at the university. There was, however, room to think philosophically about an alternative frame of reference.

When I was studying in England, any new approaches in the field were brought into our seminars and discussed in relationship to the bearing they had on our understanding of psychoanalysis. In England, I had first encountered Schrodinger's (1976) *What is Life*, Shannon and Weaver's (1964) information theory, Korzybski's (1948) *Science and Sanity* and, most exciting, Tinbergen's (1963) introduction to the new field of ethology. Both Schrodinger and Shannon and Weaver's understanding of entropy gave me a framework that made immediate and intuitive sense, and became the foundation of much of my thinking from then on.

Shannon and Weaver (1964) worked as codebreakers during the war and developed a formula for maximizing information transfer, which is the goal of communication. They identified three sources of 'noise' in a communication channel: ambiguity, contradictions and redundancies. They then demonstrated that the amount of information transfer was inversely proportionate to the noise in the communication; it turned out their formula for information transfer was the inverse of the second law of thermodynamics or entropy. Their understanding of 'noise' in communication and entrophy was to have a lasting influence on my theorizing.

Tinbergen focused my clinical perception towards 'intention movements', which I wrote about in an early paper:

> Just as it is physically possible to move in only two basic directions in relationship to another person; either toward or away, so we suggest it is psychologically possible to move in only two directions, and two planes: either up or down, forward or back.
>
> It is relatively simple to ask someone to experience this. We can ask them to introspect, and tell us whether they feel closer to us, further away, or just the same, we can also ask them if they feel superior, inferior or peer in response to what we say. If we keep our messages simple, direct and congruent, it is also relatively easy for them to tell us whether they are experiencing feelings of love (positive feeling), hate (negative feelings) or fear (panic feelings). It is also relatively simple for them to identify whether their response impulse is predominately feeling or thinking. Finally, for thinking responses, it is again relatively easy for

them to tell us if their thinking response is more concrete than abstract, more abstract than concrete.

It does not require complex skills of self-awareness for this sort of insight, if we describe precisely what we want the person to focus upon, and keep the messages to which we want the response identified, simple and short. Interestingly enough, observing this exchange in operation, we notice that not only do people easily identify these levels of response in themselves, but in our observation, their introspected direction is congruent with their intention movements (I am using intention movements here in the sense of Tinbergen (1963) to describe dominant or submissive posture, aggressive or fear response, etc.). These intention movements may either involve the total body movement, like leaning forward or leaning back, or more subtle body cues that need to be analyzed by stop-motion analysis of film, as in the work of Birdwhistell (1955) and Scheflen (1963). By this simple experiment, we feel that our theoretical construct of psychological vectors in interpersonal relationship is related at a behavioral and experiential level with some degree of significance. (Agazarian 1971, pp.15–16)

While Tinbergen stimulated my interest in watching nonverbal, body cues for the communication of emotion, Korzybski (1948) oriented me to the effect of cognition on behavior. I summarized Korzybski in one of my university papers:

All day long, man is matching his experience of the outside world with the map he has of it in his head. Man is a mapmaker. From infancy to adulthood he learns how to make maps from the experiences he has in the world. If his experiences are relevant, his perceptions accurate, and his skills of organizing are efficient, then his map will reflect the territory. When the map he makes in his head accurately reflects the world, he can react appropriately to most situations, and can make good predictions about what is coming next. However, Korzybski pointed out that in order to keep pace with 'now', man has to continually revise the map he has. Every time someone is surprised ... his map needs revision ... Man can revise the map to fit the territory, or he can revise his perceptions of the territory to fit his cognitive map. The second of these two processes leaves man less well equipped to find his way around in the real world, but does preserve his more cherished thoughts and wishes. Changing perceptions so that you see the world the way you wish to see it means that you become data unamenable, that there are certain kinds of things that you must either refuse to see, or as you do see, have to distort in order to fit the picture you have already. (Agazarian 1965a, p.1)

In my university courses, I was learning Lewin (1951) whose work was to have a very major and lasting influence on me (see Chapter 4). In his field theory, Lewin postulated that reducing the restraining forces releases the inherent driving forces toward a goal. Lewin's work also fits rather nicely with Korzybski's, and in fact for many people Korzybski's descriptions often were easier to grasp than Lewin's formulas. Lewin defined the life space as a person's perception of their environment. Lewin hypothesized that by knowing the life space, we can predict behavior $[b=f(P,E)]$ or behavior is a function of the person in interaction with the environment:

> The life space map also serves to indicate the relative simplicity or complexity of the individual's perceptual organization. Take for example, two individuals approaching a rock to sit on it: one walks to the rock in front of him, turns his back to it and sits; the other walks to the rock in front of him, climbs onto it on all fours, then wriggles around to sit facing the same direction as the first individual; the same event, the same goal, two different paths. If the second individual is a child, then the system difference is a developmental one, in that a child's perceptual system is less complex than an adult's and therefore the behavior is less efficient. If both are adult, then there must be another explanation for the difference in approach. Thus to observe an individual's behavior both implies the map of the way that individual sees the world (selective perception) and indicates the relative sophistication of the perceptual organization of information and correlates with the phase or level of development. (Agazarian 1987b, p.4)

It was also somewhere in the ethology literature when I was still in England, I believe, that I encountered the idea that 'maturation was a function of discrimination and integration'. (I have never been able to locate the exact source of this seminal idea although I can see the paragraphs on the top right-hand side of a page!) Whereas my attempts to introduce information theory and ethology into my analytic seminars failed, I was encouraged to write a paper applying discrimination and integration to Freud. I chose to write about the 'Renee Case' (Sechehaye 1951a, 1951b).

The Renee Case

For those who are unfamiliar with Renee, Renee was Sechehaye's patient in classical psychoanalysis. She came to Sechehaye for treatment at the age of 18, having first sought help a year earlier. Her symptoms included severe anxiety, motor disturbances, perseverative thought processes, poor attention, loosening of associations, flight of ideas, auditory hallucinations, suicidal impulses, incoherent crying, explosive laughing, loss of interest in food, and language disturbance, including mutism, neologisms and word negativisms.

During the second year of treatment, Sechehaye, in an attempt to contain Renee's regression, took her off the couch. This was the first of many modifications in her treatment and four years later (Renee was, by this time, manifestly psychotic), she took Renee into her home. By then, Renee would eat only green vegetables and green apples 'products of mother earth (mother) and still held to the tree…symbolic of mother's milk…a symbolic food…that is a permissible way of manifesting connecting to "mother" earth' (Sechehaye 1951a, p.50). When Renee rejected 'store apples' as 'apples for big people' and wanted 'apples from mummy like that', pointing to Sechehaye's breasts, Sechehaye understood the symbolic meaning of Renee's symptoms and began to treat her in what she later called 'symbolic realization':

> I understood at last what must be done. Since the apples represent maternal milk, I must give them to her like a mother feeding her baby … Taking an apple and cutting it in two, I offer Renee a piece saying, 'It is time to drink the good milk from Mummy's apples, Mummy is going to give it to you.' Renee then leans against my shoulder, presses the apples upon my breast, and very solemnly, and with intense happiness, eats it. (Sechehaye 1951a, p.51)

This first success of Sechehaye's 'symbolic realization' was just a beginning. There were many more to come, and many more mistakes to be made (like 'store' apples) which led to many more insights into how to apply her process.[1]

---

1   For instance, in her work Sechehaye discovered that for Renee, the Balloon symbolized the maternal breast; caring for the two dolls, Moses and Ezekial, symbolized the ego functions; Gold Pieces, symbolized the anal complex; the Little Rabbit, symbol of the right to live; the Easter Egg and the Atomizer, symbols of Virility; the Hanged Cases and the Golden Balls, symbols of the brother complex.

I titled my paper (1964) on Renee: 'Sechehaye's "Renee Case" from the formula, maturation = f(discrimination, integration)'. Clearly I was already happily influenced by Lewin's equations which for me was a clear and economical way of coding my thinking. In 'pure' Lewin, maturation as a function of discrimination and integration would read M=f(D, I). (See Figure 1.1.) The paper begins:

> The process of maturation is a function of the process of differentiation and integration: in other words, the work of perceiving similarities and dissimilarities, and organizing these perceptions into an integrative system from which the individual is then able to behave in ways that are culturally acceptable and personally rewarding. The work of differentiation has two important aspects. The first is the simple differentiation between the similar and the dissimilar. The second is the finer discrimination of perceiving the dissimilar in the apparently similar, and perceiving the similar in the apparently dissimilar. Setting up this model in a Cartesian square, and using Differentiation and Integration as the two dimensions, four combinations can be elaborated. (Agazarian 1964, p.1)

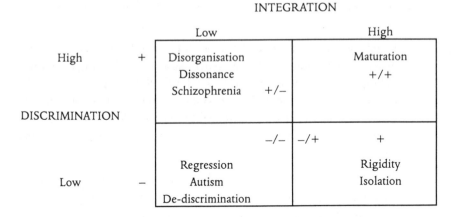

Figure 1.1 Maturation is a function of discrimination / integration: M = f (D, I)

Renee's original maturation contained discriminations of high potential dissonance, and her integration relied heavily upon the mechanisms of projection and imitation. When the disintegration set in, regression in the areas of discrimination could be traced (loss of spatial concepts, perspective, disturbance in space–time relationships). But the very process of regression of certain ego areas increased the need for a new integration, which could organize the different levels of discriminated experience. The point I want to emphasize is that the process of psychotic delusional system (called 'the system') in Renee's case was still subordinated to the organizing principal. Thus, in these first two phases, organization (integration) was still a function of Renee's process of discrimination. Whereas in her treatment, I suggest that the analyst and the process of discrimination offered an integrative model. (Agazarian 1964, p.3)

In Renee's original development, her primal introject was depriving. Therefore, in the very earliest stages of discrimination, during which the infant needs to make the primary distinction between the kinesthetic hallucinated breast feeding and the partial-object relationship with the real breast in space and time, the very process of discrimination was painful. This is graphically, subjectively described in terms of the primary guilt arising from 'affective realism' which summarized goes: 'Mama does not feed me because she doesn't want to feed me. Consequently, it is wicked to keep on wanting the mother feeding that is denied me. To be angry about it is even more wicked'(Sechehaye, 1951b, p.119). Translated into terms of differentiation dissonance, it goes: 'To want hurts…to want mother to feed me hurts more, to be angry about wanting mother to feed me hurts even more.' The greater the stages of discrimination, the greater the pain. And, already, the dissonance[2] is integrated into a system of primal guilt. And from this integration the basic behavioral model is destructive, in a culture where destructive behavior is unrewarded…and will thus create more dissonance.

Finally, the discriminatory organization between Renee and the outside world, always malfunctioning, breaks down completely, and through naive projection, Renee hears the wind in the trees carrying a message of misfortune, a naive projection that characterizes both the child's maturation process and the schizophrenic regressive progress. What is left of the organized ego attempts to project and localize Renee's destructive impulses into an 'integrated' system. Already, in the middle of

2   'Perceptual dissonance 'hurts', and the hurt itself increases the dissonance within the total person. A vicious circle is set up, in which the greater the internal dissonance, the greater the need for discrimination and integration, and the greater the strain on these processes' (Agazarian 1964, p.4).

a process of disintegration and de-discrimination, there is also the maturation process of discrimination and integration. But this time, it is based on the more naive discrimination mechanism of the similar to the similar, the dissimilar to the dissimilar. Thus, the system becomes 'outside' Renee, dissimilar to herself, and the 'personage' becomes the other half of the duality based on similarity.

It is in the *Autobiography of a Schizophrenic Girl* that Sechehaye makes perhaps one of the most crucial statements of her book: 'The certainty was then clear that if the method were to succeed, it was absolutely vital to consider the level of regression ... and not to exceed it unless the patient herself signified willingness' (Sechehaye 1951b, pp.124–125).[3]

What seems particularly crucial in this process is that Sechehaye seems to have reversed the whole maturation experience for Renee. Her primary discriminations do not bring pain, as they did in her original maturation, but peace and harmony.

It seems that from here, Sechehaye's systematized symbolism was more than a 'symbolic' reconstruction of a psychotic ego ... but that it was actually a difference in process from normal maturation. Whereas the child spontaneously related his discriminatory and integrative processes through his maturation stages, Renee was offered an integrative model by Sechehaye to both encourage discriminatory processes and to organize them.

There are two points that seem crucial in the treatment of psychotics from this model. The first is the relationship between the process of discrimination and dissonance. If the very process of perception is associated predominately with dissonance, it would seem that discrimination and integration must always be disturbed.

Second is the offering of a model for integration that is directly appropriate to the potentialities of discrimination that exist at that particular time for the patient. To the extent that perceptual discriminations, both internal and external and the organizational model for these perceptions are in harmony, there is minimal threat of the experience of dissonance which triggers de-differentiation and psychotic integration.

---

3   My attention to this aspect of Sechehaye's treatment foreshadows my interest in phases of development and the importance of context in therapy for what work can and cannot be done at any point in time.

I question whether or not on this basis, it would be possible to achieve the same success with patients who have not regressed to the stage of autism that Renee had regressed. From the apparent success of the green apples it would seem possible, but crucially different in the process. At the stage of the green apples, it would seem, from this argument, that Sechehaye was combating Renee's psychotic integration with a therapeutic integrative model, but that the process of discrimination was still basically associated pathogenically. Whereas, the process of discrimination and integration after Renee's complete regression was based on a reversal of the pathogenic trend.

The possibilities that do seem to open up, from this argument, however, are the possibilities of relating developmental stage symbolic integrative models to the most de-differentiated stage of the psychotic regression. This supports the cause of working with the ego, and not with the psychosis, but implies that at least one aspect of the work needs to be directed to the most regressed parts of the ego ... perhaps even instead of directing therapy to the remnants of the healthy ego. (Agazarian 1964, pp.3–9)

My article on Renee was the first of many attempts to build a bridge between my psychoanalytic self and my researcher/observer/theoretician/and finally systems-centered self. Different from my relationship to the traditional god, my 'atheism' with psychoanalysis was comparatively short-lived. I was briefly shocked into rejecting psychoanalytic methods when I wrote the discussion of Sampson and Weiss's paper (see Chapter 5). And I wisely refused to think about psychoanalysis while I was developing systems-centered practice. My 'researcher' was thus freed to discover that the unconscious processes which emerged in the process of systems-centered therapy are the same as those that emerge in psychoanalysis. This is no surprise of course. Dynamics *are*, however they are discovered. It is nonetheless rewarding that my psychoanalytic training has contributed to my being able to discriminate when the dynamics that I was seeing in the systems- centered process were similar and when they were different from those I would have expected from my earlier psychoanalytic frame. This has enabled me to ask questions about what it is in the process that makes the difference in the dynamics.

By 1965, I completed my work at the psychoanalytic institute although I had not yet finished my control cases, and I had finished at Temple 'all but the dissertation' (which I was to complete in 1968). Clinically, I was working with a therapy group using a group dynamics approach, and with all my individual patients I was using psychodynamically oriented therapy. My interests were still predominantly in theory and I had little trouble conceptualizing the therapeutic work I was doing from the theoretical concepts I had learned.

I was in for a rude awakening. I joined the Pennsylvania Hospital to work with the new community mental health movement in 1965 and prepared to continue to practice – setting up groups that would enable the members to get insight into their responses to authority and intimacy and to work with individuals so that they could get insight into how their early developmental vicissitudes affected their present. I was in no way prepared for the realities that my patients brought to me. So I started going out into the community, discovering, for example, that the fear of going to light the furnace in the basement was not a simple fear of descending into the unconscious but a fear of rats. In the groups that I started, I imported many of the group dynamics skills that I used to design workshops with specific goals. We set up role plays between the patients, so that they could practice presenting their issues to their social workers with more effectiveness. The patients themselves role played their social workers with great skill and gave each other excellent practice in trying to survive and even effectively use the system. Thus some patients were able to move into better housing; others to get an increased allowance for food. As they reported their successes, other patients were motivated to try, and still others to bring in issues that they would like to practice. We formed a 'depressed' group in which patients kept an eye on each other between groups. One of the most successful innovations was to arrange the medication clinic as a recreation and group afternoon, where patients could either play dominoes, checkers or chess, or work with practical issues in groups. As the groups became popular, my programs became seriously understaffed. Although my title was Director of Group Services, I was the only staff member.

I started to give group dynamic seminars, open to anyone in the center who was interested. As these also became popular, I made contact with the directors of the different departments and bargained to train their staff in group dynamics in return for the staff working four hours a week in the 'Group Services Department'. The bargain worked well. The staff members spent one hour in an experiential training group, one hour leading a patient group, one hour in group supervision and one hour doing intake interviews, patient disposition and notes. By the time I left the center in 1970, the Group Services Department saw more patients than the outpatient department, and I was still the only formal staff member!

These were the early days of the community mental health movement, and all of us were deeply involved and motivated. Our enthusiasm and idealism enabled us to work together with a spirit of innovation and dedication that had not yet burnt out on reality.

There was support for innovating and for trying something different if a more traditional approach did not work. For example, Bill, the Director of the Outpatient Department, and I spent one afternoon following a psychotic woman with her baby through the streets until she walked quietly with us into the inpatient unit. As babies were not allowed on the unit, I stopped at the maternity ward on the way up and pushed a cot, diapers and bottles into the elevator, so that we could keep the child with her in the room. Another time, when there was no more room in the inpatient unit, I took a suicidal patient to the general hospital. Startled at the conditions, I refused to leave her there, preparing to stay all night if necessary. When, at Bill's request, the director of the unit came and asked me what the problem was, I facetiously said that if he didn't know, then there was no point in me talking to him. Bill found a bed back on our unit and the patient and I 'came home'.

The Case of Sarah

With a few of the individual patients, I was able to practice in the ways that I had been trained. With many I had to innovate. For example, when I was too frightened of one paranoid and violent man, I arranged to see him in the cafeteria where others were around. With many of the adolescents we walked and talked. With a particular patient, whom we shall call Sarah, I specifically used the idea of discrimination and integration that I had applied in understanding Sechehaye. The excerpts below are from a case presentation on Sarah that I gave for grand rounds.

Sarah had been seeing Cass, our social worker, and had not been doing well, becoming very tearful, frightened and insisting on being hospitalized. As an alternative to hospitalization (again our idealism!), it was agreed that Cass and I would give her daily supportive therapy.

Reviewing the article I wrote about Sarah, it is clear that one of the values we shared at our center was to maintain patients in the community and avoid hospitalization if possible. It is true in Sarah's case that she did manage to 'get better' without hospitalization (and without the medication which she refused to take), yet in looking back, perhaps she had more clinical acumen than we did in asking to be hospitalized:

> Sarah presented two sorts of behavior in therapy: for most of the time she was depressed, crying and frightened. She was afraid to eat – was losing weight – and her sleep was filled with dreams, which precipitated her wakefulness. She described a continual headache at the back of her head and talked of it 'killing her'. During what she called 'her spells', she described a pounding in her head and was afraid her head would explode. At the onset of her 'spells', she would break into a cold sweat all over.
>
> In this sort of state, Sarah could not verbalize coherently what she was afraid of. When asked, she would say 'something harmful', that she was afraid she would put 'something harmful' in the food, 'something that didn't belong there'. Then she would stare at her hands and say with intensity, 'What do you have on your hands?' She would refer to her fear of 'dirty work', and on questioning, would answer 'ketchup or lye; coffee, Mercurochrome, medication, cleaning fluids, machine oil, foot powder and cosmetics; staples, pins, nails, scissors, razors'.
>
> Underlying her fears of 'something harmful' was a less tangible structure. These were her fears of 'something dirty' which had to do with 'sweepings' and the bathroom. She was afraid that she would put 'something dirty' in the food or in her mouth. She was afraid of the bathroom and would not urinate, retaining her urine until physical pain forced her to it. The woman was not only in a state of terror at the alien thoughts that she felt invaded by and driven by, but could make no distinction between thinking and doing ... To protect the food in the refrigerator, she kept a chair against it, so that she wouldn't do her 'dirty work'. At night she tied herself in bed, so that she wouldn't get up and 'do her funny business in her sleep'. (p.4)
>
> During the first few days of intensive therapy, she was able to give little more than monosyllabic replies, cried a good deal and avoided eye contact, except for those occasional quick, sharp glances. She appeared to be less disturbed if I did not change my position when I was seeing her. It was difficult to obtain enough information from her to get some picture of what her particular thinking system was; at the time, in her

monosyllabic replies, there appeared to be a smattering of severely regressed material that I felt needed to be re-repressed if there was not to be further decompensation. Asking her questions appeared to upset her, as did sitting in silence. She would beg for help, but the help she begged for was in the form of either hospitalization or magical cure, in which I would take the thoughts away. (p.7)

At first, when Sarah would speak fragments of her fears about her thoughts, I would say 'thinking is different from doing'. After some time, she would verbalize this same phrase; the words appeared meaningless to her, but comforting. Later, she developed it into a song, so that she could sing 'thinking is different than doing' to herself on buses or at work, without 'looking crazy'. When she would stare at her hands and say, 'What have you got in your hands?' I would put my hands on her palms and say, 'You have nothing in your hands, my hands are in your hands.' From then on she would say that to herself as a ritual to ward off her panic.

After three months, Sarah had been able to describe most of the thoughts that bothered her and also to tell us the precautions that she took against them, tying herself in bed, avoiding a whole range of objects that might be harmful, keeping a chair in front of the refrigerator and avoiding all stores, etc. She was finally able to verbalize her fear that harmful things were 'p-o-i-s-o-n', and finally, to say the word 'poison'. She had exclaimed, 'If my mother were alive, I wouldn't be this way,' and she recognized that much of what she did that disturbed her so much now, she had done before as part of her everyday routine of cleanliness and her precautions of double checking anything that might be unsafe. She was less depressed and more impatient and aggressive. Her appearance improved, she shaved her legs, started to wear jewelry and continue to go to the hairdresser every week, in spite of her fears of 'bottles'. (p.6)

This program was not without wear and tear on the therapists. Both Cass and I started to feel hounded by the telephone and thoroughly dominated and manipulated. Sarah successfully got appointments that we had previously refused and also succeeded in being seen on Saturdays and Sundays. She became more insistently demanding of a quick cure, threatened suicide frequently, with much more aggression and less depression, finally accepted medication reluctantly and then rejected it because it made her feel drowsy. She was also becoming impatient with the restrictions that some of her symptoms placed on her particularly with the discomfort of her nights. Tying herself in bed left her uncomfortable and restricted, tore her nightclothes and woke her up repeatedly.

By the end of the third month, she was able to give up tying herself in bed and could sleep through the night without being bothered by horrendous dreams and without having to start her day by four in the morning to get to work. (p.8)

From then on, her progress was slowly upwards, with many regressions. First, she would describe 'clear moments' – meaning, literally, 'clear', a 'haze going from in front of her eyes, and being able to see clearly'. She complained that the changes were killing her – good moments following bad moments, backwards and forwards. The frequency of good moments and bad moments intensified and the good moments lengthened and merged into good days, following bad days and finally good periods and the occasional half a day or a few hours of 'spells'. (p.10)

I do not want to give the impression that this progress was a smooth curve. Sarah reduced her sessions to once a week, supplemented some weeks by occasional phone calls. She was occasionally disturbed over her thoughts and reacted with sweats and panic, and needed reassurance. She had some insight that she 'has kept all her feelings inside all her life' and expressed them in thoughts in her head. She recognized that she was bothered by thoughts, either after some event that had disturbed her in some way, or by suddenly seeing something that reminded her of 'when she was sick'. She was somewhat concerned that one day she might get sick again and was very resistant to any suggestion that she may be ready to do without therapy. However, she said, 'You want me to go out and have a good time rather than seeing you next week?' and thus reduced her sessions to about three a month.

In spring, when the bushes were in bloom, we walked out onto the steps and she gasped and said, 'Oh, how beautiful!' Then she smiled and asked, 'Do you remember when you tried to get me to look at a tree and all I would do is hold onto your arm?'

I do not claim to know why she improved as she did, nor even whether she may not have made the same gains in response to the real life pressures that she experienced without therapy. She had never entirely lost contact with practical issues.

However, dynamically, it seems to me that any of several theoretical orientations could lead to an explanation of what was happening to her and the process of recuperation. I would like to present a bare skeleton of theory here, which does not seem to me to contradict other theoretical orientations, even when they are as dissimilar as Freud or Ellis.

One of the major adaptive mechanisms is the ability to perceive differences and integrate the perception of differences into some sort of rational framework which explains our experience. In both psychotic and neurotic perception, there appears a deficiency in two aspects of this process. One is the difficulty in perceiving and integrating these perceptual differences into a framework which is useful in dealing with everyday life so that the problems of living are approached rather than avoided.

The work of perceiving and integrating differences implies a period of disorganization because existing closure must be disrupted before it can be remade. Things that are different are not immediately explainable or acceptable and for as long as there is no framework into which they can be organized, the person engaged in this work experiences some stress or frustration. As soon as the focus of perception is turned toward the stress, the 'reality problem' situation becomes secondary.

The process of differentiation and interpretation was behind much of my behavior. I deliberately attempted to reduce the stress of the present situation by presenting her with as few 'new differences' as possible – even to abstaining from 'different' movements. Second, I attempted to help her tolerate some primal differences that appeared, as her use of language indicated, to have become de-differentiated. I attempted to help her accept the difference between myself and her. Since it appeared that at the verbal level, the discrimination between thoughts, feelings and actions also appeared de-differentiated, I relied mainly on the contact of my hand with her hand, while I verbalized the difference in a hope of reinforcing the separation, and connecting words to the physical sensation of presence and absence.

Further attempts to encourage the differentiations that are the basis of reality testing were made, when we would go over, again and again, the difference between thinking about something and doing it. She would 'think' about standing up and describe the experience. She would then, at my request, stand up and describe it as different. I often felt that she was inferring what I wanted to hear, rather than actually experiencing the difference.

With a different emphasis, I also encouraged her to 'experience' her body as an entity that did not change, and that she could rely on. I would encourage her to feel her own weight on her feet, to feel her own solidity, to recognize that her body was there, whether she 'thought' about it or not. (Agazarian 1965b, pp.12–15)

First Steps with Driving and Restraining Forces

In addition to working with the principle of discrimination/integration, I was also importing Lewin's field theory to the practical realities I was facing, to see if thinking through theoretically made a difference in what I could do. Excerpts from a 1966 paper, 'Preliminary Analysis of some of the Driving and Restraining Forces in the Process of Change', illustrate some of these early attempts at making sense:

> One of the problems that patients have when they first come in, is they don't know what is wrong, they don't have any sort of a structure picture of their life space as it exists here and now ... In Lewinian language what we can say is that reality problems in the here and now life space are solved either by regression to past reality, behavior in terms of past reality, or fantasy solutions at the level of irreality. We would also say that coordinates between present life space and future life space are unclear and tend to exist at the irreality level and also that any type of goal and path-to-goal clarity tends to be missing ... Therefore, one of the things that is going to have to happen initially, is that the present differentiation will need to dedifferentiate (in psychoanalytic language, regression) in order for closure to be broken and some sort of new structuring to occur that will allow for a greater degree of adaptive behavior. This process is inevitably uncomfortable because what we will be asking patients to do is to dedifferentiate, break closure and experience more sharply the aspect of the unknown and also to experience more sharply the feelings that they have of their own lack of power and mastery. The immediate question in my mind is, what conditions can we arrange so that the maximum driving forces towards rewarding and adaptive change can be induced at the same time minimizing the restraining forces against change. We have here conceptually, the classic force field model. (Agazarian 1966, p.1)

I am working here with Lewin's force field which, as I later adapted it, would provide the underpinnings for developing the defense modification in systems-centered therapy. I was also beginning to focus on identifying the conditions that will facilitate change and the problem of having enough containment to tolerate the unknown. I was clearly starting to understand that learning to tolerate the unknown is necessary for something different to happen. Today systems-centered therapists routinely work to normalize, legitimize and make more bearable the discomfort we all have 'sitting at the edge of the unknown' and in uncertainty. My paper continued:

Resistances to change: Opposing forces

The first two resistances to change that I want to have a look at are the lack of skills in doing things differently, and the feelings of frustration being experienced when they attempt to move into the unknown, unstructured areas or aspects of their life space. The need for skills and understandings that they do not have presumably can only generate strong feelings of frustration in people who already have maladaptive mechanisms in handling their feelings of frustration. Therefore the first question in my mind is, how can we teach new skills and what conditions do we need to teach these new skills, in such a way that the immediate experience of learning these skills is rewarding, both in terms of feelings of comfort and also in immediate perceptual feedback. The first requisite for modifying the resistances to change will be conditions in which new adaptive skills are taught in such a way that they become immediately positively reinforced both alloplastically and autoplastically. Thus the main opposing force can be summed up as the unstructured aspect of the life space and the main modifications of the opposing force can be summed up as ways of structuring the unstructured areas of the life space in a process that is immediately rewarding and positively reinforcing. (Agazarian 1966, p.2)

As I work here with the restraining force to change, I am working with three aspects that would remain important in my work, the issue of frustration, the problem of lack of skills, and the question of how to build a structure that is rewarding and useful to work within. I continued:

Driving forces: Motivation to change

The main driving force is power. Feelings of power can easily be equated with feelings of autonomy, feelings of effectiveness, and a psychological set that is geared to expectation of success. Lewin suggests that achievement expectation is a function of 1) the perceptual clarity of the goal itself plus most importantly expectations of achieving that goal, 2) expectations of goal achievement are in their turn a function of past experience of achievement.

Predictably the problem that we will find is that past experience of an achievement has been basically negative, therefore the next important point here is that success experiences for them need to come in small, clear increments... And how can we most efficiently and effectively influence the group norms so that the norms of the group are themselves a rewarding interpersonal experience. By this I mean quite precisely, how soon, how fast, and how can we help influence norms of interaction that are supportive rather than defensive. Therefore again, if we can start our group with prior training in behaviors that tend towards the development of a non-defensive trusting and warm climate we have automatic conditions set up for individuals which are conducive to emotional maintenance and the potential for channeling frustration into changed energy. We also have a climate in which excess frustration that cannot be channeled, can be discharged without the negative reinforcement that usually follows frustration. The next important point in the type of norms that we hope to influence would be norms of problem solving, behavioral experimentation and creative interdependence. (Agazarian 1966, p.3)

Some years later I built on this understanding that I seemed to have an inkling of here, of channeling frustration into change energy. As I developed systems-centered therapy, it was quite important to me to find a way to create the conditions in which potential energy (and frustration is potential energy for work) could be contained rather than defended against so that the potential energy could be transformed to actual energy when used for work. I am also here beginning to work explicitly with the importance of group norms and the problem of how to influence the group norms. Continuing with what I wrote in 1966:

We [also] want to look at the goal orientation and clarity of the life space that does not yet exist for the individuals and can be developed both for the individuals and for the group via problem solving technique... One of the first and basic learnings that we are going to work with is the discrimination between the data at the descriptive level and the evaluative level... In terms then of the three resistances to change that we can predict, a) lack of skill, b) thresholds of frustration tolerance and maladaptive mechanism to frustration, and c) the unstructured aspect of the life space, we can see three quite precise ways of reducing the particular change resistances.

In terms of skill, we can design very specific skill training exercises which are immediately rewarding and are part of the total process of learning effective autoplastic and alloplastic problem solving behaviors and experiences. In terms of minimizing the opposing force of frust-ration tolerance, we can see the creation of maintenance skills and a climate of trust which will allow, first of all frustration discharge without punishment, and second, group support that can serve the function of added borrowed ego strength for each individual while they are in the process of developing ego strength. And finally in terms of the unstruc-tured aspect of the here and now life space plus the tendency toward past reality and irreality levels with poor perspective on future reality levels, we can see group norms of problem solving and group pressures toward problem solving behavior as directly functional in terms of the struc-turing of a life space and the increasing range and flexibility of alternative paths to a goal.

Another important point is that to the extent the goal of the group can quite clearly be problem solving toward interdependent interaction and relationships, to that extent the goal of the group can be weaned away from interaction in terms of pathology. This is another aspect that seems very important to me as I strongly suspect that there is an inverse relationship between reinforcing use of resources, understanding of resources, emphasis on resources, development of resource potentiality at an operational level, and emphasis on pathology, understanding pathology, and describing pathology. (Agazarian 1966, p.4)

Yes!!! This clearly proved to be true, even more than I then knew, and presaged a major orientation today in systems-centered therapy where depathologizing and legitimizing human experience helps change the often very painful relationships we have with ourselves when we pathologize ourselves or relate to our experience defensively. The last focus in my 1966 paper was on establishing the norm of emphasizing observable data rather than the speculation and intellectualizing that 'why' often induces:

In other words, one of the norms that I would like to see develop in the groups is the 'what' rather than the 'why' – what is happening now, how and what do we do to change group experiences in ways that make sense to us. Observation of the behaviors and behavioral consequences, feedback techniques, techniques for validation, techniques for decisions by consensus, and techniques for group autonomy, all of these are aspects of here and now analysis and operationality and away from the intellectual 'why' of the problem. (Agazarian 1966, p.5)

These early excerpts show many of the important threads with which I was working and my steadfast focus on applying theory to clinical practice.

Though I had not yet integrated much of this, this early work contains many of the 'information bits' that I would later integrate into my theory and practice. For instance, I later developed the principle of maturation, maturation as a function of discrimination and integration $[M = f(D,I)]$, as the definition of function in the theory of living human systems. Adapting Lewin's force field and working with the driving and restraining forces would turn out to be an important model in developing the defense modification in systems-centered practice.

CHAPTER 2

The First Try at Theory

Discovering Group Dynamics

Concurrent with my psychoanalytic studies, I was enrolled in the Group Dynamics Department of Temple University (1961). Discovering group dynamics (a word and a concept I had never heard of!) was one of those happy accidents that was to change the course of my life. I had arrived intending to enter the psychology department. This was fraught with anxiety as I had been told that Temple psychology department was heavily experimental and did not look favorably on the clinical ambitions of their students. I was already deviant from the medical psychoanalysts' point of view who (until recently) did not allow lay analysts into their training institutions. I was therefore in analytic training in the Psychoanalytic Studies Institute with other lay analysts and interning with the osteopathic psychiatrists where I was already seeing patients.

'Losing my way', or at least the way I thought I was headed, took me to group dynamics. I was looking for the Psychology Department, went to the wrong building and found myself in the Group Dynamics Center where I met Art Blumberg who was to be one of my mentors for many years.[1] Motivated by him, I took my first T-Group course (Sensitivity Training) two weeks later in the summer semester and by the following summer I was teaching in the department.

---

[1]   Art Blumberg and Dave Jenkins were my major mentors in my group dynamics program. My work with Dave is described in Chapter 4.

T-groups

My first T-group experience was utterly bewildering to me. Not unusual for analysts in training, I gathered my data about the group by diagnosing the pathology of its individual members. These were early days when diagnosis was a relatively simple method of choosing between hysteric, obsessive, psychotic and borderline. (Incidentally the definition of normal in our text was almost exactly the same as the definition for borderlines!) I had no trouble dividing the group members between hysterics and obsessives, and even (as I got increasingly frustrated with her) discovered a Bettelheim schizogenic personality in the group.

However, I had a major problem. My T-group trainer was Art Blumberg – a man I liked and respected. Yet, every time he said anything, he made absolutely no sense to me. He appeared at ease, he did not appear to be psychotic to my 'in-training' eye, yet his words did not make sense. Because as a T-group trainer he did not answer questions, I had to try to answer them myself. The experience felt very like my struggle with God – but with God I never did come to an answer and had finally converted to atheism. What was different in the T-group setting, however, was that everyone else in the group was as bewildered as me.

For those who are unfamiliar with T-groups (the 'T' stands for 'training'), they emerged from Bion's work with the group-as-a-whole. They began in the formal classroom climate of the pre-1960s. Students entered the class-room to find not a row of chairs facing a podium but a circle with their teacher sitting in it. Once seated, they uneasily waited in vain for the teacher to teach. The teacher stayed silent. This created a power vacuum and elicited ever more chaotic responses from the group members. In the chaos, Bion's 'basic assumptions' (that groups avoid chaos by flight/fight, pairing and dependency responses) are highlighted so that they can be more easily studied, 'as if' in a laboratory. (This method and adaptations of this method are used effectively to this day in Tavistock and A.K. Rice training.)

Bennis and Shepard (1956), early pioneers in using this method of T-group training, observed that their groups (which met for 15 weeks) not only manifested Bion's basic assumptions, but also consistently progressed through observable and predictable sequences. They identified three phases. They noticed that their groups were preoccupied with authority, power and control in the beginning, next became preoccupied with the enchantments and disenchantments in intimacy and were finally able to work. From these observations they developed the theory of group development in which they synchronized Bion's basic assumptions with the phases of development: describing how groups predictably begin in flight, move into fight and, after scapegoating the leader in a fulcrum event, shift into phase two of intimacy where they explore their dependency. The work phase is reached when the group has developed consensually validated communication.

You can imagine what a relief it was to read Bennis and Shepard's (1956) paper on phases of development, which we were given toward the end of the course – not at the beginning. Had it been at the beginning and had I had a framework for understanding the process, my life might have been very different. I can remember trying to let in what Art said without instantly translating it into my own frame: it was literally like trying to hold open an iron hoop, like the hoops around a barrel, with all my strength. And it hurt, it literally hurt my head physically. Later I was to learn about Festinger's (1957) theory of cognitive dissonance which helped me understand the experience. It also helped me later to endure the same experience when I was developing my own theory: holding it together, discovering something that did not make sense and experiencing a similar pain as it all fell apart.

The T-group was a significant experience for me. I can remember one session when, in absolute despair, I threatened the group with a communication exercise because nothing was making sense. I came into the next group and to my own and everyone else's surprise, the group cooperated with my exercise. Alas, when we looked at the results, still nothing made sense. During the course, in my term paper I wrote:

> Steinbeck, in his *Sea of Cortez*, talks of fish. He tells of how the shoal, when attacked, reorganizes. How the weaker, most expendable members form the vanguard and how the stronger and younger take the spearhead and central positions so that both direction and survival are better ensured for the species.
>
> Steinbeck is perhaps fortunate. From a relatively simple observation of behavior he is able, a priori, to generalize into fascinating speculation about group consciousness in fish, animals and humans.
>
> Not quite so fortunate am I, the creator of the following, a posteriori, speculations. For I write from the position of one of a human shoal that continually organized and reorganized against the phantom attacks it spawned itself. Even after five weeks of such maneuvers, I still have but a

shadowy idea as to my relative size and position within the group (Agazarian 1962, p.1).

Looking back at this paper, it is clear that I was already incubating ideas about the group-as-a-whole as a system – but was far from knowing it. However I had learned that trying to explain group behavior from my psychoanalytic understandings of individual dynamics made no sense.

I wrote in my course paper a year later that I was looking for 'a hypothesis that is broad enough to spell out group dynamics theory so that the direction and goals of the operational procedures could be made more explicit... Research could become, not only a process of making available more tested information, but also operate on a construct validity level' (Agazarian 1963a, p.1). To this end, and building on Lewin's work (that the whole is different from the sum of its parts), I was beginning to work with the idea 'that parts in interaction are a different phenomenon than the part in interaction with itself' (Agazarian 1963a, p.2). I defined 'social' phenomenon (individuals or groups) as 'a pattern of parts in interaction'.

Dave Jenkins's influence on my work is apparent by this point (discussed in detail in Chapter 4). I had asked him, 'Why isn't there a common definition of group, when, without it, it is not possible to generalize from group research, and why isn't there a definition that would discriminate between group and individual dynamics and also make it possible to explain how they interact?' Dave challenged me and encouraged me to formulate one.

I was in my element in my 'observation of a T-Group' course where I had my first experience of trying to collect objective observational data. Anita Simon, a fellow student in the program, was keenly interested in understanding human behavior by coding communication – and this was another idea that I took to like a duck takes to water. We became good friends and worked together to develop SAVI (pronounced 'savvy'), an observation system for coding verbal communications.

Developing SAVI

SAVI[2] (System for Analyzing Verbal Interaction) began one afternoon when Anita and I were having coffee. Anita was telling me the difficulty she was having in her 'observation of a T-group' course. She could not tell whether, objectively, the trainer (it was Art) was scapegoating the members or whether she was subjectively distorting her perceptions. I knew that Art couldn't possibly scapegoat members because he had been my trainer! And I knew Art had been Anita's trainer the year before in her T-group course. Instantly, the psychoanalyst in me leaped into the conversation. I immediately responded (and I'm afraid interpreted) that she was in negative transference, left over from unresolved feelings from her previous group which would make it almost impossible to collect data objectively. What's more, she was observing a group that was grappling with their relationship to authority, which easily arouses strong feelings in both group members and the observers. I suggested that we develop some form of a system that she could use to code her observation data objectively.

This was, in fact, a very good idea as we were both interested in comm-unication. Anita was doing research with classroom interaction systems (Bales 1950; Flanders 1965) and I was deeply immersed in developing a theory of group communication. For me, SAVI was my first attempt to make operational my theory of group 'as a function of interdependence of parts', that I began wrestling with after Dave Jenkins's encouragement and challenge to me.

With SAVI (Simon and Agazarian 1967) we developed an observation system for verbal communication that codes and maps the dissonance or noise in communication that arises from ambiguities and contradictions in the communications. We assumed that every communication has both a topic and a personal component: the topic component is what is being said and the personal component is how it is being said and draws attention away from the topic towards the person who is doing the communicating. Both the topic and personal components are interdependent and vary inversely: the

2   SAVI was originally an acronym for a Sequential Analysis of Verbal Interaction (we coded our data in a matrix of sequence pairs, a very labor intensive method before computer!). when later we discovered that entering our data into a frequency count matrix not only saved us hours of intensive labor, but also served to give immediate, visual snapshots of the ststus of the communication we were coding, SAVI became a System for Analyzing Verbal Interaction – which it is to this day.

more the emphasis on the topic, the less the emphasis on the personal component in the communication and vice versa. For example, 'I think that is a good idea' communicates reinforcement. If this is said with a lot of enthusiasm it communicates an interpersonal message. If said without any inflection at all it might raise anxiety, and when said with sarcasm the topic component easily gets lost altogether.

The relative weight of the two components in a communication determines whether it is classified in SAVI as a topic or person communication. Topic communications are further discriminated as primarily factual or orienting (Figure 2.1).

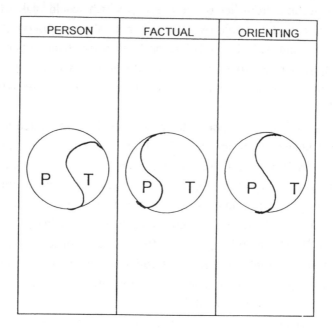

Figure 2.1 Topic and person communication

Ambiguity or contradiction within either the topic or the personal component of the message, or between these two components of the message, results in dissonance or 'noise' in the communication. When either component is unclear, ambiguity is introduced into the communication channel; ambiguity stimulates dissonance and the communication then orients towards managing the dissonance. In the SAVI coding, noisy communication is classified as avoidance behavior in relationship to the goal of communication which is information transfer. Communications that are consonant or relatively free from noise are classified as approach. The third category, contingent communications, can be either approach or avoidance, dependent on the overall communication climate (Figure 2.2).

We then worked with this categorization using a 3 x 3 grid, with 'person', 'topic' and 'orienting' behaviors identifying the columns, and 'avoidance', 'contingent' and 'approach' behaviors identifying the rows. This resulted in nine categories of behavior (Figure 2.3).

The SAVI grid that results then provides a way to look at the relative amount of dissonance in a communication system and a matrix of the group verbal behavior: the more avoidance behaviors the more dissonance, the more approach behaviors the less dissonance and the higher the probability that the information contained in the communication will be heard.

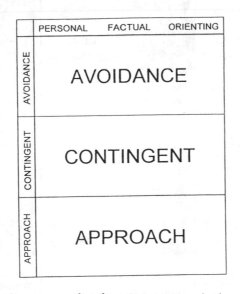

Figure 2.2 Avoidance, approach and contingent communications

Group as Interdependence of Parts

In my 1963 university paper I had defined 'all social phenomena as a pattern of parts in interaction' (Agazarian 1963 p.20), with 'social phenomenon' having 'random information bits' as its 'raw material.' 'These information bits are

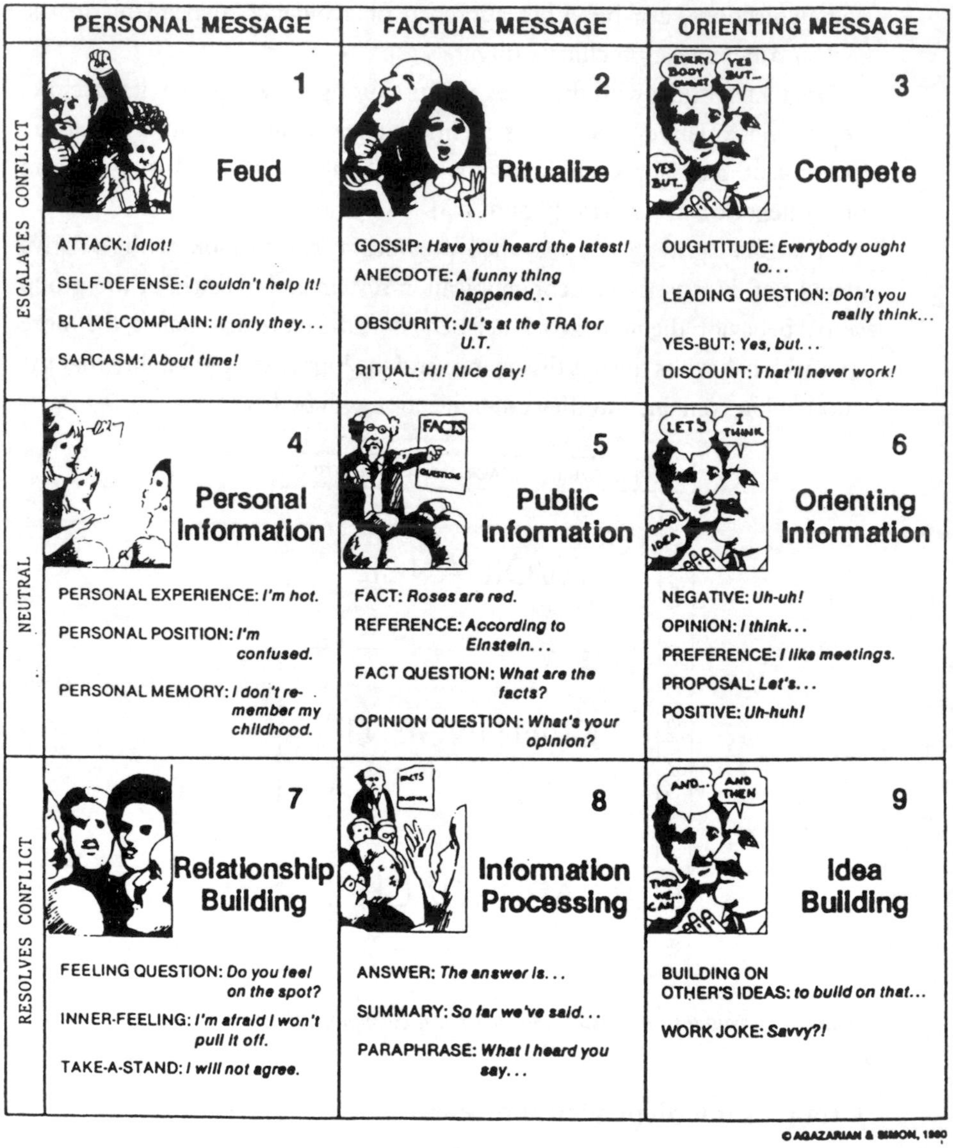

	PERSONAL MESSAGE	FACTUAL MESSAGE	ORIENTING MESSAGE
ESCALATES CONFLICT	**1** **Feud** ATTACK: *Idiot!* SELF-DEFENSE: *I couldn't help it!* BLAME-COMPLAIN: *If only they. . .* SARCASM: *About time!*	**2** **Ritualize** GOSSIP: *Have you heard the latest!* ANECDOTE: *A funny thing happened. . .* OBSCURITY: *JL's at the TRA for U.T.* RITUAL: *Hi! Nice day!*	**3** **Compete** OUGHTITUDE: *Everybody ought to. . .* LEADING QUESTION: *Don't you really think. . .* YES-BUT: *Yes, but. . .* DISCOUNT: *That'll never work!*
NEUTRAL	**4** **Personal Information** PERSONAL EXPERIENCE: *I'm hot.* PERSONAL POSITION: *I'm confused.* PERSONAL MEMORY: *I don't remember my childhood.*	**5** **Public Information** FACT: *Roses are red.* REFERENCE: *According to Einstein. . .* FACT QUESTION: *What are the facts?* OPINION QUESTION: *What's your opinion?*	**6** **Orienting Information** NEGATIVE: *Uh-uh!* OPINION: *I think. . .* PREFERENCE: *I like meetings.* PROPOSAL: *Let's. . .* POSITIVE: *Uh-huh!*
RESOLVES CONFLICT	**7** **Relationship Building** FEELING QUESTION: *Do you feel on the spot?* INNER-FEELING: *I'm afraid I won't pull it off.* TAKE-A-STAND: *I will not agree.*	**8** **Information Processing** ANSWER: *The answer is. . .* SUMMARY: *So far we've said. . .* PARAPHRASE: *What I heard you say. . .*	**9** **Idea Building** BUILDING ON OTHER'S IDEAS: *to build on that. . .* WORK JOKE: *Savvy?!*

© AGAZARIAN & SIMON, 1980

Figure 2.3 SAVI: System for Analyzing Verbal Interaction

organized structurally into a part (of a whole)' (p.23). I defined part as role.[3] (I had just taken a course in sociology.) The smallest part, I suggested, was the 'simplest' role played within an individual (foreshadowing intrasystem subgroups). The ability of individuals to direct these intrapersonal 'parts' into interpersonal work (inter-system subgroups) relates to the goal and to the map of the territory. I illustrated this idea by saying:

> Take a 'simple' example, an individual sleeping is a pattern of parts moving towards the goal of regeneration. In the movement towards this goal, only certain of the range of parts within the individual have a 'role.' To the extent a part is not playing a 'role' (operational either consciously or unconsciously) to that extent the part 'does not exist' for this particular moment in time (Agazarian 1963, p.19).

I then go on to think about 'parts' as information bits (I had not yet equated information with energy).

> An individual is made up of a quantity of information bits. The inform-ation bits are organized into 'role.' The parts or roles of the individual are organized from the information bits – and each role is structurally different. [In the appendix, I noted 'role is not bounded by 'individual'. Thus role may be specific interactive behaviors from several individuals.'] The determinant of the structure of the roles (past the strictly physio-logical level) at any one time is the 'map' (or perception now) of the territory (what's out there).[4] The structure of the interaction is dependent upon movement towards goal. To the extent the goal is explicit, to the extent the individual is able to predict consequences of movement (behavior), then to that extent there is the potential for the individual to organize and modify the interaction of roles more meaningfully ... thus movement towards goal becomes a matter of both internal and external modification of role interaction. (Agazarian 1963, p.20)

Role was a seminal construct – defined as a constellation of behaviors, which could be identified independent of individuals. Thus, the role of leader or member were defined socially in terms of their social position, whereas

---

3   Looking back, the definition of group as 'an interdependence of parts' contained all the elements that would lead to a theory of living human systems. Indeed, I used my definition of 'role as a bridge construct between the individual and the group' in my first book (Agazarian and Peters 1981).

4   I am working here with Korzybski's (1948) concept of the map and the territory (see Chapter 1).

functionally I defined them in terms of leadership or membership behaviors. As Anita and I worked, I began to get confidence in a way that had previously been impossible, that my definition of group might mean something more than just an idea. To reiterate, I had defined 'the degree of groupness that exists in any one time as a function of the degree of interdependence of parts [group^0 = f(interdependence^0 of parts)].' Communication behavior was the specific variable chosen. SAVI was the method for testing this, my first definition of theory. Thus, the SAVI sequential matrix became the operational definition of 'the degree of groupness' existing at the time of the coding.

What SAVI enabled me to do was to frame 'interdependence of parts' in terms of communication behavior. Up until then, I had defined 'parts' as clusters of behavior that defined a person's role. With the development of SAVI, I could demonstrate the relationship between patterns of behavior and the roles that people played in the group. By using SAVI data, I could also define the patterns that identified the different stages in the development of the group and discriminate the group communication pattern from the individual patterns. Thus, being able to operationally define group as an interdependence of parts was a major step toward demonstrating the isomorphy between the individual and the group as living human systems – whose similarity in structure and function could be illustrated by the SAVI data.

Theoretical Foundations of SAVI

We built SAVI from theory and SAVI then enabled us to test our hypothesis about the problems inherent in the process of communication. Using SAVI data made it possible to test the hypothesis that to the extent 'noise' in communication is reduced, so information related to solving the problems will be used to approach, rather than avoid, the problems that have to be solved by groups and individuals.

Coding SAVI categories into a frequency matrix results in recognizable patterns of communication that can be used to predict the probability of change occurring for the system generating the patterns. This has then enabled us to test the hypothesis that reducing the restraining force of noise in the communications between, among and within human systems increases the strength of the vector toward the inherent goals of survival, development and transformation.[5]

The assumptions basic to SAVI were built from the work of several theorists. The SAVI construct of approach and avoidance has two derivations – Lewin's force field and the work of Howard and Scott. Lewin perceived approach and avoidance forces as a diagnosis of the system equilibrium in relationship to implicit and explicit goals. Howard and Scott introduced the important concept that approach and avoidance relate implicitly to the overall goal and explicitly to the management of the problems that are encountered on the path to goal. This supported an important extra dimension in our thinking: before communication can address the explicit goal, the problems in the communication must first be addressed. In other words, how to communicate comes before what to communicate (Agazarian 1968).

In defining his life space as (the map of) a person's perceptions of their environment, Lewin hypothesized that to know the life space map was to be able to predict behavior. Reciprocally, to observe behavior is to infer the life space map. Just as Lewin's life space is a map of observable behaviors from which predictions can be made, so SAVI provides a map of verbal behavior from which predictions can be made (Agazarian 1986a). SAVI-generated grids can serve as a map upon which to plot the course of change by deliberately modifying avoidance communication behavior and introducing or reinforcing approach behavior.

Shannon and Weaver (1964), in their information theory, postulated an inverse relationship between 'noise' or entropic behavior (defined as ambiguity, contradiction and redundancy) in the communication channel and the probability that the information in the communication will be transferred. In SAVI language, we call these noisy, entropic behaviors 'avoidance' behaviors because they move away from the direction of solving the problems inherent in the communication process. Avoidance behaviors both increase the noise

5   This is based on the several assumptions, first group-as-a-whole dynamics are a function of subgroup interactions; and subgroup interactions are a function of group member interactions. We also see the primary developmental task of a group as developing a problem solving communication pattern; this is developed until the potential for information transfer and resolution of problems is so low, that regardless of the content, the group will remain fixated and unlikely to work' (Simon and Agazarian 2000).

problem within the communication process and also decrease the probability that the information in the communication will be transferred from sender to receiver. The reverse is true of the behaviors we call 'approach'.

In identifying avoidance behaviors we used Gibb's (1961) criteria for defensive behaviors and his discriminations between description and opinion and Shannon and Weaver's 'noise'. For our own formulation of ambiguity and/or contradiction between affect and content we built on Raven and Rietsama (1957) who had compared the topic information and the feeling content of a message, finding that the lower the consonance in the two aspects of a communication, the greater the tension and the more avoidance behaviors took precedence over problem-solving activities. The criteria for approach behaviors was 'demonstrated congruence between the affect and content components in the verbal behavior' (when the words match the music), or 'evidence that a transfer of information has taken place', as, for example, an 'answer' to a question (Agazarian 1969a).

By using ambiguity, redundancy and contradiction between the two information components in a communication (personal and factual) as theoretical criteria for SAVI coding, the SAVI generated matrix of communication is then also an operational definition of the Information Theory hypothesis, that noise in the communication channel reduces the potential that the information contained in the communication will be transferred. The hypothesis generated by the Theory of Stress is that all human behavior can be seen as either approaching or avoiding the problems (that lie on the path to the goal). Approach and avoidance behavior is defined by SAVI in terms of the probability that a specified class of behaviors will predominantly transfer noise (avoidant behavior) or information (approach behavior). Avoidance and approach behaviors are defined as isomorphic to the driving and restraining forces of a Lewinian force field. Thus SAVI categories are also used to define the force field of driving and restraining forces in communication as they relate to the goals of survival, development and transformation postulated by a Theory of Living Human Systems.

Using SAVI

Anita and I were very excited as we began using SAVI. I was teaching in the Group Dynamics Department as a teaching fellow at this time and could rely on at least four classes a year in which both to demonstrate group dynamics and collect data for SAVI analysis. Anita and I developed a series of designs. In one design, I applied Lewin, Lippitt and White's findings on leadership (1939) by changing my style of leadership as I led a volunteer group from my class. We not only replicated their study, but also demonstrated how the communication patterns varied, not only from style to style, but also in sequence: thus, for example, when a laissez-faire group began the sequence, it went into flight, whereas when a laissez-faire group followed an autocratic group, it went directly into fight.

In another design, I led a volunteer group of the class through six, ten-minute sections with a two-minute break in between. Miraculously, the group demonstrated the behavioral characteristics of the phases of group development, some groups reaching the scapegoating of the leader, other groups reaching the phase of intimacy and other groups remaining fixated in flight or fight. From this we were able to generate the SAVI patterns for flight, fight and the barometric event, as shown in Figures 2.4, 2.5 and 2.6. Later I was to take the SAVI pattern of a group and compare the individual patterns in relationship to the group pattern (Figure 2.7, p.57).

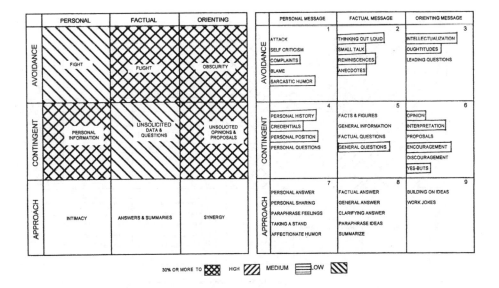

Figure 2.4 Flight

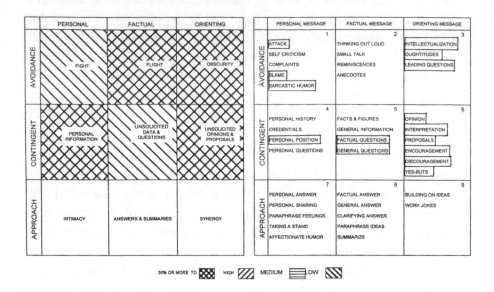

Figure 2.5 Fight

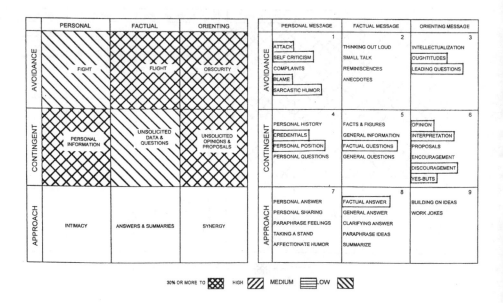

Figure 2.6 Barometric event

EXTENDED GROUP COMMUNICATION

		AVOIDANCE			CONTINGENT			APPROACH		
		1	2	3	4	5	6	7	8	9
AVOIDANCE	1	X	X							
	2									
	3	X		X		X	X			
CONTINGENT	4									
	5			X		X	X		X	
	6	X		X		X	X			
APPROACH	7									
	8					X			X	
	9									

OUTPUT FROM GROUP INPUT TO INDIVIDUAL

		AVOIDANCE			CONTINGENT			APPROACH		
		1	2	3	4	5	6	7	8	9
AVOIDANCE	1	X								
	2									
	3									
CONTINGENT	4									
	5									
	6									
APPROACH	7									
	8									
	9									

OUTPUT FROM INDIVIDUAL INPUT TO GROUP

		AVOIDANCE			CONTINGENT			APPROACH		
		1	2	3	4	5	6	7	8	9
AVOIDANCE	1			X						
	2									
	3									
CONTINGENT	4									
	5									
	6									
APPROACH	7									
	8									
	9									

EXTENDED INDIVIDUAL COMMUNICATION

		AVOIDANCE			CONTINGENT			APPROACH		
		1	2	3	4	5	6	7	8	9
AVOIDANCE	1	X		X						
	2									
	3	X		X						
CONTINGENT	4									
	5					X	X			
	6					X	X			
APPROACH	7									
	8									
	9									

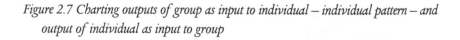

Figure 2.7 Charting outputs of group as input to individual – individual pattern – and output of individual as input to group

In one very interesting study, I first coded the entire group, and then took four sections, one from the middle ten minutes of each quartile, and compared the individual patterns to the group pattern to see what effect different individuals' patterns of communication might have on the overall group pattern. My first surprise was that in every case the section from each quartile mirrored the group-as-a-whole pattern (Figure 2.7, p.57).

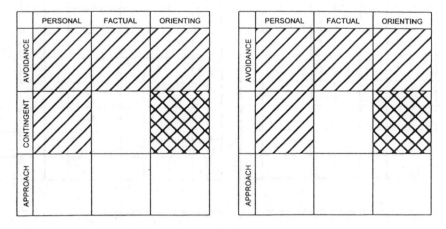

SAVI PATTERN

SECTION OF GROUP   WHOLE SESSION OF GROUP

	PERSONAL	FACTUAL	ORIENTING
AVOIDANCE	17	15	10
CONTINGENT	15	3	32
APPROACH	1	4	2

	PERSONAL	FACTUAL	ORIENTING
AVOIDANCE	16	14	11
CONTINGENT	17	3	32
APPROACH	1	5	2

PERCENTAGE MATRICES

Figure 2.8 Contrast of the SAVI pattern of the psychotherapy group section with the whole session of the group

My second, even greater, surprise, was that though individual patterns changed in each quartile, they changed in such a way that the group pattern was stabilized. Even, for example, in one quartile where, when the group communication pattern gave brief evidence of 'work', the therapist re-equilibrated the group into flight/fight (Figure 2.9, p.60).

There is another way of observing the communication process as it is displayed by SAVI and that is in a time-sequence graph (referred to informally as 'taking a talk for a walk'). A SAVI graph looks rather like a musical score, and from it can be read, not only whether the words match the music, but exactly how and in what way the information flow is maintained and monitored in the direction of approach or avoidance (Figure 2.10, p.61).

This lent strong support to my idea that the group dynamics determined what individual dynamics were manifested in a group in other words, as I later understood, who one can be in a group has more to do with the group than with oneself. One cannot take responsibility for the effect on a group of what one says in the group, in that the group may respond to the same communication in one way at one time and another way at another time. At the same time, one is completely responsible for what one does not say in a group, in that the group does not have the opportunity of addressing the information. I was certainly on my way to a group-as-a-whole view.

It was not until 1971 that I used SAVI as a major change variable in my consultation to Devereux Schools for Children. In my consultation to the staff on the adolescent unit, I taught the staff the SAVI patterns for noise-free communications: a decrease in jargon and critical language, cross-purpose talk, generalizations, rhetorical and vague questions and an increase in their ability to discriminate opinion from description. In fact, 'avoidance' communications did decrease. It was quite exciting to demonstrate that we had operationally defined the theory[6] in a way that easily translated into behavior and that the constructs could be related to specific behavioral responses on the unit. For instance, one of the goals of the unit was to encourage checking reality with others and to create an environment that

6   In my dissertation (Agazarian 1968), I discuss the conceptualization of the communication problem as of a different order and as primary compared to the other problems studied in groups. The detailed theoretical rationale for the work I did with Devereux is in the paper 'SAVI Applied to Staff Training in the Milieu' (Agazarian 1972).

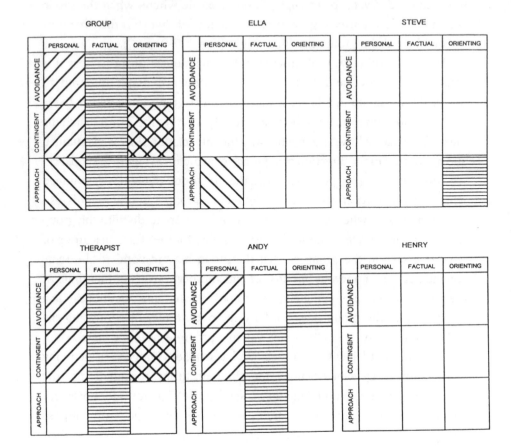

Figure 2.9 Group-as-a-whole and individual SAVI communication patterns, showing therapist re-establishing group norm after fight/flight

encouraged the adolescents to become aware of their maladaptive responses. To this end, the more the communication was non-ambiguous and non-contradictory, the more the environment would be likely to encourage experimentation with adaptive responses and getting feedback.

Ambiguity and contradiction introduce dissonance and the reactions that develop in response to the dissonance. These reactions can go one of two ways: towards reality testing and collecting reality information or a flight

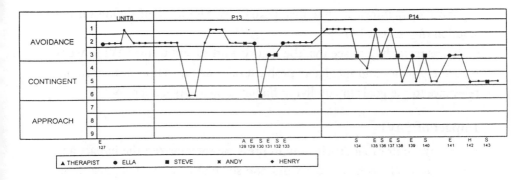

Unit 8 starts with Ella talking: here she is complaining (the accusative aggression of the pas-
sive-aggressive) telling a long story about telephoning her father. Someone coughs, Steve
makes a half-joking interpretation (130) 'Hey, your father went into therapy', gets dis-
counted ('My father's never been in therapy in his life'), tries again to interrupt (132) but
Ella pre-empts him and continues with her story, shifting back into complaining until
Steve again interrupts (134). As this is the first serious power struggle, we might take a
close look: Steve interrupts with 'I have a suggestion'. Ella won't be interrupted. Steve tries
again, 'Do you want a suggestion?' (136). Ella continues as if he has said nothing. Steve
interrupts a third time, 'Seriously, call them collect, I mean, seriously.' (He's tried twice to
negotiate a proposal, twice been turned down. The probability that he will get heard is
low.) He doesn't. Ella says, 'They didn't call me collect, my brother called me collect
(139). Steve, 'Well, you can call your brother collect and let him take the message.' Ella, 'I
did that, and he didn't accept the call (141). The group laugh, 'It's almost like a joke', 'It's
almost funny.' (Ella at this point has her head in her hands.) Communication has failed and
Ella takes off back into complaining.

Figure 2.10 SAVI time-sequence graph

into wishes or fears. The higher the degree of congruence in staff
interactions, the less the ambiguity, the less dissonance, the more likely the
task of reality testing will be accomplished.

In collaboration with the staff, the overall goals for the adolescent unit
were defined as moving the students from: fantasy to reality, irresponsibility
to responsibility and dependence to independence. I then operationally

defined the goals in terms of verbal behaviors: checking perceptions; differentiating data based on wishes or fears from descriptions of what is happening; collecting information; formulating questions and facilitating answers – in short, using the behaviors that facilitate the transfer and organization of information so that it can be used for problem definition and solution (Agazarian 1972).

It was rewarding to see that the theory worked and using SAVI to work with the primary and inevitable problem of communication has enormous relevance to the goals in any living human system (Agazarian 1972).

Impact of SAVI

In an early draft of an article now in press we summarized the impact and usefulness SAVI has had in our work and some of its current applications.[7]

Most theories of group assume that the underlying dynamics of the group-as-a-whole are reflected in the communication patterns of the group. As SAVI is a content-free observation system, it can be used to collect information about any model of group psychotherapy.

SAVI analysis is of verbal communication. Change in communication patterns can be charted at any system level, within, between and among the systems of members, subgroups or the group-as-a-whole.

The advantage of developing a common definition for the dynamics of both the group-as-a-whole and its members is that research can become generalizable between different theories of group. For both Anita and me, SAVI was designed to fill the need for a tool that:

- focused on communication as a system output rather than as a characteristic of an individual;

- allowed examination of group properties rather than just individual properties;

- allowed for a definition of group in terms of its potential communication resources rather than as a collection of discrete individuals.

7   The passages that follow are cut from several earlier versions of an article recently published (Simon and Agazarian 2000).

We also used SAVI to predict, from the SAVI grid communication pattern, the probability for the transfer of information. In this, we used SAVI both as a diagnostic of the potential for therapeutic change, a measure of therapeutic change and also as a map for how to increase the probability for therapeutic change.

Possibly the most important benefit that SAVI has brought to us is its use as an informal guide to our own and others' leadership behavior in a group. This informal research has had a significant influence, in clarifying our own understanding of the dynamics of the phases of development in groups, the recognition of the clusters of verbal behaviors that characterize them and the leadership communications that contribute to modifying defenses that would otherwise fixate the group in a phase.

It has also been invaluable for making discriminations between different styles of communication in otherwise similar patterns, for example, between the group-as-a-whole communication patterns to deviant that result in creating the identified patient from those that create the scapegoat (Agazarian 1992c).

Later, using SAVI enabled me to formulate the theory of living human systems in operational definitions in the hierarchy of defense modification and to select specific sets of verbal behaviors that translate the overall methods into the techniques for practice (Agazarian 1997). For example, the SAVI-generated matrix of communication patterns was specifically used to adapt the techniques of defense analysis practiced in Short Term Dynamic Psychotherapy (Davanloo 1987) into the techniques for systems-centered defense modification (see Chapter 5). Therapist interpretative opinions, for example, were replaced by data – from the 'opinion' (square 6) to 'description' (square five). Thus the goals of the therapeutic communications remained unchanged, while the route of the 'path to goal' was changed after charting it on a SAVI map to make it compatible with the systems-centered values of legitimizing, depathologizing and normalizing the human dynamics in group and individual therapy.

Finally, without having SAVI as a method for discriminating between different communication patterns, it is unlikely that we would have been able to define the communications that characterize each phase of group development as the context which determines which defenses can be modified and which defenses cannot. (For example, attempting to modify defenses against the retaliatory impulse in the phase of flight increases rather than decreases flight defenses, whereas modifying them in the fight phase successfully undoes depression and releases energy for exploring the impulse to scapegoat.) Having made these discriminations, it was a relatively simple matter to define the restraining forces that, when modified, release the driving forces in the group (and its individual members) towards the goals of group development. It was being able to define so clearly the sequence of these restraining forces in the context of each phase and subphase of group development that resulted in developing the hierarchy of defense modification for systems-centered practice (see Chapter 6).

For myself, developing the theory behind SAVI and using the SAVI system to collect data both formally and informally has had a significant impact on my ability to think isomorphically about the different system levels in groups. Practically, SAVI has a unique potential for enabling the input and output communications between systems to be observed (like the systems of member, subgroup and group-as-a-whole) while simultaneously making it possible to identify the communication patterns that are specific to each system level involved.

For Anita, a priority has been to bring the process of research into clinical practice by introducing a tool which can be used by both therapists and clients. She has tried various ways of introducing the SAVI-generated communication matrix to clients as a map upon which they can trace what happens in their relationships with themselves and others as they try different strategies. For example, she redefined the categories of avoidance as 'red light' behaviors and the categories of approach as 'green light' behaviors. This was almost instantly successful, both in her therapy sessions and in outside settings.

One of the more exciting things that we have discovered is that people intuitively know the SAVI grid – when asked to generate communication within the nine squares, they spontaneously develop a system sufficiently close to ours to be equivalent. What is more, people intuitively know the pattern of 'the worst' communicator – but are not so clear about the 'best'. Interestingly enough, we discovered that people quite easily recognize the difference between how they are communicating and what they are communicating. However, although they intuitively 'know' which categories give them trouble, they do not know which categories get them out of trouble. Training in the underlying theory of non-defensive (low noise) communication allows them to learn how to both recognize 'noisy' communications and how to reduce them.

SAVI Communication Patterns: Identified Patient and Scapegoat

One last example of using SAVI illustrates the range of its versatility. In 1992, I participated in a panel at the American Group Psychotherapy Association's Conference where I was one of three panelists discussing a videotape of Irv Yalom's interpersonal approach to group therapy (Agazarian 1992c). My task was to compare Dr Yalom's interpersonal approach (Yalom 1995) to a group-as-a-whole, systems-centered approach.

I did a SAVI analysis of the communication pattern in each of the two sections of tape to compare the individual communication patterns against the group matrix. Dr Yalom's interpersonal approach lends itself particularly well to analyzing the communication patterns to deviant as the style itself encourages the group to give feedback to a series of elected deviants. Using a SAVI analysis, I concluded that in both tapes the basic communication pattern was indeed that of 'communication to deviant': in the first tape it was to the identified patient; in the second tape it was to the scapegoat. I discussed these findings on the panel:

The identified patient

Watching Dr. Yalom's first tape, I see through my systems eyes a group that has managed its conflict by splitting and disowning one half of it and now having the problem of how to reorganize.

Volunteering an identified patient to the therapists to treat gives the group-as-a-whole a common focus, as well as a container for the dependency that was split off at the beginning of the group. Alice is a well-chosen identified patient. Like the group's dependency she is 'on the outside looking in,' quiet, and afraid of what others will think, anxious to please, and full of good, if unrealistic wishes, as she talks of bringing coffee and cake for the group. The therapists accept the group offering of Alice as an identified patient and by asking her if she wants to work on how she is 'on the outside looking in, both in her life and in the group.'

The communication pattern derived from a 'who speaks to whom' chart tells the story: of the next 18 communications, 8 (45%) are directed to Alice and 7 (38%) are Alice's responses to the group. The remaining 3 (16%) communications, though not directly engaging Alice, were related to Alice: Allan defending Alice from Bob, Bob attacking Allan, and the therapist re-directing the attention back to Alice.

Through my systems-centered eyes what happens next is interesting, in that when the therapist asks Alice if she wants to work on how she is 'on the outside looking in,' Alice refuses! 'Yes,' she says, 'but not today!' Immediately, the group volunteers another member to the therapist for the role of identified patient: 'I was a little concerned about Kathy...' However, Kathy also avoids the invitation. The possibility that the group is making a transition from the identified patient role (flight phase) to the scapegoat role (the fight phase) is reinforced when Kathy offers the group a scapegoating target instead, by volunteering the men. 'Well, I don't want to offend anyone but I have to be truthful – I was a little bit put out by the men in the group. Especially you two guys'. 'Which two?' asks Dr. Yalom, reinforcing the group direction. There is an immediate, enthusiastic sub-grouping by Darlene, Betty and Kathy around displeasure with the men: 'I'm put out by the men'...'top dog or something'...'I feel competition in here'...'don't feel so safe right now.' With this transition, the group has crossed the boundary from the flight phase (in which the identified patient carries the group yearning to be 'cured' by the therapist) to the fight phase (in which the group scapegoats members as a preliminary step to scapegoating the therapist).

In Dr. Yalom's second episode this communication to deviant pattern is repeated, only this time with a scapegoat (Dan) instead of an identified patient (Alice).

The scapegoat

When the communication pattern is analyzed by SAVI, it is clearly typical of the fight phase, so it is no surprise that every communication provokes more fight: 'You jumped right in'...'You're taking it wrong'...'You always have the last word'...'What were you trying to prove?'... This is a traditional scapegoating; 43 per cent of the work is being done in 'attack,' of which the female subgroup contributes 68 per cent in 'direct attack' and 'indirect blame' and the attacked subgroup (two of the men) respond with 31 per cent in self-defense.

Contrasting the SAVI patterns of identified patient and scapegoat

Once the communication pattern to deviant is established, the next question is, what kind of deviant? Using the SAVI analysis of verbal behavior, it is relatively easy to tell whether the deviant is an identified patient or a scapegoat. For example, a pattern made up of 'questions' from the group and 'personal information' from the deviant would infer an identified patient. This was the pattern we saw in the episode with Alice in the first tape, where 89 per cent of the group communication was to or about Alice; with all the questions coming from the group and all the personal information coming from Alice.

In Dan's case, 27 per cent of the group communication was in fight – 18 per cent of which was group 'attack' and 'blame,' and 64 per cent of which was Dan's response in 'self-defense' and 'complain.' This data shows a group attack with the scapegoat on the run. It is interesting to note that so strong is group influence on individual communication patterns, that 'coffee and cake' Alice (whose first pattern was personal and responsive) contributes 20 per cent to the group's attack! (Agazarian 1992c, pp.2–4)

Group life is frustrating, and frustration makes people irritable, tense and anxious. Therefore, learning how to contain the energy in frustration, rather than discharging it defensively, is an important task in a therapy group. The goal in systems groups is to learn to manage frustration energy, rather than to discharge it in irritable blaming and complaining, anxious worrying, suspicious or depressing thoughts, or tension and psychosomatic symptoms. When frustrated feelings are sidetracked into symptoms, the symptoms in turn generate a secondary set of feelings. For example, the Dan session was frustrating, and the irritability engendered by the frustration was acted out in scapegoating which then generated a secondary set of feelings elicited by the acting out. I framed this idea of contagion with the audience who had watched the videotape of the episodes we discussed above, and asked them:

When watching the episode with Dan just now, I wonder how many of you found yourselves becoming frustrated or irritable with Dan, or perhaps with the group or perhaps even with the therapists? There is a high probability that scapegoating is contagious. Complaining elicits more complaining, blaming elicits more blaming, attack and self-defense elicits more attack/self-defense.

In the episode with Dan, a systems therapist would make the group conscious of the way it had unconsciously split the two sides of a conflict – the group giving solutions and blaming, Dan resisting solutions and complaining. By owning and exploring both sides of Dan's role instead of scapegoating it, the members of the group can join whichever of the two subgroups has more salience for them. With subgroup exploration, it is more than probable that the group would discover that the stubborn fight against everyone and everything is the attempt to save the essential self. It is through a group level exploration that the group makes stubbornness ego-alien, as the members of the subgroups recognize that stubbornness costs them, not only their relationship with others but also their relationship with themselves. It seems to me that the group's energy would have been better spent exploring this group issue rather than playing it out in the kind of Mexican standoff that is familiar to everyone from the age of two-and-a-half.

In his discussion at the end of the presentation, Dr. Yalom talked of encouraging group autonomy. I would very much agree with his goal. My difference with his interpersonal therapy is not in goals, but method. In a systems therapy group, no inter-member feedback would be attempted until the group had learned to explore their own impulses with other members of a subgroup instead of acting them out by interpreting each other's motives and behavior. Thus, Alice would have had a subgroup exploring the impulse to please the group, Darlene, Betty and Kathy would explore their impulse to scapegoat men, and Dan would have worked on one side of the group conflict: the impulse to scapegoat and the impulse to volunteer to be scapegoated.

There are several hypotheses underlying the systems approach to influencing a therapy group. One is that *how* people talk to each other and to themselves is more important to the outcome of therapy than *what* they talk about.[8] A second is that how people communicate determines the potential in the group for solving the different problems that come between it and its goals. A third is that a problem-solving communication pattern in the group-as-a-whole increases the group's ability to discriminate and integrate differences and that systems development and transformation occurs through the integration of different communications. Differences, however, are frustrating and cause conflicts in

8   This led to the systems-centered hypothesis that more therapy will take place if members use 'exploring' language rather than 'explaining' language.

integration. Systems tend to manage differences by splitting them off and projecting them into containing subsystems. (Agazarian 1992c, pp.7–8)

For this reason, systems therapists discourage a group from splitting off and projecting frustrating differences into an identified patient or scapegoat. Instead, members are encouraged to take back their projections, and to explore the inner experiences of conflict. In a systems group, the two sides of a conflict are deliberately contained in the group-as-a-whole, split between two explicitly working subgroups, instead of worked on alone by the individual member. This method deliberately uses subgrouping as a containing function for the projective identifications that occur at all levels of group: the member, the subgroup and the group-as-a-whole. (See Chapters 5 and 6.)

CHAPTER 3

Second Theory: Theory of the Invisible Group
Bridge Construct of Role Between the Individual and the Group

After five years in community mental health I 'burnt out' (before we called it that) from a collision between my ideals and reality which left me irritable, restless, unable to see any contributions I had made and prone to illness.

'If one can't do, then one can teach!' I returned to the Philadelphia Mental Health Clinic as Director of the Group Program, joined Research for Better Schools as a consultant, began at Devereux School for Children as a once-a-week consultant to the adolescent unit and started in private practice by buying a condominium office in Philadelphia.

Devereux

At Devereux I had my most explicit confrontation between my psychodynamic and group dynamic orientations. For example, the first problem presented to me was that the children did not speak up at the weekly meetings with their teachers, housemothers, phys-ed instructors and psychologists. The meeting was held in the gym and each group gathered together at separate ends of the gym and looked at each other. It seemed to me that the problem was simple. The groups were too far apart to hear each other. I happily reported this and was sternly told, 'Don't give us geography, we want to understand the psychodynamics!'

This began two years of some important successes and important failures. Most importantly, however hard I tried, I failed to communicate what was so clear to me: that the group itself had dynamics that influenced the behavior of its members. I warned the unit that if the children were not involved in the issues around drugs, they would not co-operate with the staff. I cautioned one of our most empathic psychologists that if he were to take over a unit that had been managed in a high authoritarian style, he would have to maintain the pre-existing structure, and introduce his more humane approaches very gradually. I attempted to import the idea that scapegoating on the unit and among the staff members was a group phenomenon that was a response to deviance, and that deviance often contained resources which the group needed. I warned senior staff that there was a norm, that one way to achieve status was through a heart attack – a norm that was consistently reinforced by the emotional and financial rewards offered the heart-attack victim. All of my warnings were in vain and I helplessly watched as the events happened in the way that I had tried so hard to prevent. I was confronted with the continuing challenge of how to communicate formally the interdependence between the dynamics of the individual and the group.

In contrast, my work with the interns, the children and with the individual staff members was rewarding and successful. Particularly with the interns, there seemed to be an intuitive grasp of the principles that I was introducing – and an interest in the less familiar concepts of group structure, goals and cohesiveness. I wrote many short pieces for the seminars that I gave every week and, without being aware of it, I was laying the foundation for the book I started writing about five years later (Agazarian and Peters 1981).

During this time at Devereux, I reluctantly learned that it was not necessary for members in a change process to understand the concepts that governed it and that what mattered was not the theory but whether or not it was useful in practice. (This was, and continues to be, a very painful reality for me!) Fortunately and unfortunately, the results of my consultation with the adolescent milieu unit were a great deal more successful than my ability to communicate the concepts behind the work.

Two years later, when my consultancy ended, I was still coming to understand that my success in practice was not necessarily reflected in my communications to upper management. By that time, the director who had hired me had died (sadly, of a heart attack) and a new, three-person management team was in place, introducing 'The New Model'. In my 70-page report to this new 'triumvirate', I wrote:

There are some crucial differences in conceptualizing change from the framework of group dynamics. As these differences may not be familiar to organizational administrators, the following paragraphs attempt to make explicit some of the principles underlying the change strategy that I developed for the Adolescent Unit.

The most usual approach to organizational change is to influence individuals' dynamics with the expectation that this will change the organization's output. In contrast is the approach that influences, not the individuals in the group, but the norms of the group (group norms govern the kind of behavior that is acceptable or unacceptable in a group). The latter is the approach that I use in my work at Devereux, with the expectation that changes in individual, goal-oriented behavior occur as a consequence of effective norm changing. (Agazarian 1970, pp.2–3))

I attempted to spell this out in my report summary:

By June of 1970, the following is an assessment of changes in particular groups in the Hall-Manor unit. The group of people who attended the seminar to the end are able to produce the behaviors of a consensually valid group in setting goals and reaching them.

The management team have changed their norms of behavior to include both task and maintenance interactions, have developed and used mechanisms for checking out contradictions and for defining generalizations at the data level, and are experimenting with models for decision-making that would be pertinent to specific demands of the unit.

The group of teachers have engaged in participatory problem solving, and have defined a set of problems they considered relevant to their job performance, and formulated problem solutions that would be available for implementation in the following year.

The recreation staff continue to be characterized by implicit subgroup function, and have two contradictory frames of reference within which to approach their work. One frame of reference implies concern with implementing 'the new model' and the other frame of reference implies concern with abandoning 'the old model.' Some specific problems relevant to their job function have been identified, but no specific problem-solving steps have been defined for the following year.

The houseparent staff made public the conflict between feeling frustrated at things they felt helpless to change, and the time and energy investment that change would demand. Problems relevant in their job have been identified, one problem solution has emerged but not been implemented, and no specific change steps are outlined for next year.

It appears that at the management level, and in the seminar, significant changes have occurred in the communication pattern, communication behavior and content, and some changes in the decision-making pattern. This was a step, therefore, in the overall strategy goal of influencing the management group to serve as a microcosm from which the behaviors could be modeled and generalized to the rest of the subgroups in the unit.

At the subgroup level of the teaching and recreation and houseparent groups, some changes occurred along some variables in some groups, but no significant change was achieved in clarifying the change channels between subgroups or between subgroups and the management group.

Thus, the level of ambiguity, redundancy and contradiction appears to be reduced within some groups, but this change is not reflected in the communication channels between groups. Therefore the processing of information relevant to the achievement of the goals of Hall-Manor remain a priority concern. (Agazarian 1970, pp.53–54)

My final recommendation to the 'New Model' management was that 'the strategy of change be implemented at a more consistent change level, or reduced to focus on a more circumscribed and more achievable goal level.' My contract with Devereux was not renewed. I never knew whether the deciding factor was the change in management or whether my change goals had been too ambitious, and the actual changes were too different from the Devereux management's norms to be integrated.

Certainly I had overlooked a crucial change factor. At that time, 1970, I was not sufficiently aware how important it is, when introducing change into a subsystem, to do it in such a way that the system that one is changing does not become deviant from the organizational norms in the larger system. Although I was highly aware of monitoring the communication behavior within the subsystems, I failed to pay sufficient attention to the communications between the systems. For example, training middle management to ask direct questions of each other significantly increased their ability to co-operate with each other. Yet when the middle management, quite naturally generalizing, began to question upper management, it created friction in the communication between the two systems. Looking back, it seems so obvious now, but then I was not yet consistently thinking from a systems frame, and I was having difficulty managing to keep in mind all the systems levels at once. It is easy to see, retrospectively, that I had many of the ingredients for understanding the interdependence of systems, but I had not yet integrated what I knew and was not at the time able to formulate the difficulty I was having in implementing what I knew.

The Problem

From then until I finally published *The Visible and Invisible Group* (Agazarian and Peters 1981) I wrestled with the problem of how to address both individual dynamics and group dynamics at the same time:

> Two major issues in the teaching of group psychotherapy are: 1) how to apply different personality theories to the practice of group psychotherapy, and 2) how to differentiate between doing individual therapy in a group setting and doing therapy with the group-as-a-whole. These issues are particularly challenging when teaching group therapists from different theoretical backgrounds who are already experienced as individual therapists. Two important points are relevant here: 1) teaching group dynamics from a multi-dimensional perspective does not conflict with disparate theoretical orientations, like, for example, psychoanalytic, cognitive, interpersonal or behavioral; 2) conceptualizing group and individual levels as separate systems requires the trainee to differentiate between them, and to decide when (not if!) it is therapeutically appropriate to work with the individual in the group setting, when to work with the group-as-a-whole, and when to work with both. (Agazarian 1983b, p.245)

The journey between the work at Devereux and developing what I was to call 'the theory of the invisible group' felt very much like marking theoretical time. I worked in my private practice, gave seminars in group dynamics, gave SAVI workshops with my colleagues Anita Simon and Claudia Byram, wrestled with Lewin's concepts as they applied specifically to groups (see Chapter 4) and, in my mind, like a dog with a bone, incessantly worried at the problem of the interdependence of individual and group dynamics.

The Exploration

I went looking. I went to as many conferences as I could in Group Analysis and Tavistock. I was looking for someone who had already developed the theory that would be either a solution, or the key to a solution. I was continually frustrated that I could not find the umbrella theory I so wanted to discover. Yet the search itself would prove invaluable; my learnings were significant and I developed important lifelong friendships.

I spent time working with Harold Bridger in his workshop at Minster Lovell (a truly beautiful small English village in the Cotswolds whose access was across an old stone bridge only just big enough for a car.) Harold's emphasis was on the importance of clear group goals (Bridger 1946, 1990). Looking at groups through his framework, I understood the chaos that inevitably arises when groups are not clear about their goals. This was revolutionary to me at the time, as I had always waited for the goals to emerge from the group, and specifically avoided 'doing their work for them!' Working with Harold, I took a large step towards seeing group process in a time context which fits with the phases of group development.

During my search I was also lucky enough, while I was in England in 1975, to go to a weekend on Group Analysis with Foulkes himself as the convener. I was charmed and felt in the presence of a master. I was also impressed with the gentleness of Foulkes and the tender affection that those around him communicated. I was not as sure about group analysis – it had no umbrella theory and I missed the clear emphasis on theory and its connection to practice that my Lewinian training with Dave Jenkins had given me. My curiosity however was sufficiently aroused, and I signed up for the five-day group analytic workshop in London the following January. Here I was also lucky as I was assigned to Dr Holmes's group (pronounced Hume), another gentle and supportive conductor. When my turn came for supervision, I discussed the group I was most worried about whose members managed their everyday life with great difficulty, and who I felt sure could get more from group if I knew more about how to make that possible. To my surprise, I was encouraged instead to appreciate how well I was doing with a difficult population and to accept that the members were already doing as well as could be reasonably expected.

On the plane back to the USA I looked out of the window at the clouds and tried to accept the wisdom of 'cutting my coat according to my cloth'. I felt sad and deflated, not liking the reality that I was trying to face. It seemed impossible. I went over again in my mind the Bennis and Shepard phases of development. Was it really true that my group would never integrate aggression and be permanently fixated in the early stages of flight/fight?

The more I tried to accept this, the more I felt the familiar rebellion rising within me.

My first night back in group, I told them that I thought we were not tackling all we could in the group. I went on to say that I knew that the group and I worked well together, but I wondered about the times when group did not go quite so well and whether there were sometimes reactions to those times that the group did not say to me. The group agreed. I asked the members what conditions we could set up so that we could work with the negative as well as the positive feelings in group. The group decided that we should try an experiment for six weeks – but no more than six weeks – that I was not to say a word. During this time, the group would tell me if they needed me to intervene. (Incredibly enough they had laid out the structure for dealing with the authority issue. A. K. Rice training, Tavistock and our own advanced systems-centered training use the structure of a silent, inactive leader as the context for the group to explore issues with authority.)

As the weeks passed, I became more and more impressed by the group's ability to name the things that I did which were not helpful and how they felt about them – and balance those attributes with how they felt when I was helpful. The group appeared to gain confidence and so did I. It was quite clear that the group did not split as I had been warned it might and could in fact recognize and integrate both good and bad into a whole relationship with me and with the group.

Their ability to act autonomously was demonstrated over a real life incident. A member had to leave early one night. We were working in a building which was locked at night and it required a key and a journey through a dark and empty building to let her out. With difficulty I held my tongue while the group worked it out. They went into my office and got the key from my desk. They decided that two of them would go to let the member out so that no one had to come back through the building alone. When they returned, they put the key back and the group continued to work. I was over the moon, both at the group's ability to solve real problems and also at having my conviction validated that if one can find the right conditions, groups can continue to develop their capacity to solve problems.

I presented this in a short paper at the First Conference of the International Association of Group Psychotherapy (IAGP) that was held (miracle of miracles) in Philadelphia in 1976. I was able to host several of the group analytic members and began a close association with many of them that has continued to this day. It was also the beginning of some important professional work for me. I was to publish my first book, *The Visible and Invisible Group*, at the invitation of Malcolm Pines, who was editor of the International Library of Group Psychotherapy and Group Process. I was later honored by an invitation to do the Foulkes lecture in London in 1988. In 1993 I put together an article on the large group from taped interviews with three important group analysts: Pat de Maré, Earl Hopper and Lionel Kreeger (Agazarian and Carter 1993). In 1985 I joined the Board of the IAGP where I worked with Malcolm Pines and Earl Hopper for ten years.

Another avenue of significant training was with Tavistock in England and A.K. Rice in the USA. I learned more about group dynamics than I could have thought possible as I survived weekend after frustrating weekend. Each workshop sharpened the connection between what happened in groups and the group dynamic principles in which I had been immersed at Temple University.

In spite of all that I was learning in the Tavistock and A.K. Rice workshops, I was once again intensely frustrated by their failing either to account for a theory of group development (Bennis and Shepard 1956) or to integrate phase-specific influences on the phenomena that kept erupting, weekend after weekend. From my own framework of group development phases, the chaotic acting out was absolutely predictable and typical of the authority issue subphase, in which preoccupations around power and control, and defiance and compliance in relationship to authority, dominate behavior.

For example, in the A.K. Rice small groups in the 1980s in which I participated, the consultant would walk in the minute the group was to begin, sit down in the chair and remain, with a blank and unresponsive face, looking at the floor or ceiling or walls, avoiding any contact with the individual members, and walk out again the minute time was up. Interpretations were to the group-as-a-whole and focused on the different ways that the group was acting out their conflicts by avoiding them (flight), fighting over them (fight) or pairing up to ward them off. In spite of the fact that the consultants spoke to the group and not to the members, it was impossible for the members not to take what they said personally. Feeling personally chastised led to members feeling regressed, scolded, childlike, infuriated or depressed and to react either with strong feelings of worship or hatred towards the consultant. Inevitably, the members acted these feelings out on each other with extremes of caretaking or scapegoating. These reactions are predicted by Bennis and Shepard (1956), in which they connected the probability of their resolution to the demeanor and personality of the trainer. In their summary of the first phase of group development, they wrote:

> The very word development implies not only movement through time but also a definite order of progression. The group must traverse (subphases 1, 2 and 3) before it can move into Phase II … Blocking and regression occur frequently, and the group may be 'stuck' at a certain phase of development. It would, of course, be difficult to imagine a group remaining long in subphase 3! [exclamation point mine!] – the situation is too tense to be permanent…in short, groups do not inevitably develop through the resolution of the dependence phase to Phase II. This movement may be retarded indefinitely. Obviously much depends upon the trainer's role. In fact the whole dependence modality may be submerged by certain styles of trainer behavior …The personality and training philosophy of the trainer determine his interest in introducing or avoiding explicit consideration of dependency. (Bennis and Shepard 1956, pp.426–427)

Another frustration of mine was the failure of the small-group consultants to re-orient 'bewildered groups' to their goals, a principle fundamental in the research of Lewin and his students in their work on clarifying the path to goal (Raven and Rietsema 1957) and whose effect Harold Bridger had not only demonstrated in his clinical work but specifically emphasized in the conferences that he directed.

The chaotic acting out that characterized the small group work in these training events was easily escalated in the institutional event, in which all the members of the conference came together to develop an institution. These institutional events were built into both the weekend and the ten-day conferences. In the weekends, the chaos was somewhat contained by time – there was not the time to develop the full panic and irrationality that characterized the longer conferences. In my first conference, before I understood how serious were the implications of the irrational behavior that I found so amusing, I had the whole 50 members of the conference running in a panic from one end of the building to the other, simply by saying to the running members who were leading the pack that the 'meeting with the staff' had been changed to room X, and then telling the members at the tail that it had been changed back to room Y.

By the time I attended the ten-day conference, I no longer considered any aspect of the irrationality amusing. The structure of the conference was tight in its boundaries of time and place. The consistent absence of personal support from the staff promoted strong competitive cliques and regressive and stereotype responses. In the ten-day conference, not as infrequently as one would wish, a member would have a psychotic episode (perhaps indeed elected by the group to contain the chaos). For example, in the conference I attended, the designated member erupted in the large group and fled from the building pursued by the 'psychiatrist' subgroup and the 'psychologist' subgroup, who caught him on the lawn in front of the large group room windows and literally fought over him, one group pulling him by one arm and the other group pulling him by the other. In my own panic I ran 'to the authorities' attempting to explain how serious the situation was – only to be met with my own opportunity to learn that the facts that I was endeavoring to communicate were drowned out by my emotion and I failed in my attempt to influence. (This lesson had great ramifications when I later developed the hierarchy of defense modification and understood that words connected to emotional intelligence have much greater impact than words discharging uncontained emotion.)

This was not the only benefit in my own experience. The next morning, as I went out to jog around the lake, the member who had erupted the day before literally fell into my arms. I tucked him in, buttoned him up, persuaded him to sit on the steps with me and kept repeating that he did not have to be afraid of the volcano erupting, as it had already erupted and the worst was over. It was then that I caught sight of a staff member and calmly(!) called him over, so that he could see for himself how serious the problem was. He told me later that his heart sank (this was his first conference as staff) knowing that he would not be able to remain uninvolved. He told me to go off and run and I thankfully left the problem in his hands. It was thus that A.K. Rice brought me into contact with Ken Eisold who has remained a good friend over the years and whose innovations in Tavistock were quite exciting to me. As a staff member in Ken's conferences, I learned how to work with other staff so that we could take on our role responsibility to support our conference director's connection to the organizational goals. This was another learning that had great impact on my work in the future when I found myself involved in developing an organization. Today, Ken consults to our developing organization, the Systems-Centered® Training Institute.

Overwhelming as the Tavistock conference experiences sometimes were, it was clear to me that once I had experienced the underlying dynamics of groups and individuals with the intensity that they manifested in the conferences I would never again be in doubt of their existence, nor take them lightly. For example, in the ten-day Tavistock conference in Leicester, England, I was never again to doubt that without insight one was doomed to repeat one's past. I not only relived many aspects of my schooldays (including the biting cold at night and the convent food), but also responded with the same frustrated and self-defeating behavior. From this experience, I became intensely involved in discovering how to develop group norms which, rather than eliciting past behavior, enabled responses appropriate to the present, so that the tendency to repeat old role relationships could be experienced and explored rather than acted out.

This was another experience that guided me later into formulating a major technique in the development of the hierarchy of defense modification: the discrimination between when going to the past is a flight from look-alike conflicts in present and when going to the past is in the service of getting information to solve the problems of the present. As I was to discover, redirecting energy from the past back into the present is a simple matter of how the question is framed. 'How is the present different from the past?' undoes the flight from the present, whereas 'How is the present similar to your past?' directs attention away from the present and into the past.

I continued in a love–hate relationship to Tavistock. I was enormously frustrated with what I considered the poverty of theory on the one hand, yet could imagine no better training experience in group dynamics. In other words, while I did not doubt Tavistock's effectiveness, I was unwittingly challenging the tenets of its laboratory training. I addressed the background of Tavistock in the paper I presented as a guest lecturer to Harvard Medical School, 'Bion, the Tavistock Method and the Group-as-a-whole' (Agazarian 1987a):

My charter with you today is to talk to you about the group-as-a-whole perspective as it is grounded in the Bion–Tavistock approach. I shall therefore start by discussing the contributions of Bion and Tavistock to group theory, practice and training [and] continue with the model derived from my own theory (called the theory of the invisible group) ... Bion (1959, 1985) first started to work with groups during World War II as director of the rehabilitation center of a military psychiatric hospital. It was the ideas that he began to develop there, and later took to the Tavistock clinic, that served as the foundation of what developed into the Tavistock approach. Bion perceived groups, not in terms of individuals, but as a discrete entity which he called 'the group.' One thing that was quite clear to him was that while people in groups 'claimed' to be working, as a group they often behaved in ways that were quite antithetical to work. It also appeared to him that the individuals in the group appeared quite bewildered by the experience, as if they were helplessly in the grip of forces that they could not account for, and that Bion himself could not attribute simply to individual unconscious motivation. It was thus that Bion came to formulate assumptions about the dynamics of the group-as-a-whole.

Bion observed that when the energy of the group was directed in ways that seemed to be antithetical to work, the behavior was in fact not random, but appeared to be organized and directional. It appeared to be purposeful. He made assumptions that the non-work behavior that he observed was in fact a defensive organization at the group level. He asked himself what the group was defending itself from, and postulated that the group had a terrifying chaotic chore. These group level defenses appeared to him to take identifiable forms: Group Dependency, in which the group attempts to create someone, usually the group leader, as a savior, whose goodness and wisdom would protect, nurture and save it. Group Flight–Fight, in which an evil enemy was created who must either be attacked and annihilated, or avoided and placated. Group Pairing, in which the group treated two of its members as the chosen couple whose union would result in the birth of a messianic rescue in the form of some solution to the group's helplessness and hopelessness. He called these three defensive solutions Basic Assumption Cultures: Dependency, Fight–Flight and Pairing. When Bion worked with groups, it was to these group level issues that he addressed himself, rather than to the issues of the individual.

The Tavistock method, as applied for some years following Bion's formulation, was used to treat psychotherapy patients in groups with the therapist paying attention to the dynamics of the group-as-a-whole. Parenthetically, let me stress here that the pure 'Tavistock method' has not generally worked well as a method for conducting psychotherapy groups, but perhaps not for the reasons given. The narcissistic pain engendered in patients by the pure group-as-a-whole interpretations leaves them feeling diminished and dehumanized (Malan *et al.* 1976). In my experience, however, even a minor modification like making supportive eye contact with individual patients changed the outcome for group patients. Adding group-as-a-whole interventions to individual interpretations resulted in a very powerful additional dimension to the practice of group psychotherapy and has worked very well.

The assault on individual narcissism by the group-as-a-whole approach is by no means confined to psychotherapy group patients. Certainly in training groups of professionals, one of the major issues that the trainees struggle with is the experience of narcissistic pain when they confront the effect of group dynamics upon their individual behavior. Post-Freud, there is a general acceptance of the originally unbearable idea that we are relative puppets on the strings of our unconscious dynamics (hence the importance of making the unconscious conscious), but post-Bion we have by no means accepted that in groups, we are relative puppets on the strings of unconscious group dynamics. We come but slowly into a Copernican world.

Let us now turn to human relations training. While the Tavistock method was being used in clinical practice, the group-as-a-whole focus was also being used as a core construct in the human relations training groups, or T-Groups, which were used in different aspects of training both in England and in the United States. Two practitioners in the United States, Herb Shepard and Warren Bennis (1956), observed the sequence of happenings in T-groups over several years of a university course in which students 'discovered' group dynamics by the participant-observer method which required them to observe the dynamics of the developing group as they were participating in its development. In these groups the leader behaved in the Tavistock method of consulting to the group-as-a-whole rather than to the individuals in the group, or to the group-of-individuals. This was in the 1950s when university professors were expected to behave in a predictably didactic fashion. The student's expectations were violated by the non-directive leadership, and a power vacuum was created. There is some criticism that the developmental sequence that Bennis and Shepard observed was a function of this artificial condition rather than a natural process that could be attributed to group dynamics, and that their developmental theory could not, therefore, be applied to groups in general. It has since become clear, however, that in fact the power vacuum did not create dynamics that would not already exist, but rather highlighted a natural process of development, as well as emphasizing natural trends towards regression that occur in all groups when the socialized defenses do not maintain the group equilibrium and the primitive core becomes exposed.

As we have said, Bion called these primal forces psychotic-like. Being a psychoanalyst, studying patient groups, predisposed Bion (and future 'Bionists') to interpret these primal group forces as pathological. Although, in fact, much that can be observed of the manifestation of this core is characteristic of psychosis, to label it as pathological is, to my mind, limiting and misleading. For example, it is important to note that certain core processes like conceptual condensations, paradoxical insights, concretizations and contradictions are common both to unconscious and conscious processes. It is just as valid to frame these mechanisms as the raw material of group work and creativity as it is to frame them as basic group states that in and of themselves need to be defined and feared and treated as intrinsically pathological.

I would therefore propose to reframe Bion's Basic Assumptions as core emotional response states that serve the group much as ego defense mechanisms serve the individual, and which are aroused in a group by the primal fears and frustrations that underlie the process of all work: work which entails the collision between the fantasies, wishes, fears, hopes and ideals and reality. In reality, reaching work goals means adjusting to reality demands, and struggling to work through the concomitant frustration, jealousies, competition, and other painful human social responses that working generates. At the group level, as at the individual level, a work culture requires that compatibility be developed between the system's implicit and explicit goals (Agazarian 1987a, pp.4–5).

Bion's work was quite important to me and equally important was discriminating the differences between my own work and Bion's which I further elaborated in a 1989 presentation to the Human Relations Conference of the A.K. Rice Institute, called 'Reframing the group-as-a-whole' (proceedings published Agazarian 1993):

The defensive function of basic assumption behavior is subsumed under a general assumption that all human behavior can be described in terms of its approach and avoidance character in relation to the problems that must be solved along the path to implicit and explicit goals (Howard and Scott). Thus the defensive nature of the basic assumption behavior is interpreted in relationship to the secondary goals and understood in relation to the primary goals.

[In] the relationship of basic assumption behavior to the primordial terror of the underlying chaotic group core ... Man has an instinctive compulsion to 'make sense' of the unknown. Primary 'sense' is primitive sense, archaic, anthropomorphizing, primordial, chaotic, often experienced as psychotic. Thus each new experience arouses 'terror' of the unknown combined with curiosity about it, which fuels the impulse to explore, organize and master. The underlying chaos which arouses the group basic assumption defenses, I reframed in terms of 'noise' (Shannon and Weaver). 'Noise' is the entropic resultant of the ambiguities, contradictions and redundancies inherent in man's communication with man. Reframing chaos in terms of noise frames chaos as a researchable construct which reflects the universal rhythm of organization and disorganization, matter and mass, entropy and negative entropy. (Agazarian 1993, pp.165–166)

In my 1987 lecture at Harvard, quoted earlier, I also highlighted the work of Bennis and Shepard and the Tavistock training process, both of which influenced my thinking and work:

Let us now return to Bennis and Shepard. Observing a consistent and predictable sequence of events in the T-groups, they developed their theory of group development (1956), using Sullivanian interpersonal theory and Bion's constructs of dependency, flight–fight and pairing as their underlying framework. Bennis and Shepard divided group development into two discrete phases, separated by an important fulcrum event. The first phase is dominated by 1) issues of power and control in which the group used all its energy to seduce the leader into being a good, nurturing protector of its dependency needs in order to defend it from the underlying chaos, and 2) the primitive competitiveness that is aroused in the work life of the group. When this is frustrated, a flight–fight culture is precipitated in which spasmodic inter-member scapegoating finally coalesces into a ritualized attack upon the leader. When this attack is successful, the group resolves its conflict about good and evil by splitting, locating 'evil' in the 'bad' leader, and 'good' in the group. This is called the barometric event in that after a successful confrontation of the leader, the group energy is freed from the absorbing struggle with the leader for power and control and is turned, instead, into issues of intimacy.

Just as in the first phase, where the manner in which the dependency and flight–fight phases are resolved is influenced by the balance of conformist (dependent) and rebellious (counterdependent) members, so in the second phase, the resolution of the issues in intimacy is influenced by the balance between counterpersonal and overpersonal members. The heavier the weighting of overpersonals, the more cohesively symbiotic the group will become and the stronger the enchantment myth that the group provides something close to heaven. The more the weighting of counterpersonals, the more the group cohesiveness will be tempered by paranoid-schizoid fears of loss of identity in the group, which finally precipitates the group into a phase of disenchantment that is close to hell.

The final phase of group development is reached through the hard work of learning to reality test, and it is this work that leads to the final stage of consensual validation, in which the group develops a culture for work, with insight into the characteristic manifestations of its defensive dependency, flight–fight and pairing dynamics.

Each group is unique. The resolution of the conflict between dependent/counterdependent and between overpersonal/ counterpersonal forces will be specific to the composition of the group, the responses of the leader and the vicissitudes in the group development. When a working consensual validation is reached, the group has developed a therapeutic milieu in which the recurring developmental issues are triggered by current group events rather than by the developmental process itself.

The most usual fixation points for groups led by those who are not familiar with the specific requirements of leadership of a developing group is the barometric event. The barometric event is the fulcrum event in which the group, by temporarily freeing itself from the bondage of its projections onto authority, can cross from a group culture dominated by power politics into a culture in which relationships based on intimacy can be explored, an essential step towards being able to use information as data, rather than in the service of power politics. This crossing requires understanding on the part of the group therapist. Serving the group by containing the projective identification of the group demon is not an easy task. It is, for example, very important that the therapist knows enough not to take it personally (which would be hard on the self-image), and not to retaliate (which would be hard on the group). Because of the inescapable vicissitudes in the process of development, trauma and fixations in development apply to group development just as they apply to individual and social development. It is no coincidence that culturally our most salient issues are issues around authority. Therefore it is no coincidence that groups are often fixated, either at, or in regression from, the barometric event.

Issues with authority are not only fundamental to most of the therapeutic work that patients must do in group therapy, they are also fundamental to the work that group therapists must do if they are to use transference and countertransference experience as information for the performance of the task, and if they are not to act out their own authority issues in the organizational setting in which they work: clinics, hospitals, communities.

The Tavistock Institute for Human Relations in England and the A.K. Rice Institute in the States offer weekend, five-day, ten-day and two-week conferences on the relationship between authority, leadership and organization. The task is to explore individual issues around authority at the level of the individual, the small group and the organization. It is interesting that the definition of authority in these conferences is in terms of the ability to work, and all that implies about the relationship between the conscious intention to work on the task and the unconscious intention to defend against the primitive anxieties aroused by the task. These conferences provide the opportunity to observe and experience the conflict between work goals and basic assumption goals in two settings. The first is in the context of a small study group and the second is in the context of an organization. The small group is made up of approximately twelve people with the goal of studying group dynamics. The staff member serves as a consultant to the group-as-a-whole and at no time addresses an individual. The workshop design results in intense contextual pressure at both the individual and the group system level, which serves to intensify the manifestations of the basic assumption cultures. The workshop thus provides an excellent arena for the participant-observation of fight, flight, pairing and dependency dynamics. For group psychotherapists in particular, there is the opportunity to observe the similarity between the response of the conference members, as they attempt to get the consultant to gratify their dependency, to the attempts of group psychotherapy patients to get the therapist to provide their cure. These similar dynamics have implications that apply not only to the management of psychotherapy groups, but also to mental health institutions, as will be discussed below.

The second context is an inter-group event in which the membership is invited to learn about institutional dynamics by setting up an institution in which they can study issues of authority between groups. Three roles are available to the members: observer, delegate and plenipotentiary. The role of the observer is to 'observe' and collect information. The role of the delegate is like a manager that transfers information. The role of the plenipotentiary is to negotiate as a 'voice' that is in synchronicity with the group that the plenipotentiary represents. The staff serve as a consultant group and work in a fish-bowl format. The membership are free to observe the staff work and to request consultations from them on their work.

As can be expected when one predicts from the knowledge of the relationship between the basic assumption culture and work, the formation of groups, allocation of roles, and interchanges with the staff in the intergroup exercise are expressed in Dependency, Flight–Fight and Pairing, rather than in the behavioral requirements of the task. And again there is a parallel between the behavior in the inter-group event of the Tavistock conference, and the patient in group psychotherapy who 'depends' upon the therapist to magically cure under the guise of work. Thus, there is an isomorphy (a similarity of structure and function) between: the basic assumption and work goals in the institution, the small group and the individual. These authority conflicts tend to be typical, for the individual conference member, of personal difficulties in their own institution, in their own small groups, and within themselves. For this reason, Tavistock conferences serve as a particularly good training ground for group psychotherapists. (Agazarian 1987a, pp.5–7)

An Interim Theory

By the mid-1970s I had gone as far as I could in understanding and integrating some of the major approaches in the fields of group and individual dynamics. I had abandoned, with significant disappointment, my early formulation that group was a function of the interdependence of parts, as I could not at that time see how it could help me in my efforts to both discriminate and integrate individual and group dynamics. Looking back, of course, it appears simple. I would have solved the problem had I substituted the concept of system for group; the formula would then have applied to both the system of individual and the system of group. This, of course, is what I was ultimately going to understand when I finalized the concepts of a theory of living human systems, but at this point in my theoretical journey I was still looking for a bridge concept that would relate the two levels of group and individual.

My second major attempt to develop an integrative theory was called the theory of the invisible group. My work with Tavistock and my consultations to Devereux had helped me to be more specific about the real world which I was theorizing about.

In the paper 'Role as a Bridge Construct in Understanding the Relationship between the Individual and the Group' that I gave at the 1980 Copenhagen Conference of the International Association of Group Psychotherapy, I start by defining the difference between the visible and the invisible group:

> The invisible group cannot be seen. The invisible group is a construct, deduced from theory and induced from the dynamics and processes that exist at the level of the group-as-a-whole which cannot be adequately explained in terms of the dynamics of the individual members whose interactions make up the group.

Theory of the invisible group

In my presentation of the invisible group, let me first define what it is not, by defining the visible group. The visible group exists in space and time – its meetings are scheduled, for a specific duration in a particular place; it has members who are present and can be counted, and whose seating can be charted. The visible group has a descriptive identity implying structure, goals and/or populations like: a long-term or short-term, open-ended or closed therapy group or training group or work group. Information about the visible group is public. It can be acquired by observation or by asking.

It is the visible group that the individual patient joins, experiences, and labels as his psychotherapy group. For the majority of group psychotherapists, the visible group is the group whose process they watch, whose dynamics they seek to understand. Most significant of all, perhaps is the fact that it is not necessary to have a group theory in order to make sense of the visible group process or to explain the visible group dynamics. It is only necessary to observe, describe and use common sense.

The invisible group, on the other hand, cannot be seen. It can only be inferred from behavior and must be defined by theory. The first formulation of the invisible group will be published in February in the book of that title which I wrote with my co-therapist, Richard Peters. Presented here are some aspects of the theory that are necessary to the understanding of roles. (Agazarian 1982, p.182)

In the 'Theory of the Invisible Group Applied to Individual and Group-as-a-whole Interpretations' (Agazarian 1983a), I again addressed the difference between the visible and invisible group:

The 'invisible group' was developed to explain the dynamics of the behavior that occurs among the visible and observable group of people who comprise a therapy group.

One of the challenges facing group psychotherapy today has been to differentiate individual therapy in a group setting from group therapy. This differentiation is not just a matter of splitting hairs. If group therapy is no more than doing individual therapy in a group setting, then the therapist needs no more than his understanding of individual dynamics to become a group therapist. If, however, group therapy is different from doing individual therapy in a group setting, then the group therapist needs to know more than individual dynamics. A knowledge of group dynamics is also essential.

Although much has been written about this issue, there is still much controversy, not to mention serious doubts and questions as to whether group dynamics is in fact different from the sum of individual dynamics. One of the best single references on the group-as-a-whole approach, Leonard Horwitz (1977 'A group-centered approach to group psychotherapy') reviews the major literature, insists that every group therapist must come to terms with the individual–group dialectic, and dismisses as invalid objections to the group approach.

Theorists who have addressed this question tend to compromise, committing themselves neither to the position that claims that group behavior can be explained as a function of individual behavior (Wolf and Schwartz 1963), nor to the position that claims that all individual behavior in a group is a function of the group (Bion 1959; Foulkes 1965).[1] Dr. Foulkes (1965) states 'It is assumed that the individual

---

1   An important exception is Durkin (1972) who presents the fundamental principles of systems theory that are germane to group therapy and proposes that the two approaches are compatible and complementary.

patient and even the nature of his disturbance is only a symptom of conflicts and tensions within his group. Psychopathological and psychotherapeutic processes arise from various configurations within the total dynamic field of this group'. (p. 291)

Although the extremes encourage conflict of an all-or-nothing nature, to attempt to solve the dichotomy by explaining that the truth lies somewhere in between blurs the importance of the opposing arguments and denies the seriousness of the underlying dichotomy. Kurt Lewin was one of the first to point out the seriousness of the underlying conceptual issues in this controversy when he emphasized that the whole was neither equal to nor greater than the sum of its parts. Rather, the whole was different from the sum of its parts. Lewin thus changed a quantitative notion into a qualitative, dynamic concept, central to the development of this field theory (Lewin 1951).

The theory of the invisible group (Agazarian and Peters 1981) is indebted to field theory (Lewin 1951) and also deeply indebted to general systems theory (Bertalanffy 1968; Durkin 1972). In systems thinking, both the whole and parts can be defined as system. Invisible group theory explains individual dynamics in terms of a discrete individual system and separates it from the equally discrete group system which explains group dynamics. The individual system has two sub-systems – *person* and *member*. The group system has two sub-systems – *group-role* and *group-as-a-whole*. All four systems are in hierarchical relationship and their structure and function are, through their principle of isomorphy, related. (Agazarian 1983a, pp.27–28)

Formulating definitions for these four constructs was to be a big step towards the final formulations that I developed for a theory of living human systems some fifteen years later. First I looked at each as a discrete system. Next, I formulated the dynamics relevant for that system level. From the Person system perspective, dynamics are a function of personal genetic inheritance, history, development and environmental influences. From the Member system perspective, dynamics are manifested in the group member's current group role, through which he repeats, acts out, or modifies his past role relationships. Group-Role system dynamics are manifested in group-level role relationships. Group-as-a-whole system dynamics are a function of the particular group composition, history, development and environmental influence.

For example, in a group when 'Sherry' relates to 'Mary Beth' as if she were her mother, this is in the person system and based on Sherry's past experience. Her member system relationship with Mary Beth is influenced by not only her person system experience from the past but also her experience and perception of Mary Beth and the group in the present as they relate together in the group. Both the person and member systems have to do with the individual perspective.

Group role has to do with the group perspective and influences the member behavior. Which aspects of Sherry's behavior the group reinforces or encourages will depend on which of Sherry's behaviors best serve the goal of the role that is most salient for the group-as-a-whole at that time. So that if Sherry is angry with Mary Beth and the group is beginning to work with scapegoating impulses, the group will encourage any scapegoating behaviors

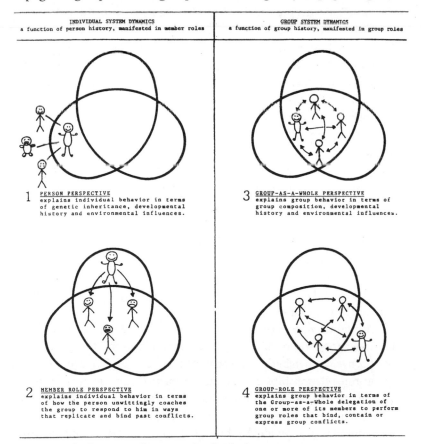

Figure 3.1 *The dynamics of group and individual systems*
Source: Adapted from Agazarian and Peters (1981)

that Sherry displays, thus encouraging Sherry in the role of acting out scapegoating for the group-as-a-whole. Group role is a function of the group more than a function of the individual system dynamics. I have included a drawing from my article 'The difficult patient, the difficult group' (Agazarian 1987f) (Figure 3.1).

Referring again to the 1983 paper, 'Some Advantages of Applying Multi-dimensional Thinking to the Teaching, Practice and Outcome of Group Psychotherapy', I restate the advantages of conceptualizing group and individual dynamics, and explain the function of role as a fulcrum concept:

> In this paper I join the trend in the field to reconceptualize group psychotherapy from two perspectives: one from the individual point of view and the other from the point of view of the group-as-a-whole. In this task I am deeply indebted to the challenge and thinking of the people on the General Systems Theory Committee of the American Group Psychotherapy Association (Durkin 1981). Multi-dimensional theories explain how the impact that the group-as-a-whole has upon its individual members is dynamically different from the impact that individual members have upon one another, or from the impact that members have separately upon the group.
>
> Invisible group theory was developed…to explain group dynamics and individual dynamics as separate systems (Agazarian and Peters 1981). The individual system is defined in terms of two component systems: person and member…The group system is defined in terms of two component systems: group-role and group-as-a-whole. All four systems – person, member, group-role and group-as-a-whole – co-exist conceptually in a hierarchical relationship and their structure and function are, through the principle of isomorphy, related. In short, individual dynamics are a function of personal history and are manifested in member roles. Group dynamics are a function of group history and are manifested in group-roles.
>
> This framework permits common events in group psychotherapy to be understood from two levels. For example, from the group level perspective, a member's scapegoat role is seen in terms of how the group-role relationships between the scapegoat and the group acts out, for the group, conflicts in the group. This is different from viewing a scapegoating event from the individual level. In fact, unless individuals [or subgroups of individuals] through whom group-roles are expressed

are sophisticated, they will probably be unaware of how strongly their behavior is influenced by the group, and unaware that they are containing for the group its group-as-a-whole conflicts.

Applying multi-dimensional thinking to theory

Another advantage of multi-dimensional thinking is that it makes clear that disagreements between theoreticians are often due to confusion of the levels of abstraction rather than to incompatible views of the same reality. The importance of keeping one's frame of reference in focus is well demonstrated by the paradox of the barber. The statement goes, 'The barber, in a small village, shaves every man who doesn't shave himself. Who shaves the barber?' The paradox lies in the fact that the meaning of a word is dependent upon its context and that context is determined conceptually by the level of abstraction: for example, the 'general' level is the context for the 'particular' roles in that level. Hence, when the barber shaves other men, he is a 'barber' and when the barber shaves himself he is a 'man'. When the levels of abstraction are confused, so are barber (role in a general context) and barber (particular person who has taken up the role). It is the man in the barber who shaves himself, and the barber is the man who shaves every one else.

Interestingly enough, it is the human difficulty in discriminating between the role as a function and the person who functions in the role that has given so many of us our surnames – barber, smith, tailor, cooper, etc.

For example, in her comprehensive work of researching and explaining phases of group development, Ariadne Beck (1981) has formulated a theory which delineates four specific leadership roles (Scapegoat, Defiant, Emotional and Task leaders) which she defines as critical in articulating and resolving group level issues in the phases of group development. When she identifies these roles at the individual level, and does not see them as interchangeable among members, Dr. Beck takes a theoretical position different from mine. From the multi-dimensional perspective there is difference, but not disagreement. In fact, we share the same view of group dynamics from the Individual System perspective. The difference lies in conceptualizing from the Group System perspective, from which Group-Roles serve a group-as-a-whole function and are therefore independent of people and interchangeable. For example, if one scapegoat leaves, the group will find a substitute.

Applying multi-dimensional thinking to the practice of group psychotherapy

Multi-dimensional thinking has implications for the practice of group psychotherapy and the outcome for the patient. This is the area where understanding the dynamics of interaction between the patient and the group is most critical. For example, interpreting to a scapegoat without being aware of the group level issues will reinforce the group scape-goating trend. At best the therapist helps to create an identified patient whom he will help the group to cure. At worst, he will join the group in stuffing unwanted aspects of both personal and group conflicts into the group member who has been chosen to contain them. The therapist who is unaware of the group level will be dangerously blind to his or her part in it.

Seeing from both the individual and the group perspective enables the therapist to address the role concept at both levels. He asks not only what intrapersonal and interpersonal dynamics is the individual acting out by taking the scapegoat role but also what is the group-as-a-whole acting out through him by assigning the role to him.

Because scapegoating serves a group function, people in the scapegoat role are at risk. However, when the therapist recognizes that working through must take place both within and between the group and individual levels, resolution of scapegoating has a positive outcome for both the group-as-a-whole and the individual patient. (Agazarian 1983b, pp.243–246)[2]

I continue to build on the importance of the construct of Role in the 'Role as a bridge construct' paper (1982):

Notice the shift in perspective. At the individual level one asks what role is the group playing for the individual? From the group perspective one asks what role is the individual playing for the group? It is in this sense that role is the bridge construct in understanding the individual's

2   'This multi-dimensional perspective on 'working through' in group psychotherapy is particularly important when dealing with the difficult group patient. A major source of the problems that therapists and groups experience with these patients (frequently borderlines) can be attributed to a failure to understand the dynamics at the level of the group-as-a-whole. Working through the transition between the borderline patient and the group, for example, entails working through not only the projective identifications that other group members and the group-as-a-whole contain for the patient, but also the projective identifications that the difficult patient contains for the group-as-a-whole.' (Agazarian 1983b, p.246).

relationship to the group both from the individual perspective and from the group perspective ... just as it is necessary to know the dynamics and history of the individual member to make individual interpretations that result in insight on the individual level, so it is necessary to know the dynamics and history of the group to make interpretations that result in insight at the group level...concept of role [is]...a function of the group-as-a-whole, and I hypothesize that the behavior of a person in a group has more to do with the group than it does with his individuality. In other words...group role is a function of group dynamics (p.3).

In order to 'see' the invisible group-as-a-whole, one observes the complementary relationship between group dynamics and group role. We ask ourselves different kinds of questions, make different kinds of connections, view things from a different perspective, and the result is a different understanding of the group, and the definition of a different system: the group system. (Agazarian 1982, p.15)

And finally I conclude with my address to group therapists, hoping that they would join me in seeing the significance of role in the way that I did:

What may not be so familiar to therapists in general (although certainly familiar to practitioners whose training has included Tavistock, A.K. Rice, or Group Analytic method) is the concept of the acting out of group conflicts at the group-as-a-whole level by using a member or sub-group as a container for the denied aspects of group life.

Group is a social microcosm. Using a member or subgroup as a container is equivalent to the social dynamic of getting rid of the elements that are undesirable in society by stuffing them into a conveniently stereotyped minority. Interpreting the individual aspect of this problem without recognizing its social purpose is rather like interpreting to a Jew in Nazi Germany the personality dynamics of his problem with the expectation that individual insight will solve it.

For therapists whose understanding and interpretations are confined to the individual level, there cannot be any formal understanding of the group system, or of how the group-role contains important developmental issues for the group-as-a-whole. Nor can it be clear to him how individual therapy is better served if the person can understand his or her part in the group-role, rather than confining insight to the individual level.

The therapist who is unaware of the group level will be blind to it and his role in it. He has no choice but to experience and interpret scapegoating for example at the individual level. By doing so, he unwittingly joins the group in the scapegoating trend, at best helping the group to create a patient whom he and the group will attempt to cure; at worst, joining the group in stuffing unwanted aspects of his own and group life into the person who has been chosen by the group to contain them. (Agazarian1983a, p.29)

Scapegoat Role

The major factor that focused my attention on the role people played for the group was my sensitivity to the role of the scapegoat, both in my reactions to those who volunteered for it and the keen awareness I had to avoid volunteering myself or being volunteered into the role because of the differences in my thinking and being. In a sense I became an 'expert' in recognizing when groups were reacting, not only to scapegoats in particular, but also to deviance in general. As the Foulkes Lecturer for the year of 1988 (Agazarian 1989c), I addressed these issues around deviance:

> The group communication pattern to deviant is an unfailing signal that the group is in the process of splitting off and denying information. The success of this pattern in maintaining the split rests in the fact that by its very nature it prevents true informational exchange between the group-as-a-whole and the role. When the group 'mascot' is indulged, the group 'hero' is idealized, the group 'patient' is cured, or when the group 'scapegoat' is scapegoated, the group has successfully dealt with difference by institutionalizing it in a stereotyped role-relationship. The advantage is that the system remains in homeostatic equilibrium. The disadvantage is that the development of system complexity requires the integration of differences, and maturation potential is restricted when integration does not take place.
>
> Applying this understanding of splitting and containing at the group level led me to understand and intervene in the process by which groups 'contain' deviance in a way that was quite different from my understanding and intervention style when I looked only at the individual. For example, it was a great surprise to me as a group therapist to recognize how often both the group and I created a patient to cure when I, and/or the group, were stuck. It was not until I understood what the dynamics were that I could recognize that we were attempting to solve one group repetition compulsion with a different repetition compulsion and could then work to exchange this repetitive solution for group problem solving.

One of the most important applications of this theory to therapy is, perhaps, in the management of deviance and scapegoating. From the individual perspective, scapegoating is a pathological event. An acting out, usually repetitively, of an old role relationship, usually originating in the family group. From the group perspective, scapegoating serves a maturational function in the early phases of group development, containing differences which the group is not mature enough to integrate. There is an apparent anomaly in that 'acting out' of scapegoating is pathological for the individual system and developmentally potentiating for the group system. However, the early stages of group development (like the early stages of individual development), are not governed by the repetition compulsion, and therefore the potential for reintegration when the system has matured remains. If, however, there is a fixation in development around the scapegoating issue, then the group system will mirror the problems of the individual system in repetitively containing in a scapegoat role an attempted solution to disequilibrium.

The diagnosis of a group-as-a-whole scapegoating solution to deviant information is best made through observing the communication pattern. The scapegoating pattern has three phases – in the first phase, the scapegoat is ignored (he is breaking the group norm and the group is signaling non-verbally that ostracism is the penalty for non-conformity). The group typically avoids looking at him or addressing him, and he is responded to only cursorily if at all. The communication pattern looks like a five-pointed star, with a sixth point that is not connected by any lines. If the scapegoat gets the message and conforms, the group has solved its problem. If his deviant behavior continues, the second phase of scapegoating is initiated and the group puts overt pressure on him to conform. All communications in the group focus on him (the pattern is like a fan, each rib connecting a member in the group directly with the hub of the fan, which is the position the scapegoat is in.) Members support each other with glances, smiles, shrugs, nods and whispers, while a small subgroup will take the role of grand inquisitor and pressure for a conversion, sometimes by reason, sometimes by seduction, sometimes by bullying. In the third and final phase, the communication pattern looks very like the first phase. The scapegoat is ignored, isolated, treated as if he does not exist – only this time, and different from the first phase, the group pressure on him to 'disappear' from the group is so great that he typically does – either psychologically or physically.

The second phase of scapegoating arouses many therapists to mount a rescue attempt. I well remember intervening energetically to get the scapegoat off the hook, sometimes by punishing the group for scape-goating, more often by attempting to 'cure' the scapegoat by getting him to see how and why he volunteered for the role. I was often surprised at how fervently I intervened, almost as if I was trying to stuff the insight into the patient. From the group perspective, of course, my 'therapeutic' fervor is now clear. Moved by the dynamics of the group, I had actively joined the 'communication pattern to deviant' and was serving the group-role of repressing the difference that the scapegoat contained. It comes as a shock to recognize that the familiar solution of the 'identified patient' in psychotherapy groups is a form of scapegoating in disguise!

The second important dynamic issue that is well illustrated in the phenomenon of scapegoating is group level projective identification. When this is understood in the context of the dynamic function of splitting off difference, and, in this case containing it encapsulated in the scapegoat, then the therapist's intervention of choice is to address the dynamic process at the group level. In making the group conscious that the scapegoat is serving a function for the group, and making each individual member conscious of what, particularly, he is projecting into the scapegoat's chair that he himself does not want to own, undoes both the individual and the group dynamic of projective identification. (Agazarian 1989c, pp.365–368)

Discovering the Symbol

I was understanding more and more about role. Yet as the deadline for the book on *The Visible and Invisible Group* drew near, I continued to struggle with the theory chapter. Many of the earlier papers that I had written for various seminars served as excellent first drafts for the beginning chapters. I had written the first version of what became the chapter on phases of development in 1967 for the group section at Pennsylvania Hospital. (It is no accident that the chapters on group development and the levels of group process are practical guides as well as discussions of the issues that they raised as these chapters were originally written for members of the community mental health center staff.) The chapter on group dynamics was a joy to write. The theory chapter, however, would not catch fire.

It was as if I had a collection of fragments – like having discovered a broken piece of valuable porcelain. I could almost hold the fragments together in my mind and get a glimpse of what I was knowing, and then everything would fall apart and I was again left with the bits and pieces: role, deviance, container, dissonance, noise, SAVI, the force field, person, member, group, group-as-a-whole. This was a period of tremendous frustration. It was not only that the deadline for the book was drawing near, it was also that in my most despairing moments I was afraid that I would never be able to define the gestalt that I was so sure I already knew.

I woke up one night with a wave of excitement and a symbol in my head (like, but not like, the three rings that advertise a beer). I had no idea what it meant, but I knew it was important. I got up and drew it on the back of the nearest piece of paper (a bill). Then I took it into the other room and pondered. My feelings were very mixed – the symbol reminded me of fragments of symbols that I had experienced before; a bright curve, a brush stroke of light, an 's' which was not an 's'. I 'knew' that each one was important, had no idea of how they were important and had been left to contain them, as a series of tantalizing images which never quite left and which might never reveal their meaning – if they had a meaning. Some of my dread was that this was more of the same. Some of my excitement was that this time, the symbol was not a fragment but a coherent whole.

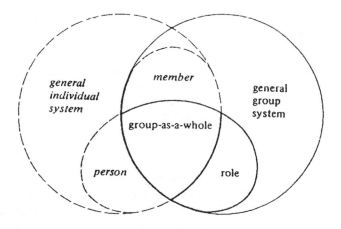

Figure 3.2 The visible and invisible group
Source: Agazarian and Peters (1981)

What the symbol gave me was a structure in which I could compare and contrast the levels of abstractions that I was trying to integrate between the individual and the group. It also gave me a frame from which I was later able to develop a theory of living human systems. Figure 3.2 is the version of the symbol that I included in the book I co-authored with Dick Peters, *The Visible and Invisible Group* (1981).

As I wrote in *The Visible and Invisible Group:*

> This leads us to define the first of our two theoretical perspectives which we call the individual perspective.
>
> From the individual perspective, 'group' is a collection-of-individuals, and its dynamics can be discussed in the language of individual and social psychology when group is defined in terms of 'the sum of' or 'greater than the sum of' its individual members.
>
> When we observe group from the individual perspective, we are observing the stimulus of individual behavior upon group behavior. When we view group from the second of our two theoretical perspectives, however, we observe the obverse of this. We call the second perspective the group perspective, where group is the stimulus to individual behavior. It is from this perspective that Foulkes writes: 'The individual patient and his disturbance is only a symptom of the conflicts and tensions within his group' (Foulkes 1965, p.291).
>
> The group systems perspective...in contrast to the individual perspective group is called the group-as-a-whole and its dynamics can be discussed in the language of group psychology when, and only when, group psychology defines group as different from or other than the sum of its parts. (Agazarian and Peters 1981, pp.65–66)

With this gestalt, I then came to understand role:

> Role behavior, therefore, contains the potential for both defensive and problem-solving communications: defensive, when the implicit goal of the system is to maintain internal equilibrium by keeping certain non-integrated information separately contained (maintaining the split), problem solving when the goal of the system is to mediate with the environment (discriminate and integrate the input/output communications between the system and the environment) and move along the path to its explicit goal.
>
> Role behavior thus serves as the major bridge construct in defining the systems of individual and group isomorphically. It is in this sense that

system role behavior signals the internal state of the system, and permits the therapist to monitor the balance of defensive behavior (which signals system homeostasis) and problem-solving behavior (which signals system re-equilibration). (Agazarian 1989c, p.363)

CHAPTER 4

Theory of the Group-as-a-Whole

It is impossible for me to talk about group-as-a-whole theory without talking about Dave Jenkins who studied with Kurt Lewin in Chicago.[1] I have mentioned Dave Jenkins briefly in Chapter 2 as 'my other mentor', but I have not yet communicated how important he was to me both as a person and to the development of my conceptual discipline. Dave was the chairman of the Temple University Group Dynamics Center and had been away for the summer when I joined the department. I did not take any courses with him until a year later when I had finished my masters and joined the doctoral program. He noticed me in my first research class, when he asked for an example of generalizing from the particular and I answered that 'one swallow does not a summer make'. Dave talked to me after class, told me that he had a good report of my work from Art Blumberg and asked if I would like to join his theory seminar that met one evening a week.

With great apprehension, I joined. It is hard to remember the shy side of me in those days, the side that was given to stage fright and significantly inarticulate if I had to talk about theory. Strangely enough, this has not changed. I can talk to my heart's content, and sometimes others' discontent, about conceptual frameworks that I have already understood and developed, but talking about ideas that are still in the ether for me is practically impossible.

---

1   It is equally impossible to talk about the development of group-as-a-whole theory and its transformation into a theory of living human systems without remembering the significance to me and my development of Helen Durkin's General Systems Theory Committee of the American Group Psychotherapy Association. I talk about this in Chapter 5.

This has its driving and restraining forces. The drive is that my work is mine, has developed from whatever process it is that compels me to keep part of my head worrying at a concept until its formulation has some sort of integrity that satisfies me. The restraining forces (and I feel them keenly) are that I have few conversations with my peers and have had to reinvent many wheels, some of which were out-of-date by the time I had reinvented them. This is also true of some of the motivators that have fired my conceptual rebellions. All too often, by the time I have found an alternative orientation to that against which I was rebelling, the original orientation has also changed – sometimes, curiously and humorously enough, in the same direction that I have taken.

When Dave asked me to join his theory group, however, I had no idea (or confidence) that I would ever learn to find words to say what I thought, or to find anyone who would be interested in hearing them. Dave's seminar was the beginning of a long journey. He would encourage me to say what I thought. I would. Neither he nor the other members would understand, with the exception of Bill Underwood (lifetime friend and at the time a fellow graduate student) who would translate. 'What Yvonne means,' he would say, when I had tried to give an answer to a theoretical dilemma by saying it was the 'rings of a tree', 'is that it depends on the environmental context.'

After a few weeks Dave diagnosed my dilemma as having neither umbrella concepts nor a language adequate to my thoughts. He offered to tutor me in addition to the seminar. I met with him every Thursday afternoon and was in my element. The Group Dynamics Center's theoretical orientation was Lewin's field theory. As soon as Dave introduced me to Lewin's life space and the concept of permeable boundaries and barriers and barrier behavior, I was in conceptual heaven. I related immediately to the idea of a tension system between the person and the goal and the concept that as soon as the goal region was reached the tension system no longer operated. I loved group dynamics research. It was my first exposure to how research worked and I was awed by the creativity of the solutions to link the abstract ideas of theory to pragmatic tests. For example, Zeigarnick's (Lewin 1927) simple design left me in no doubt that uncompleted tasks would be remembered where completed tasks would be forgotten because the tension system between the person and the goal still operated for uncompleted tasks. I understood that one of the major purposes of research was to demonstrate the obvious that had not been so obvious before field theory had simplified the issues. (I think it is very sad that today so few clinicians and organizational development specialists read Cartwright and Zander's *Group Dynamics* 1960).

Dave had great respect for and love of research methodology. He was particularly rigorous about defining a clear set of connections between the concept, the constructs that define the concept, the operational definitions that bridge between the theory and practice, the hypotheses that the operational definitions generate and the methods and techniques that permit the hypotheses to be tested, both validating the theory and the reliability of its practice. Dave's deep influence on me is evidenced by the theory chart in Chapter 7 that displays these links between a theory of living human systems and the practice of systems-centered therapy.

All this, of course, was not without frustrations and rebellions. Dave required me to be scientific about all my thinking, even to making operational definitions for my poetry. Later, he headed the committee for my dissertation and insisted that I do a dissertation that included my theory as well as research. Dave died in 1968 just after I graduated and it was like a light going out. There is no question in my mind, however, that he and his influence is still with me, that I still follow the tenets he taught me – and that he also influences, through me, all the SCT practitioners who learn how to 'turn their researcher on'.

The Life Space and the Force Field

Under Dave's guidance, it very soon became obvious to me that Lewin's life space could apply to both the individual and the group, although I was still not certain how to demonstrate their interdependence (my very early attempts at working with this are discussed in Chapter 2 and my later work in Chapter 5). I was not to solve this until I truly understood the concept of isomorphy – comprehensively, with all its facets, and to recognize that it was the construct of interdependence itself that was standing in my way. I initially understood interdependence of parts as parts belonging to the same dimension, whereas the solution (obvious once one reached it) was to understand the interdependence of the multi-dimensional relationships at all levels of abstraction. Even though this understanding came much later, I laid much of the groundwork at this time. Paradoxically enough, it seems I knew it without knowing I knew it, as the paper suggests that I presented at the 'The Lewin Legacy' Symposium at the American Psychological Association meeting (Agazarian 1987b):

> One advantage of defining the life space for both the individual and the group in General System Theory terms is that GST explicitly states what is implicit in field theory, and that is the principle of isomorphy. The isomorphic principle requires that operational definitions of the structure and function of any one system in a hierarchy can be applied to other systems in the same hierarchy. When system structures and functions are described comparably at different system levels, then what is learned about the dynamics of any one system can contribute to understanding the dynamics of all other systems in the same hierarchy. (Agazarian 1987b, p.1)

In the same paper I wrote:

> This paper is part of an ongoing formulation of theory I have been engaged in since 1962, when David Jenkins, a student of Kurt Lewin's and then Director of the Group Dynamics Center, Temple University, first encouraged me to formalize my thoughts about the difference between the group and the individual life spaces.
>
> In 1962, there was no generally accepted operational definition of group in the field and therefore no criteria for deciding when research results related to group-as-a-whole dynamics, when to individual dynamics, and when to the relationship between the two.
>
> What is more, there were no clear criteria for operationalizing the difference between group dynamics and individual dynamics. Even where constructs were clearly a property of the group (for example, group cohesiveness) they were most typically represented as the result of individual dynamics (defined, for example, as the sum of individual attractedness to the group). Group dynamics were explained interchangeably as the sum of individual dynamics or as greater than the sum of individual dynamics as if there were no significant difference between the two explanations. This, in spite of the fact that one of Lewin's most fundamental theoretical contributions was the reformulation of the quantitative Gestalt equation (the whole is greater than the sum of its parts) into a dynamic equation (the whole is different from the sum of its parts).
>
> My ambition therefore became to define the difference that made the difference: to apply Lewin's reformulation that the whole is different

from the sum of its parts to the task of understanding the group-as-a-whole as a separate and discrete phenomenon from the individuals who are the members and to operationalize the dynamics of the difference.

Since 1962, therefore, I have been involved in an ongoing effort towards formulating the dynamics of the group-as-a-whole as different from the sum of individual dynamics, which I first presented as the theory of the invisible group (1981). The theory of the invisible group describes the invisible inner dynamics and the visible external behavior of living systems, which I then applied to understanding and interpreting small group phenomenon.

Some of the major theoreticians whose constructs and concepts I have turned to in my work are: Kurt Lewin (Field Theory) and Von Bertalanffy (General Systems Theory); Bowlby (An Alternative Model for Instinct Theory); Festinger (Cognitive Dissonance Theory); Howard and Scott (Problem Solving Theory); Shannon and Weaver (Information Theory); Korzybski (General Semantics); and I am deeply indebted to Schrodinger (*What is Life*); Klein (Projective Identification and Containment); Bion (Group Dynamics, Basic Assumptions and Containment); Bennis and Shepard (Theory of Group Development); Freud (Psychoanalytic Theory); Tinbergen and Lorenz (Ethology); Mahler (Rapprochement); Horwitz, for his regular reviews of the literature; and Helen Durkin and my colleagues on the General Systems Theory Committee of the AGPA for their commitment to making theory operational.

I present two discrete but complementary definitions for group, one in terms of individual system dynamics and one in terms of group system dynamics. These two systems are hierarchically and isomorphically related as described below. As you will see, there are two important steps: to define 'individual' and 'group' in terms of the Lewinian life space, and to translate Lewin's life space concept into general systems theory terms.

Lewin states that behavior is a function of the life space. The life space depicts the person's interaction in his perceived environment. In other words, the life space is the implicit mental representation or map that is drawn from the person's interaction with the environment as he perceives it.

Thus observations of an individual's behavior imply the individual's life space, as do the observations of group behavior. The life space serves as: a snapshot of the system organization; a diagnosis of system sophistication and response potential; and a predictor of response probability (Lewin said that 'behavior now' is a predictor of 'behavior next').

Lewin also states that all behavior is goal directed, in that there is a motivational tension or driving force that connects the person to his goal. Thus to depict a person's life space is not only to draw the map but also to predict the path that the person will take in the direction of his goal: through the regions that he perceives as having permeable barriers, and around those that are perceived as impermeable. In other words, the map of the person's life space charts, predicts and explains why he behaves as he does as he journeys from one end of his day to the other. (Agazarian 1987b, pp.1–3)

A great value of Lewin's life space maps is their simplicity. They depict the obvious path that a person will take in order to reach the goal. In *The Visible and Invisible Group* (Agazarian and Peters 1981, pp.34–36) I used a series of life space maps of a donkey's dilemmas. In the first map (Figure 4.1(a)) the donkey's goal is to get to the carrots in the next field and have his supper. His 'tension system' (in Lewin's language) is related directly to his goal and the boundary between him and his supper is permeable (the gate is open). Equally predictable is the second map (Figure 4.1(b)), in which the donkey is in his 'goal region' after he has eaten his supper: no carrots, no hunger, no tension system. The donkey is satiated and so, in Lewin's language, is the goal region.

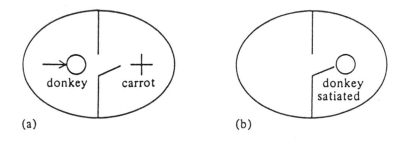

(a)   (b)

Figure 4.1 The donkey's goal

The next five maps (Figure 4.2) show the life space of the same donkey in relationship to the carrot and the stick (negative and positive valences).

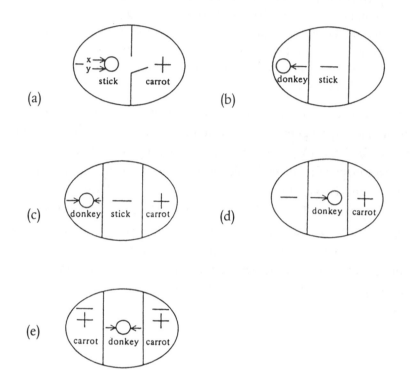

Figure 4.2 Life space of the donkey in relationship to the carrot and stick (negative and positive valences)

In Figure 4.2 (a) it is equally predictable that the donkey will move towards the carrots and away from the stick: towards the region of positive valence and away from the region of negative valence. Figure 4.2 (b) shows the donkey simply moving away from the negative valence of the stick (he doesn't see any carrots!). In Figure 4.2(c) the stick is between the donkey and the carrot (the region of negative valence is between him and the region of positive valence). If the donkey does not see the carrot he will not be in conflict and there will be no tension system between him and the goal. He will be in conflict, however, if he does see the carrot. He will be caught between the negative valence of the stick and the positive valence of the carrot. If he is hungry, then the tension system between him and the goal region will allow him to move towards it, as in Figure 4.2(d). In Figure 4.2(e) the poor donkey is immobilized between equal and opposite valences: if he moves towards one carrot he moves further away from the other. His movement toward one is helped by the nature of the driving force (the closer to the goal, the greater the attraction). However, his movement is also hindered by the nature of the restraining force (the closer to the aversive goal, the greater the resistance).

Lewin represented this conflict as a force field. Lewin's force field of driving and restraining forces became one of the central constructs in the practice of system's centered therapy, in which change is initiated through reducing the restraining forces rather than increasing the driving forces. The force field illustration of the donkey's dilemma is given in the adapted format which we have used (Figure 4.3).

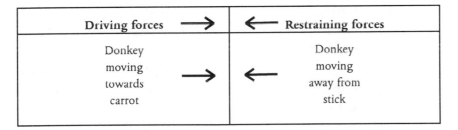

Figure 4.3 Driving and restraining forces

At the Third International Lewin Conference in 1988 I built on my 1987 paper and described my adaptation of Lewin's force field (Agazarian 1988b):

> In the paper 'Towards the formulation of group-as-a-whole theory,' I defined the group-as-a-whole and the individuals who are its members as two isomorphic systems that co-exist at two different hierarchical conceptual levels, similar in structure and function, and defined by two different formulations of the Lewinian life space. In it, I said ... 'In translating field theory into general systems theory terms, where the living system described can be as small as a cell or as large as society, Lewin's life space has been reformulated to apply to living systems in

general. The advantage of this for formulating group-as-a-whole theory is that the life space serves as an operational definition of the behavioral path of all living systems of a defined hierarchy and can be applied isomorphically to either of the two system levels of group that I have defined: the system of the individual and the system of the group-as-a-whole.'

Because of the general systems principle of isomorphy, the life space concept can be used to describe the behavior of either the individual system or the group system, depending upon which system the observer wishes to analyze. The life space equation can thus be used both to underline the isomorphic relationship between the systems in the hierarchy and at the same time delineate the differences between them. A separate but related life space equation of the group[2] and the individual[3] systems thus describes each as a discrete, hierarchically related system whose dynamic field of force is similar in structure and function.[4]

Thus two apparently contradictory statements can be made, both of which are true, and each of which applies contemporaneously to the same group event:

1) the behavior in this event can be explained by understanding the individual dynamics in the group and without referring to the group dynamics.

2) the behavior in this event can be explained by understanding the group dynamics in this group and without referring to individual dynamics.

As both of these statements are true, which explanation one uses at any one particular time depends upon the purpose for which an explanation is required. For example, when one is attempting to understand individual behavior in a group, sometimes it is sufficient to formulate the individual dynamics inferred by a life space in order to explain individual

---

2      $[Gsb = f(GS,E)]$: Group system behavior is a function of the group systems in relationship to its environment. Group behavior is a function of group dynamics.

3      $[Isb = f(IS,E)]$: Individual system behavior is a function of the individual system in relationship to its environment. 'Group' behavior, from this perspective, is defined as a function of individual dynamics.

4      $[Sb = f(S,E)]$: System behavior is a function of the system in relationship to its environment. System behavior is a function of system dynamics in relationship to its environment.

behavior. At other times, it needs to be framed in the context of the group life space if the apparent contradictions are to be explained.

Central to understanding the many apparent contradictions that occur in group behavior is the ability to compare and contrast explicit goals (those goals that are explicitly and publicly formulated) with implicit goals (those goals that can be implied from the behavior manifested by those in goal directed activity). Sometimes the goals implied by the way goal activity is being conducted are congruent with the explicit goals, sometimes they are contradictory. Congruence or contradictions between the direction of behavior and the direction of the goal exists at both the individual and the group level, and between group goals and individual goals.

One of Lewin's most useful constructs in analyzing goal directed behavior in the life space is the field of force which represents the constellation of forces that impinge upon a person and result in locomotion in a predictable direction. Thus, a representation of the current field of force generates a series of hypotheses about:

1. the probable direction of locomotion;

2. the apparent congruence or incongruence between the direction of locomotion and the explicit goal region;

3. inferences that the explicit goal and the implicit goal exist in different regions when the direction of locomotion is directed away from the explicit goal region;

4. the current level of equilibrium of the system or subsystem (defined as you will see as the implicit, or 'as if' goal).

One fortunate alliance of concepts from the field is the combining of Lewin's concept of the life space, Korzybski's formulation of man as a map maker whose behavior can be understood in terms of the specific map of the world that he has drawn (and the tendency to revise perceptions of the world before he revises his map), and Festinger's theory of cognitive dissonance.

What this permits us to do is to use the reasoning of Korzybski's map-making model to illustrate life space equations. In their original form, Lewin's equations can appear daunting to those who do not share his knowledge of physics and its application to social science. The addition of Festinger's understanding of the dissonance that results from the impact of the discrepancy between the mental map of the territory and the territory itself provides a presentation of ideas that are a clear alternative to the more complex psychodynamic formulations more usually used to explain the conscious, preconscious and unconscious workings of the psyche.

Particularly useful is the fact that an 'as if' map explains the path a system takes without implying intentionality; whether the system is 'group' or 'individual,' or for that matter, 'organization' or 'nation' or any other system–subsystem relationship in the world. In other words, locomotion by perceived map (whether the map is conscious or unconscious) is functionally predictable, and explains behavior that would otherwise appear diametrically opposed to its announced intention.

Howard and Scott, in their short and brilliant article defining their theory of stress (1965) suggest that all behavior is directional, moving either towards or away from the problem to be solved. As Lewinians, we would add, 'problems to be solved along the path to goal'. The goal concept is a fundamental one for Lewin, as without it, there can be no tension system, and therefore no locomotion potential in the life space. The relationship between person (or system) and the tension system in relationship to goal that explains and predicts movement is the life space. The status of locomotion at any one time is formulated by the resultant field of force.

'As if' goals, then, are the goals that are implicit in the behavior of the system. The implicit goals may be congruent or incongruent with explicit goals, but, as they are empirically implied by behavior, they have face validity. Explicit goals, on the other hand, exist only in the realms of intentionality until they are reached, thus, the frequent discrepancy between words and deeds. As it is dynamically clear that when implicit and explicit goals lie in different directions, locomotion is towards the implicit goal region rather than towards the explicit goal region, then it can be said that for a system to reach the explicit goal, it must lie in a direction congruent with the implicit goal.

As we know, task achievement is heavily influenced by how compatible the nature of the task is with the basic assumption culture. For example: war is best waged in a fight culture, organizations produce most successfully in a dependency culture and social goals are reached best in a pairing or flight culture.

Once we have assumed that behavior is goal-directed, we have postulated a relationship between behavior and goals, whether they are explicit or implicit.

As we have said, implicit, or 'AS IF' goals are the goals that are implied by the behavior of the system. Behavior can be seen as an output of the system, and output is a function of system equilibrium. System equilibrium is also depicted in Lewin's field of force. We now have all the building blocks necessary to operationalize the use of a modified force field to the diagnosis of system goals.

There are some modifications to the force field that I have made for the sake of simplicity. Kurt Lewin called the forces towards or away from a region 'driving forces;' and forces not to enter a region 'restraining forces.' Thus for Lewin, driving forces had to do with locomotion, and 'restraining forces' had to do with barriers or boundary conditions (Agazarian 1988b, pp. 1–3).

The innovation that I made was to see driving and restraining forces in a dynamic equilibrium related to opposing goals like, for example, to move towards or to move away. Thus restraining forces were not simply barriers to the driving forces, but goal-oriented forces of their own – whose implicit goal could be intuited by observing their behavioral implications. Redefining Lewin's force field concept makes it compatible with the approach and avoidance forces of SAVI and links Lewin's concept to both Shannon and Weaver (1964) and Howard and Scott (1965). Defining my adaptations of Lewin's model, I write:

> In the modification of the force field that I have made in order to operationalize Lewin's construct as an instrument, I have kept the locomotor character of driving forces, but have made an important discrimination between driving forces that move towards the explicit goal and those forces that move away. This then differentiates between the directions of approach and avoidance.
>
> The label 'driving force' then refers only to those forces that move the system in the direction of the explicit goal; and the label 'opposing, or restraining force' refers only to those forces that move the system in the direction away from the explicit goal.
>
> The most important purpose of carefully differentiating between driving and opposing forces is, that when forces are defined in terms of behavior, and when it is clear that the driving forces relate to the explicit goal, then it can be argued that an analysis of the constellation of opposing (restraining) forces relate to the implicit goal to the extent the implicit goal is in a direction that is incongruent with the explicit goal. (Agazarian 1988b, p. 5)

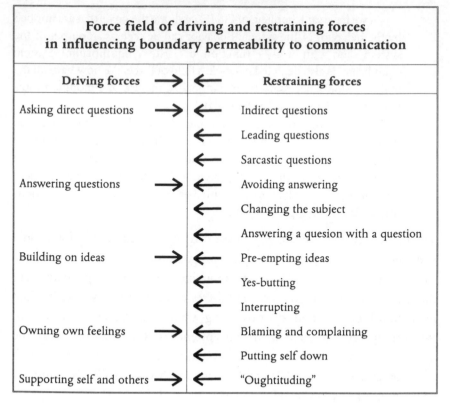

Figure 4.4 Force field of driving and restraining forces to communication adapted from SAVI

I have included here a force field of the driving and restraining forces in communication adapted from SAVI (Figure 4.4).

I was not to know fully until I developed systems-centered therapy from a theory of living human systems how important Lewin's force field and my adaptation of it was to be. Much much later, in the 1990s, this adaptation was to become the fulcrum of systems-centered therapy, which is organized to reduce the restraining, defensive forces (in context) which then releases the inherent driving forces towards the system goals of survival, development and transformation, which are synonymous with the goals of therapy.

Role and Listening to the Voice of the Group

The construct of role as a bridge construct between the individual and the group in my invisible group theory was no less important in orienting myself to the group-as-a-whole.

> In formulating group-as-a-whole theory, the construct 'role' is used isomorphically to describe the external, visible behavior that arises from the dynamics of the living system in context. Thus the word 'role' is reserved as a descriptor for behaviors that, when observed, can be identified as having a function in relationship to the two basic requirements of every living system: system maintenance and system locomotion in relationship to system goals.
>
> 'Role' applies to the behavior of all system levels in the hierarchy. When 'role' is used to describe individual system behavior it is called 'member-role,' and applies specifically to a particular individual level system behavior in the context of the group. When 'role' is used to describe group behavior, it is called 'group-role' and in this paper applies specifically to the particular group level system behavior in the context of the group-as-a-whole. (Agazarian 1987b, p.2)

> The group-as-a-whole system perspective defines a group as having a genetic inheritance, composition, developmental history and maturational experience which is similar, at a different hierarchical level of abstraction, to the person system. Group behavior is an expression of the dynamics of the group, and just as individual behavior serves to keep the individual system in functioning equilibrium, so group behavior serves an equilibrating function for the group. How this is accomplished is by the allocation of group differences to group roles. (Agazarian 1987f, p.208)

Using the construct of 'role' and attempting to understand it as a bridge construct was to have a profound impact on my observation of levels in group. As I worked to understand the construct and what it meant in reality, I began to see what I had only cursorily noticed before. Indeed, my apperception of role led me to listen to the voice of the group in a different way, first in seeing the implicit role voices coming together in implicit subgroups, and then in understanding how following the different voices actually defined different roles that performed different functions for the group.

I will start with the paper that I wrote for an American Group Psychotherapy Association panel in 1985 on 'The Difficult Patient, the Difficult Group' (Agazarian 1987f). We were fortunate as panelists in having the videotape of the group to watch to prepare our papers. The group was indeed composed of 'difficult' patients and, as so many difficult patients are, they were sensitive in relationship to each other and very moving to watch.

I started my paper with some theory, which leads directly into an example of the members' sensitivity:

> An individual may carry a particular and important developmental role for the group. For example, a crucial and continuing maturation process in groups is the ability to integrate similarities and differences at all levels, an ongoing task of perceiving the similar in the apparently different, and the different in the apparently similar. For all humans, this is a relatively painful activity. Our wish is not to have to change our perceptions; we'd like to keep the map we have already to fit the territory. But as the territory is changing all the time, our map has to be revised all the time. This is a core issue in the dynamics of a developing group.
>
> As we know from individual therapy, when a patient is unable to integrate certain kinds of differences, then there is a dynamic that we call projective identification by which the therapist contains for the patient what the patient has unconsciously split off and denied in order to maintain his equilibrium. At some point later in the therapy the patient re-introjects and makes conscious differences that were impossible for him before. The same phenomenon happens in group. In group, sometimes the therapist contains for the group those differences that the group needs to repress and deny; other times a member or a subgroup serves as the container. Most frequently, but not exclusively, group projective identification is expressed through the dynamics of group deviance manifested in the scapegoat and defiant roles.
>
> In the process of reintegrating the deviant, the group develops the necessary tolerance of the previously intolerable differences, and thus increases its potential resources.
>
> Understanding projective identification as a function of group dynamics allows the therapist to observe how the group-role serves as the container for the group of those dynamics that are upsetting the group equilibrium. Conceptually, understanding lies in recognizing the isomorphy between member roles (individual system) and group roles (group-as-a-whole system). Thus, group roles serve an equilibrating

function that maintains the viability of the group by balancing forces which might otherwise disrupt it, even though, as in this group, the very mechanisms that keep the group equilibrium also fixate it and preclude further development.

For example, two of the members contain two sides of the defensive isolation that characterizes the group, with one consistently containing affect, and the other containing thought.

Member 1:   You know, I spill…and the person who spills the most gets hurt the most.

Member 2:   [*puzzled*] It doesn't make sense…you are very intelligent…

Member 1:   Course I know it doesn't make sense…

Member 2:   [*suddenly understanding*] So that's why…it's emotionally …I see what you mean.[5]

As a subgroup, these two also illustrate the reciprocal group role containment of the isolation of thought and affect which serves a defensive function for the whole group…with Member 1 containing and expressing the 'spilling over' feelings for the group and Member 2 containing the 'making sense' for the group.

Listening to the group-as-a-whole

Listening at the group level permits you to help therapy happen in a way that isn't possible if you confine your listening to the individual level.

Let us turn now to thinking about group-as-a-whole interventions. This group of difficult patients is an excellent example of why group-as-a-whole interventions are essential if members of the group are going to reach some of the goals of group psychotherapy. Let us hypothesize that the most important goal for these patients is to accept the realities of their condition and to make the best adaptation they can.

The realities that these patients face are indeed difficult, both for these patients and for the therapists. The potential for therapeutic gain is limited by their psychological and sociological resources. Their psychosomatic symptoms, by and large, are probably a better adaptation than the deterioration that might ensue if the problems were not bound at the level of the body ego. These are the facts of this difficult group that

5   This is also a nice example of integrating discriminations.

the therapists must face if they are going to hear enough of what is going on to help the patients face their realities.

The voice of the group cries out in metaphor and simile what cannot be said in plain language. The following is an excellent example from the beginning of the group session of the group voicing its wish to communicate to the world in general and to the therapists in particular. Implicit in what they say is the cry that there is a part of the group that is not being heard and is alone and lonely. The part of the group for which 'medication' is not the treatment of choice, the part for whom the act of communicating is in itself therapy. It is not a fantasy to say that this group voice speaks as much for the helplessness and loneliness of the therapists as it does for the patients.

At the beginning of this group session, the group talks about telephoning. Bess has just finished telling the group that she has sinned again, and that her son has taken her to task for talking inappropriately on the phone. 'Too much telephoning,' she says. The group responds:

> 'It happens because you are lonely, know what I mean, and you don't have no one to talk to.'

> 'And you get someone on the phone, and you say, "Let me talk."' 'It will happen eventually, you know, because sometimes it happens to me.'

> 'It's a terrible thing to be lonely.'

> 'Yea, terrible.'

> 'Yea, I never get used to it.'

> 'No matter who calls you, even if it's a wrong number, sometimes it's better than nothing.'

> 'Is this an obscene call? Huh, don't mistake my asthma for passion.' [laughs]

> 'Call the operator, and they hang up, and you give up.'

> 'Isn't it terrible.'

> 'Call back the second time and it's the same wrong number.'

> 'Sometimes you could go all day without talking to no one.'

> 'Sometimes you wonder, is your phone out of order.'

> 'And I get kind of panicky – and they say: Call me back!'

[From the group-as-a-whole perspective] the therapists do not attend to the group talking about the harsh facts of their loneliness outside the group, and do not legitimize bringing these feelings into group. (Is the group saying that in response to their call, the therapists hang up and they give up?)...

Certainly [a group-as-a-whole therapist would say that for this group], loneliness is an issue more serious than the jealousy that the therapists are assuming is in the group because one of the members is getting individual attention from the therapist. Jealousy is not a topic that appears cathected and loneliness is; listening to the group voice is more likely to lead to work in the group than an interpretation of expected dynamics. (Agazarian 1987f, pp.209–213)

In the next example in the article 'Group-as-a-whole systems theory, and practice', there is an opportunity to listen from two frameworks: first hearing the dialogue without a specific focus and second listening with a group-as-a-whole ear.

The episode starts with a knock on the door. A late patient, Bess, enters and there is much commotion as everybody makes room and squashes their chairs together.

Therapist 1:   [a nurse] Fine, come on in...

Therapist 2:   [a resident] Why don't you...here, take this chair...

Therapist 1:   Watch the wire...

Bess: Yeah...

Alice: Move the table...

Edna: The camera will break...

Alice, Bess, Clara, Edna, Doris, Glenda: [Laughing together]

Alice: It's called togetherness [as they all squash their chairs together]...

Clara: Closeness...

Bess: That's what we're all looking for...

Therapist 1:   All thinking...

Therapist 2:   Ready?...

Alice: Christmas...

Therapist 2:   We were just talking about the fact that Edna was seeing me individually for treatment of her depression. (Agazarian 1989b, p.137)

Listening to the group-as-a-whole, one can hear a duet between two subgroups, one giving voice to how to structure the group, the other giving voice to the yearning for intimacy:

Structuring Subgroup:

> 'Here, sit here,'
>
> 'Take this chair,'
>
> 'Don't trip over the wire,'
>
> 'Move the table,'
>
> 'Come on in,'
>
> 'Ready?'

Intimacy Subgroup:

> 'Come on in.'
>
> 'It's called togetherness.'
>
> 'Closeness.'
>
> 'That's what we're all looking for.'
>
> 'That's what we're all thinking.'
>
> 'It's like Christmas.' (Agazarian 1989b, p.138)

Separating the themes in this way it became clear that the implicit subgroups had come together on a common resonance and were not determined by the individual person (Alice's voice, for example, is heard in both subgroups), nor by role (both patients and the therapist contributed to both subgroups).

It is not a new idea, of course, that subgroups come together spontaneously around similarities, not only of theme, but also of stereotype similarities like race, religion, gender and status. However, as stereotype subgrouping tends to set up a 'we/they' dichotomy, the themes tend to be voiced politically rather than functionally. Functional expression in a group requires members to work in relationship to what is being explored without giving undue emphasis to race, gender, religion or status. It is important for leaders to modify stereotype subgrouping if the work is not also going to be stereotypic and redundant.

It was a step forward, therefore, to identify in the script above, the spontaneous subgrouping that was functional rather than stereotypic and which carried two important implicit goals for the group: managing the group boundaries and identifying the relevant theme for work.

Integrating Voices in the Group-as-a-Whole

The next episode illustrates how big a difference it makes when the therapist listens solely to the dynamics of individual members as they speak in the group and when the therapist listens not only to the individual members, but also to the voices of the subgroups in the group-as-a-whole. This episode is also a good illustration of how group conflicts are contained in a group in unacknowledged subgroups that maintain the split and keep the group stable. (This was to turn out to be an extremely important understanding when I was developing the methods for systems-centered therapy, and led to my discovering how to deliberately split group conflicts so that they could be worked in functional subgroups in order that an integration could take place in the group-as-a-whole. This is discussed at greater length in Chapter 6).

The transcript below is taken from a group that had been working together as a demonstration group for two days for the Eastern Group Psychotherapy Conference in 1985 (Agazarian 1988a). I was the fourth and last of the guest leaders, demonstrating the 'group-as-a-whole' approach.

As you will see, in the beginning of the group work there is only one group voice: the voice of group exhaustion. Then comes a duet between two subgroup voices: the voice of exhaustion and the voice of work energy. As long as these two subgroups contained opposite group forces, the group is effectively stalemated in relationship to its work goal. When these subgroups enter into a dialogue, reintegration takes place and the group moves into a state in which it is ready to work:

> *I had started the group with clear time boundaries and a task instruction 'to experience the group-as-a-whole.' The group's initial response was half-appreciative, half-angry, manifested first in some rather desperate sarcastic joking about past leaders.*

>> 'Well at least she spelled out our task very clearly, which none of the others did'...

>> 'Except Dr. X, who told us that we were going to be depressed and thus gave us some structure!'

> *This was followed by wry joking about the group-as-a-whole which was the label for my demonstration:*

>> 'They left a hole here!'

>> 'And we have to fill it!'

'How can we fill this hole?'

'How can we make this whole?' ...

'Well at least we have a hole if we are going to have to fill it!'

By two-thirds into the group, I had made the following interpretations, first to the 'hole':

> 'It seems to me that the stakes are very high for this group, having recognized that there is a hole in the group, the group can only count on a funny, ineffectual, irrelevant leader to help them with the job of confronting and filling that hole.'

> ...'It's very hard for the group to experience the group-as-a-whole if it remains on the understandably more comfortable level of what it might be!'

> ...'In my short exposure to this group it does seem that the group has developed some very useful defenses that keeps it safe from exploring the hole that the group is afraid it has, and intellectualization has been a very useful way of making this group experience bearable.'

I had reinforced the boundary between the group and the audience:

> 'There will be no crossing of boundaries between the audience and the group.' [Spoken to the audience, when the audience had laughed at what a group member had said.]

And I had begun to focus on the specific defenses that served as restraining forces to the group work:

> 'Again it seems to me that the group is using its valuable and useful escape into intellectualization, an escape perhaps away from the very thing the group wishes it could experience.'

> 'It's possible that another way that the group is using right now to prevent the experience is by talking very fast and maybe preventing the experience that comes up when one takes a deep breath'. (Agazarian1988a, p.3)

The excerpt below is taken from the last third of the group and demonstrates how members use fulcrum roles that help the group to maintain its equilibrium until they are no longer necessary to the group.

Male speaks to a female: 'You look so depressed.'

She replies: 'I'm pooped.'

'You're pooped?'

'Exhausted.'

'This tired you out?'

'Yeah. I wonder if the group-as-a-whole [smiles] can resonate with that? I know I'm pooped.'

Group silence.

Leader: 'Is the group going to leave all the experience of being pooped in one chair?'

This intervention assumes that the 'pooped' member is voicing the fixating affect for the group which she is containing in a group-role. It is the first step in the process of undoing a group split in order to release the affect, and restore the group's ability to work. (Incidentally, when successful, this relieves the individual member of the overload of feeling that she carries for the group, as you will see.) The first step is to identify the individual in the group-role as a voice for a subgroup, which this intervention does. The second step is to identify the subgroup function for the group-as-a-whole. The third step is to identify the group-role relationship between the subgroups in the group. The fourth step is to deduce the group goals that these subgroups have. (Are they maintenance or task goals? And are they congruent or incongruent?). And the final step is to encourage the group to make a conscious decision about how to proceed, given that the conflict that the group had previously contained in a split off subgroup-role is now consciously experienced in the group-as-a-whole.

Following the intervention, a second female member speaks up:

'No, I'm exhausted, it's been an exhausting experience. I don't know how much more I have left in me.'

Then a third female: 'I don't feel that tired. After this is over I'll probably get more tired; after yesterday I was fine, and then all of a sudden I felt tired and exhausted, so I don't feel it when it's happening...'

Then a different group voice, a male: 'I don't feel tired, I feel as though I'm getting started. I feel great and ready for a marathon!'

Subgroups are becoming identified: an 'exhausted' subgroup and a 'marathon' subgroup.

Third female: 'Are you running tomorrow?' [*The New York Marathon is the next day*]

'No, I meant a group marathon.'

Second female: 'Do you mean that?'

'Absolutely!'

'You could go on and on?'

A third male: 'I don't know if I would want to if it would keep generating a feeling of exhaustion.'

'You don't want to go on?'

'I want to go on if we feel good, I don't want to go on if we keep feeling pooped and exhausted. I figure something else better go on.'

Original female: 'Mm – you can feel exhausted and still have good feelings.'

Male: 'Mmm – I got an invitation that we have to share the exhaustion somehow.'

The member is obliquely referring to my intervention. It is at this point that I make a group-as-a-whole interpretation. You will notice that as the subgroup for 'exhaustion' voices good feelings, the 'marathon' subgroup considers taking in some exhaustion. There are therefore signs both of subgroup cross-fertilization and undoing of a split [integration, in SCT language!] and also signs of a group-as-a-whole maintenance goal which is being served by 'exhaustion.' The intervention that follows acknowledges the position of the two subgroups, and at the same time reminds the group-as-a-whole that it has the ability to set task goals that are congruent with its maintenance needs.

I say: 'I'm wondering if, for this group, it's rather as if it's run three marathons already (referring to the three previous groups) and that right now the group is trying to decide whether it's worth it to summon up the energy to run a fourth, knowing that it's a short one, and knowing that it's going to end...(locating the group within of the reality boundaries of time)...or whether the group has earned the right to sit back, experience its exhaustion, and become aware of what it has already achieved. I sort of sense that the group's not sure whether it wants to put its energy into another marathon or whether it wants to sit back and, in its exhaustion, process this experience.'

A male responds: 'In an attempt to process where we've come, I feel really good that we're a lot closer to one another now than we were in the last session. There is much less antagonism, hardly any at all.'

Group: 'Mmm.'

'For example there was a disagreement between John and Betty about termination, but I didn't see any antagonism. I feel very close to everyone. I guess I like the feeling of our being together as a group.'

The marathon subgroup is proposing the task goal of 'processing.'

A fourth female: 'Well, I'm exhausted and I like the first part of what you said, I wasn't sure I was ready for the second part, which was allowing myself to experience. That's the scary part. It makes me realize how much we tire ourselves out in avoiding things, how tired I am from trying so hard. And getting permission not to try so hard, that feels like, 'wait a minute – into space-flight – where's the anchor? – where's something to hold on to? But it could be, it could be all right.'

Another voice from the 'exhausted' subgroup is considering the marathon! This is data for the leader that making the subgroup goals explicit has shifted the group equilibrium, in that each subgroup is now processing the 'difference' that was previously contained separately. The group is now in a functional disequilibrium.

There is a long (25-second) silence.

Male: 'Not exhausted?'

Female: 'Who?'

A different male: 'The person behind you?'

The remaining male: 'Its almost as if it's catching, this exhaustion, and I don't want to catch it. I don't feel like I was exhausted, but, there's something! I kind of feel like I have to fight it off, it's either something that I'm supposed to be, supposed to feel. If all these people are feeling exhausted there's not much I can do about it, so I can either join them or leave [*small laugh*]. But maybe it doesn't have to be that way. It doesn't have to be an either/or. Maybe I can be nonexhausted and that's O.K. too.

*The marathon subgroup is working through the experience of disequilibrium,
taking back what the exhausted subgroup had contained.*

Original female: 'Well I thought we had another option which is to sit
            back and process what's been going on and I don't think
            you need to be exhausted to do that.'

The original voice for exhaustion is experiencing relief!

Female: 'Yea.'

Original female: 'You don't have to catch my exhaustion.'

Male: 'Mmm'

Original female, smiling: 'I may be getting my second wind!'

*This is a good example of how, when the group-as-whole repossesses what has been
split off and contained in a group-role, the member who has been containing for the
group experiences relief. As one member put it in another group, 'I simply don't
believe in a hydraulic system of group process, but it is certainly true, when the
group took all that back, it was as if my feelings drained away back into the group,
and I watched the group's feelings rise.'*

Male: 'Yea, I was aware…that's great.'

Original female: 'But I was wondering if I could rally my energy again a
            fourth time because this is very stressful.'

Another long group silence (25 seconds) is broken by a voice for task.

            'You're smiling Don, what are you smiling at?'

            'Well, I'm just thinking Bill, I'm very relieved to hear that
            you're not feeling exhausted?'

            'No!'

            'Glad to hear that, because I was beginning to think I was
            the only one…'

            '…ready for a group marathon?'

            'Right. Is there anyone else beside the two of us who is not
            feeling exhausted?'

A fifth female:

            'I'm not feeling exhausted. I'm feeling like I'm just being;
            just kind of experiencing, kind of wondering whether other
            people are experiencing or not. Its O.K., it just feels
            comfortable'…

This voices the group work on the assigned original task of 'experiencing' the group-as-a-whole.

> '...I feel kind of concerned about you, Pat, because you said you were so uncomfortable and you wanted to get off the stage. And this experience is not like that for me, and I'm hoping it's not going to be like that for you. I'm hoping you're going to come away with something better than just discomfort.'

The group is continuing to check out its membership. The voice for the task goal voice is much stronger, but there is still a silent subgroup whose maintenance status is not clear. Assessing its membership strength is a very important step for a group that is re-equilibrating the congruence of maintenance and task goals.

Pat answers: 'Oh right now I feel fine, I feel very relaxed.'

'So it's changed for you?'

'It changed.'

Original female: 'It's changed for me too, I think maybe getting permission not to expend all that energy changes it, some.'

It is also not unusual for an individual, who has experienced relief from the pressure of 'containing' for the group to 'explain' why she feels relieved in terms of familiar individual dynamics.

Male: 'Maybe the exhaustion has something to do with you, Marie!'

The final member is polled! 'No!' she says. The group maintenance check is now complete – every member is 'O.K.' and the group is now re-equilibrated and ready to go to work. (Agazarian 1988a, pp.4–8)

Group-as-a-Whole Theory

The scripts I have included here illustrate how I learned how to listen to the group-as-a-whole. As I worked with my group-as-a-whole 'ear' and my Lewinian background, I began to formulate my group-as-a-whole theory, which I presented in 'Group-as-a-whole Theory Applied to Scapegoating' at the Eastern Group Psychotherapy Society in 1987 (Agazarian 1987d):

> From the perspective of the group-as-a-whole, group behavior is understood as a function of the intragroup dynamics which result from the unique genetic inheritance, composition, developmental history and maturational experience of the group-as-a-group.

Group-as-a-whole interventions are designed to focus the group on its behavior to modify group level defenses. This is so both in the potentiating sense that group level defenses bind group level chaos (groups 'store' non-integratable differences in group-roles) and also in the inhibiting sense that the group level defenses limit problem solving potential. Thus, whereas splitting is fundamental to the ability of the group to maintain equilibrium it also potentiates group fixation: for this reason it is fundamentally important that the group therapist understands when to reinforce the containment of splitting as a factor in group development, and when to interpret it so that the group members can take back their projections and reintegrate the differences that have been contained.

A group-as-a-whole intervention would be something like: 'I wonder if Peter's late arrival today and the present group focus on last week may represent the conflict that the group feels about entering into the work of this week?' (The work of this week is both the boundary work that the group needs to do to form the new group as well as the membership work necessary to include the new member within the group-as-a-whole boundary).

Another group-as-a-whole intervention would be to focus the group on the function of Brian's 'puppydog' role as the container for group dependency...

I will take the opportunity at this point to expand on the framework that I use in conceptualizing group development which forms part of my rationale in interpreting to the group-as-a-whole.

The underlying dynamic common to maturation of all human systems, as small as a cell and as large as society, is the functional discrimination and integration of differences, from simple to complex. This is the process that makes order out of chaos, makes the unconscious conscious, codes information and organizes it in relation to group goals.

I therefore describe the group developmental process as a function of the rate that similarities and differences can be discriminated and integrated. The process is twofold. Similarities and differences must be perceived; both the similarities in the apparently different and differences in the apparently similar, and system equilibrium must be sufficiently maintained so that the work of integration can take place. Until discriminations are integrated they are disequilibriating, chaotic. It is this chaos that the group system must contain while the work of discrimination and integration takes place.

Thus, how far any particular group can develop is dependent upon the mechanisms that the group develops to contain chaos. The newer the group, the simpler the mechanisms. The simplest way for a group to contain chaos is to split the integratable from the non-integratable and to contain them separately. This reduces the information overload, and the group can then use the information that is 'similar enough' without being overwhelmed by information that is 'too different' to be integrated.

Thus, on the one hand, splitting is fundamental to the ability of the group to maintain the equilibrium necessary to group development, and on the other hand, splitting potentiates group fixation. For the purpose of maturation theory, the definition of maturation is 'maturation of any system is a function of the rate by which the process of discrimination and integration occurs.' The process of maturation in both groups and individuals can be described in this way. In groups, maturation starts by the splitting, and containing separately, conflicting perceptions: containing similarities in subgroups that are perceived to be 'like me and good', and containing differences in subgroups that are perceived 'not like me and bad'. Once contained, the group can continue the maturation process that enables it to integrate at a later time that which was too different to integrate at the time the conflicted perception occurred. Splitting is a system equilibrating function that permits the system to maintain an equilibrium by allocating conflicting forces to separate subsystems. In both individual and group systems, the dynamics relating to the process of splitting and containing are: isolation, denial, projection, projective identification etc., and the dynamics that occur in splitting, and reintegrating differences are: scapegoating and opening communication channels to deviance at the intra group-as-a-whole and inter-subgroup system levels as well as the intra and inter-personal individual system levels.

As it is important for a group to reintegrate differences when it has developed the ability to do so, and thus regain problem solving potential, it is fundamentally important that the group therapist understands when to reinforce the containment of splitting as a factor in group development, and when to undo it through interpretation so that the group members can take back their projections and reintegrate the differences that have been contained.

In the service of this task, there are therefore two defensive mechanisms fundamental to group development that are important for the therapist to monitor: denial and projective identification. Both of these mechanisms contribute to the group's maintenance of a functioning equilibrium, and both put the group's development at risk.

Denial is an early defense mechanism used in the service of both individual and group development. It is important to differentiate group denial (the container-source of information which the group uses when it can finally give voice to something that it 'knew all along') from group projective identification, in which the split off information (frequently coded in affect of symbol, rather than in words), is removed from group conscious awareness through repression, projected and contained in a group-role (frequently perceived by the group as deviant). (Agazarian 1987d, pp.9–10)

Implementing the Theory

Finally, in my presentation to the A.K. Rice conference in 1989 (published in Agazarian 1993), I summarized the group-as-a-whole theory and clarified my similarities and differences with Tavistock. This paper also describes some of my early work in implementing my group-as-a-whole approach with my groups:

> In practice, this means that consultant interventions frame interpretations of basic assumption behavior as but one of the types of group defense that must be modified in the process of group development. The other defenses are group tactical defenses and the character defenses: the particular constellation of defenses that characterize a particular group, much as a particular constellation of ego defenses characterize a particular individual. From the systems perspective, basic assumption, tactical and character defenses exist at the individual, subgroup and group-as-a-whole levels isomorphically, functioning contemporaneously.
>
> All group defenses influence the nature of group development, and the nature of the group's development at any one time is reflected in the group's relationship to the system's implicit primary goals of survival and maturation, as well as the system's secondary goals of mediating with its environment. The achievement of explicit task goals is inevitably influenced by the nature of the group compromise at any given moment of maturational time.
>
> The problem solving skills that the group develops are a function of this compromise. The group's ability to use those skills is a function of the dissonance or congruence arising from the relationship between the

group's implicit and explicit goals. The particular style of problem solving and decision making that each group develops affects the way the group relates to its work tasks. (Agazarian 1993d, p.166)

The group-as-a-whole system is defined as the environment for the individual system. System-role behavior serves as the conceptual frame for the behavior of both the individual and the group: framed as a sub-group containing function when behavior is viewed as a function of the system 'life-space' of the group-as-a-whole; as member-role behavior when behavior is viewed as a function of the system 'life space' of the individual (Lewin, Agazarian).

This [group-as-a-whole systems] orientation frames consultant interventions as 'consultations to system boundaries,' consultations to the boundaries of the system, within, between and among systems in the defined hierarchy. It generates the hypothesis that if the nature of the communication contributes to problem solving rather than to noise, then the system hierarchy will mature along lines in which discriminations can be made and integrated, and the potential for moving in the direction of system primary and secondary goals will be increased.

To this end, all group work whether large group or small group is either punctuated by, or immediately followed by, a period of review. I introduce the application of theory to practice with the following letter that is sent to new members of my training groups and workshops:

'The orientation of the group is from the perspective of group-as-a-whole systems theory. The goal of the group is to learn to observe and explain all behavior in the group as a function of group-as-a-whole dynamics. The proposed format for reaching this goal is that each period of experiential group-work is either punctuated by, or followed by, a processing period in which the subjective experience will be reviewed objectively and analyzed from the group-as-a-whole perspective. To this purpose, individual dynamics are relevant only to the extent that they help members to understand the impact of group dynamics upon their individual experience and behavior. Subgroups are the basic unit of the group-as-a-whole. With the exception of member selection, all decisions that affect the group; like fees, meeting dates and times, holidays, new members, etc.; are the property of the group. Members are reminded that objectively analyzing subjectively experienced behavior from the perspective of the group-as-a-whole is emotionally frustrating as well as intellectually challenging.'

Thus – the group is the environment in which members experience how their behavior is influenced by the dynamics of the group-as-a-whole. Through sharpening the skills of participant-observation, they identify how they 'contain' and 'voice' not only their own dynamics, but also group dynamics, and how the implicit and explicit goals of the group determine the boundaries of their sub-group roles. (Agazarian 1993d, pp.166–167)

Bion and the 'psychotic' core

I have reframed Bion's formulation of the group core by emphasizing its chaotic nature in contradistinction to the field's tendency to talk and behave 'as if' it is psychotic. De-pathologizing interpretations of everyday human dynamics is basic to group-as-a-whole systems theory.

All systems develop from simple to complex, and the less sophisticated the system the more primitive will be the attempts to organize chaos. Thus early phases of group development will arouse the same kind of primitive fears and conceptions of the unknown that characterize the beliefs of primitive societies. There is perhaps a tendency in writing about Tavistock dynamics to dramatize and reify this developmental stage into some 'thing' that is terrifying in and of itself, and thus to focus more on the aspects of destructive acting out and less on the methods for the organization of chaos.

In group-as-a-whole systems theory, maturation through the organization of chaos is the primary survival goal of a system: to contain the dissonance that chaos arouses, to maintain system boundaries and system equilibrium. In group-as-a-whole systems theory maturation is defined as the process of differentiating, organizing and integrating information.

A. Bion's basic assumptions of flight and fight

Bion's constructs of flight and fight then, are reframed as behavioral vectors related to the systems goals[6]: both the primary intra-system goals (the implicit goals) and the secondary explicit goals that relate to the system environment.

Thus from a group-as-a-whole systems theory perspective, Bion's basic assumptions of fight and flight are understood as defenses against the anxiety aroused by internal chaos, but most often interpreted as

6   Lewin's force field is a useful construct for mapping these.

behavioral vectors that are sometimes oriented in the direction of the relationship between the explicit (secondary) and implicit (primary) goals, and sometimes directed to the relationship between either or both the primary and secondary goals and the environment. (Howard and Scott, Lewin, and GST) Consultant interventions serve a dual function, both to help the group identify the dynamics and symptoms of defensive 'panic' behavior and to learn the kind of communication that contains the panic and organizes the chaos.

B. Bion's basic assumption of dependency

In group-as-a-whole systems theory, dependency is conceptualized as an existential dynamic common to all living systems and not as a defense.

I define dependency as a dynamic that exists on a developmental continuum with interdependence. Maturational work is an ongoing process, and inherently in itself is never a defense. Defensive functioning comes when the normal maturational conflicts around dependency cannot be contained within the system and are discharged into dependent and counterdependent behavior that acts out the unresolved conflict. (It is possible that the custom of framing dependency as a defense has contributed to giving this basic human dynamic a bad name in Tavistock work, and led to groups denying the underlying dependency forces that exist functionally in reality.)

In practice it is particularly important not to distort the group's attitude towards its dependency or encourage its denial. Phase-appropriate dependency is fundamental to developing appropriate boundary permeability which in turn is fundamental to avoiding fixations in development or a premature maturity.

For example, the management of dependency is in the service of developing intimacy. Intimacy cannot develop unless dependency can be accepted. In psychodynamics terms, dependency is the raw material of later separation individuation work. In systems terms, system maturation is dependent upon the ability to open and close boundaries to both similarities and differences.

C. Bion's basic assumption of pairing

I do not differ with Bion's definition of pairing as an unconscious fantasy that through 'pairing' a group savior will be born. However I see this Messianic fantasy as only one of many unconscious fantasies contained by the group in a 'pairing' subgroup. Again, 'pairing' is framed as an existential system dynamic, genetically and socially reinforced, that is not necessarily defensive. In practice, when pairing occurs in a group, it is a signal for a judgment call as to whether pairing is in the direction of fantasy or reality problem solving in relationship to the task required in reaching the explicit and implicit goals.

The principle of discrimination and integration

The maturational process that underlies all systems is defined in terms of the process of discrimination and integration. This concept can be applied to communication. Thus in group-as-a-whole systems theory, maturation of individual and group systems can be described in terms of the kinds of communication by which discriminations are made. Maturation of a system is a function of the system's ability to integrate information about similarities in the apparently different and the differences in the apparently similar.

In practice, then, group development is facilitated by observing subgroup interactions, without intervening, as long as the group-as-a-whole is processing information. Even when the group forms stereotyped subgroups, this in itself is not an intervention point unless the group information flow becomes redundant, ambiguous or contradictory.

Shannon and Weaver's information theory

Ambiguity, contradictions and redundancy are the source of entropic noise in the communication, according to Shannon and Weaver's information theory. This, then, is the criteria variable I use when listening to group communication.

In the following examples, the interventions are typical group-as-a-whole interventions, and it is not this aspect that I wish to draw attention to, but rather to the specific discrimination and/or integration work in group development that they are designed to encourage.

A. Ambiguity

In ambiguity, pointing out first similarities and then differences helps the group to make the necessary primary discriminations.

For example, in a new group, relief first comes when members discover that anxiety is shared. This is usually followed by the relief that occurs when a status hierarchy is built, based on the differences in the apparent 'expertise' that members appear to have.

B. Redundancy

In redundancy, the group is in fixating homogeneity. Pointing out differences in the apparently similar disequilibrates the redundancy. For example, in a comfortable but repetitive group, a functional disequilibrium can be introduced by drawing attention to the fact that a silent voice of the group is expressing an unacknowledged difference: 'There have been several yawns in the past two minutes.'

C. Contradictions

Groups frequently ignore one aspect of contradictory events, and behave 'as if' there is no contradiction. Bringing the contradictory information to the group's attention is a call for group integrational work.

For example, in a demonstration group in Japan, after an interaction in which the behavior contradicted the traditional roles, there was a sudden group silence followed by a shift of attention so abrupt that it was almost as if the group had amputated part of itself in an effort to ignore whatever had just occurred. So I described what I had just seen, and asked 'I wonder if the group work will be helped or hindered if the group agrees to ignore whatever it was that just happened?'

D. Integration

One way of facilitating the integration is to point out to the group the similarities in the apparently different and later, differences in the apparently similar.

In a group that is watching a fight, for example, the first part of the intervention brings the group's attention to the fact that the fighting pair, who are apparently on opposite sides, are in fact in the same subgroup – a 'fight' subgroup – and that the rest of the apparently uninvolved group perform the role of a supporting subgroup. Having laid the foundation, a question then directs the group to relate its behavior to the group-as-a-whole goal. For example an intervention like: 'The fighting subgroup appears to be supported by the group silence. What useful service is this serving for the group-as-a-whole?'... (Agazarian 1993d, pp.169–173)

Group-as-a-whole development

From the individual system perspective, groups are made up of individual members – but from the systems perspective, both the group system and the individual system is made up of components.

Thus, whereas looked at from the individual perspective individual group members are seen as the basic building blocks of the group, from the group system perspective, the basic building blocks are subgroups, which exist independently of the individuals whose subgroup member-ship may overlap or change from instant to instant. (This same frame can, of course, also be applied to individuals. It is relatively easy to experience the many and different subgroups 'voices' that 'talk things over' inside oneself, and to become aware of how they perform a successful defensive function that both keeps one's system in equilibrium and reflects the conflict between, shall we say, the competing id, ego and superego goals.)

Thus subgroups are the raw material of system development, and contain the group potential. They are self-generating and regenerating. Subgroups are the source of the integrating blueprint, the basic container for similarities and differences. Through subgroup interaction systems develop through predictable phases towards maturation (Agazarian 1993d, pp.175).

At the time that I was writing this paper, I had not finished discriminating between functional and stereotype subgroups: stereotype subgroups forming around similarities and attacking differences, functional subgroups coming together around similarities and integrating differences. Functional subgrouping puts into practice the process of discrimination and integration, first recognizing differences in the apparently similar and then recognizing similarities in the apparently different. How this process results in the development of the group potential from simpler to more complex is illustrated in Figure 4.5 and contrasted with stereotype subgrouping which results in maintaining the status quo.

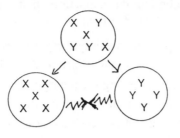

a   Stereotype subgroups form around similarities and attack differences.

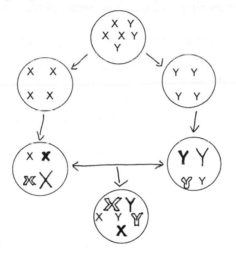

b   Functional subgroups form around similarities and integrate differences.

Figure 4.5 (a) Stereotype subgroups form around similarities and attack differences; (b) functional subgroups form around similarities and integrate differences

To continue with the 1989 paper:

> *Subgroup roles in group-as-a-whole development*
>
> Subgroups come together around similarities and separate on differences. Each matures by the process of differentiating and integrating similarities and differences within its subgroup system and between subgroup systems in the environment of the group-as-a-whole.

At each moment of group life, the group-as-a-whole system integrates all subgroup discriminations that are within its integration ability (Agazarian 1993d, p.176).

This was an important point whose implications I was not to understand fully until I was translating the theory into practice. As will be discussed at greater length in Chapter 6, by weakening the restraining forces that are specific to each particular phase of group development, the group-as-a-whole and its members not only integrate differences that would otherwise cause conflict, but by so doing reduce the restraining forces to the development of the group from one phase to another. Thus, when the members of the group use less maladaptive and more adaptive behaviors, isomorphically, so does the group.

Individual and group isomorphism in the group-as-a-whole

When an individual member of the group serves in the 'container' role for the group – he is acting out in his member-role a set of behaviors which express an internal conflict. In other words, he sets up an old, familiar, stereotype role relationship that expresses an unresolved conflict externally, thus discharging the tension which would otherwise have to be experienced, contained and integrated internally (within his individual system).

Isomorphically, from the group system perspective, the member is performing a subgroup role and containing for the group-as-a-whole a 'difference' that the system has split off and projected. This mechanism serves, at the group level, to discharge disequilibrating tension into a boundaried subsystem, which permits the group-as-a-whole to continue in a maturational process which can lead to reintegration of the difference at a later time. In the process of splitting, projecting, containing, reintrojecting and reintegrating, developmental change can occur at all system levels (Agazarian 1993d, pp.176).

It is interesting to me, looking back, to see how I was still seeing role as the bridge between the group-as-a-whole and its individual members. Although I am using the construct of isomorphism (similarity in structure and function) I have not yet developed (as I would later) clear definitions of the structure and function of the systems of the group and the member – or understood that subgroups were another system in the hierarchy (of living human systems). Next in the paper I address goals:

Primary and secondary group goals

By 'containing' in separate subgroups those differences that the group-as-a-whole is not yet sufficiently differentiated to integrate, the primary goal of the system, to maintain a viable equilibrium, is met. And so the differentiation between primary and secondary goal behavior is created. The primary system goals of survival and maturation take precedence over the secondary goals of mediating with the environment.

The maturational task of the group is to develop sufficient maturity to reopen the boundaries between subsystem roles and integrate the information (resolution of projective identification). When subgroup boundaries are impermeable to different information, and an individual is assigned a deviant containing role, the stage is set for an identified patient, a hero, a savior, a group mascot or a scapegoat. Creating a deviant role does maintain the group system in equilibrium, unless or until the group-as-a-whole becomes developmentally ready to open the system boundaries to the dissonant information. Most leaders are alert to the 'deviant' solution when it is allocated to a scapegoat, because of the nature of the scapegoating climate; less easily alerted when the solution takes the form of creating an identified patient, a hero, a savior or a group mascot. (Agazarian 1993d, pp.176–177)

As I discussed in Chapter 3, the style of leadership behavior has much to do with how the group will act on the impulses to create containing roles, and how likely it is that these roles will be acted out. Thus, leadership styles that do not help the individual member to understand how their behavior is influenced by the dynamics of the group will reinforce the interpretation that it is the primitive underlying dynamics common to human beings that cause group chaos, rather than recognizing that the communications within the group and between the group and the leader were not themselves containing. I am reaching for this argument in the paragraphs that follow:

Group-as-a-whole leadership style

It is for this reason, that group-as-a-whole consultancy has no pre-set role boundaries. Group-as-a-whole leadership behavior is related to the aspects of the developmental phase that the group is in, and is oriented to the relationship between the system equilibrium and the primary and secondary group goals. There is, however, a general guideline for the form of an intervention.

1. Whenever possible, the words are selected from the group vocabulary, reinforcing the task of consensually validating group language (Bennis and Shepard).

2. Whenever possible, a description of the group events that form the data base for the consultant's hypothesis are included in the intervention.

3. The target of the hypothesis is to influence the process of discrimination and integration of group information.

4. Certain skill building interventions 'train' the group in communication and problem solving skills, and in certain dynamics like the process of 'taking back' projections. Learning how to take back what the group has projected into the 'container' role is essential to the group-as-a-whole method in that it is the group work of undoing the containing split, and is essential to the development of the group ability to change scapegoating communication to an open communication to deviant.

5. Consultant interventions are conceptualized as consultations to the transactions across the boundaries of systems.

Consulting to boundaries

The task of the group-as-a-whole leader can be conceptualized as that of 'consulting' to the dynamics of the group-as-a-whole, and monitoring the noise in the communication transactions across the boundaries between and among all systems in the relevant hierarchy.

A general criteria for consultation to boundaries is that the information itself should mirror a problem-solving communication: in other words, contain as little noise as possible.[7] Whenever possible, this is done by grounding the communications in here-and-now reality. Here-and-now reality exists at both the primary and secondary goal levels.

The language that relates to the primary goals in the here-and-now reality of the group-as-a-whole is the language of emotion, condensations, metaphor and paradox. Primary goal communication organizes chaos in ways that can be integrated without isolating thought

---

7   I am referring here to noise as defined by Shannon and Weaver as redundances, contradictions and ambiguities in communication.

from affect. It is the language that every consultant recognizes and uses intuitively – and is very difficult to code or teach. The language that relates to the secondary goals is the language of problem solving. This language is relatively easy to teach.

Much of the thinking behind the understanding of communication as a series of input and output transactions between systems, and of consultation as acts of influence directed at these communications transactions at the boundaries of systems, has its roots in the development of SAVI, a System for Analyzing Verbal Interaction that Anita Simon and I started to develop in 1965.

In group-as-a-whole theory, goal achievement and individual change is explained as a function of group dynamics. In a developing group, the dynamics of each phase of development are available as a major force that impacts upon the individual experience. Within each member, salient developmental issues are aroused that resonate with the issues that the group is in the process of mastering. It is the group-as-a-whole leader's function to relate the developmental arousal to the explicit goal of the group. To the goals of therapy, when a therapy group, to the specific training in a training group, in conferences to the conference task: traditionally, in Tavistock conferences the leader behavior tends to highlight the fight/flight phase of development which arouses regressive dependent and counterdependent behavior. This arousal is congruent with the conference goal of exploring relationships with authority. (Agazarian 1993a, pp.178–180)

Group-as-a-whole theory provided an important equilibration for me. I had learned to listen to the group voices and subgroup voices in relationship to their functioning for the whole group and I was working with training groups in the group-as-a-whole approach. I was understanding the group's development as a function of discrimination/integration and the importance of system equilibrium for integration. All of this would later be integrated as part of systems-centered practice and functional subgrouping.

CHAPTER 5

Thinking Systems

My first encounter with systems was the weekend I spent with a chapter in a sociology book while writing 'The Agency as a Change Agent' (Agazarian 1969b). Delivering the paper had its compensations and frustrations. The greatest compensation was that I actually met Scott (of Howard and Scott 1965) although, devastatingly, I became too tongue-tied to talk to him coherently. My frustration came from my conviction that the field of the blind was very far from having an organized approach and was not yet addressing the practical issues that I, as parent of a blind child, was encountering.

I was completely unaware, when I presented my paper, that everyone did not in fact already know everything that I knew. Therefore, when I received a polite and uninterested reaction from the audience, I was not to understand until much later that it was not necessarily the ideas themselves that were the problem, but that the level of abstraction with which I dealt with them would appeal only to a very select audience. Below is the flavor of my ability (or inability?) to communicate at that time:

Systems analysis as a conceptual resource

In the face of this exponential escalation of information, system analysis seems to offer a framework which allows some generalization from the literature in the comprehensive field of social science.

First, the components of the system under analysis are defined by their relevance to the particular system under analysis and are functionally related, so that change in one implies a change in the relationships among all the components (Kuhn 1963). Second, change in the response of the system (output) is a function of change in the system of equilibrium, extraction of information from an environmental input, or both (Kuhn 1963). Third, the particular level at which the equilibrium is maintained in the system (the system goal) can be described without references to whether human desires or motivation are reflected in any way (Kuhn 1963). Finally, a component of one system can be a component of two or more different systems, and every system is functionally related either as a subsystem component in a larger system or as a system with its environment. Thus, all 'behavior' in the universe can be conceptualized as an interaction of parts of systems among themselves, or of systems with their environment of subsystems (Kuhn 1963).

This approach provides, for the agency and the person, a model that allows broader findings in the social science field to be generalized to the blind person and to the agency system. It also allows generalizations to apply to the client and to the cultural system.

Discrimination of change focus

It thus becomes possible to analyze the particular components that are relevant to the system 'blind person,' and differentiate them from components that are relevant to other systems to which 'person who is blind' belongs. This separation becomes particularly relevant when the change agent is influencing change in a person who has components both in the system 'blind person' and in the system 'dependent person.' Components relevant to the first system are different from those relevant to the second. This difference carries different implications for effective change agent behaviors. Influencing change in the system 'blind person' implies a focus upon the sorts of input from which information relevant to a blind person's social mobility can be extracted. (Agazarian 1969b, pp.388–389)

The audience's lukewarm reaction to this paper was not only because of its level of abstraction; I also failed to deal with any of the practical issues whose absence so disappointed me in the conference. I did not, however, give up immediately in my attempts to contribute to the field of the blind, even though the frustrations continued. For example, when I was asked to give a workshop at my son's blind school, I introduced an exercise in which the staff were blindfolded, with the intention of having them discover the most effective ways of communicating directions to their charges. The staff had never been blindfolded before and were only marginally interested in the activity. (This was a surprise to me, as I had spent a weekend blindfolded when I first discovered that Jack was blind.) This indeed was a different kind of frustration from my experiences when I gave workshops to a blind population, where the guide dogs were more interested than their masters and mistresses. And I had a still different frustration when Art Blumberg took me as his co-trainer (I was over the moon with pride) to the staff of one of the Offices for the Blind. In response to their 'as if' reactions, Art interrupted the meeting at coffee break, told the group that they did not have to train with us if they did not want to, and that he and I would willingly sit outside their room for the next two days (it was a two-day workshop), if they so decided, and would not report their decision to management. They decided to train, and Art pointed out to me that the group's most significant work in the workshop probably took place in the process of making that decision.

The frustrations were by no means all one-way. The critique of myself that I wrote about a 'Three-day session in human relations training for forty professional employees of the state office for the blind' (Agazarian 1963) shows another example of the gap between my aspirations and my ability:

> In the hope of increasing the experiential learning of the subjects, half were blindfolded, and volunteered to remain blindfolded throughout the hour. In order to demonstrate the frustration of 'no feedback' (inherent in blindness), specific frustrations were built into the design.
>
> Critically, this seems to have been a good basic idea but insufficiently worked out. Having induced the members to experience frustration, I omitted to resolve the frustration once it had served its purpose(!) (Agazarian 1963b, p.1).

It was clear to me that, like the challenge in bringing up Jack, I did not know enough to manage the practical realities that would have made me effective in my work for the blind. Unlike the challenges in bringing up Jack, there were not enough compensations for me to bear the frustrations of learning how to be a resource.

Systems had opened a whole new world for me, but at that stage, 1969, I was most aware of its usefulness to SAVI and the 'inputs and outputs' of communication between the SAVI group pattern and the pattern of its members. I failed to recognize the dimensions that the systems constructs were later going to add to the rest of my thinking.

It was not until the late 1970s that I refocused my interest on systems again. I went to an American Group Psychotherapy Association institute on systems, given by Helen Durkin and Don Brown. By the end of the weekend

I was deeply immersed in a way that I had not been since first encountering information theory. Information theory had revolutionized my emotional life by giving me a satisfactory 'explanation' for the universe and put to rest my search for God (neg-entropy and entropy are a good solution to good and evil, particularly as they are best pictured as a yin/yang). Systems theory revolutionized my thinking life by providing a meta-theory in which to organize the many components of my thoughts. I do not mean to convey the idea that this was an epiphany and that everything fell into place. It actually took another ten years before I developed my own version of a meta-theory (a theory of living human systems) and another five after that before I had developed a coherent application for its practice (systems-centered therapy).

General Systems Theory Committee

In 1980 I was invited by Helen Durkin to join the American Group Psychotherapy Association's General Systems Theory (GST) Committee which she chaired. At the time that I joined, the book that they had successfully written as a committee (not a camel!) was in press (J. Durkin 1981), and the members were turning their attention to how to build the bridge between theory and practice. I was somewhat disappointed with this focus, as I was still trying to build a theory that could be put into practice. And I was excited: the committee was the first time I had worked with a whole group of people all of whom were dedicated to theory. Helen Durkin had brought systems thinking into group psychotherapy (H. Durkin 1972; H. Durkin 1981) and continually urged us to push our thinking beyond our present horizons. With Jim Durkin, I became passionately involved in the differences between our theoretical approaches, and argued long and hard about our operational definitions (what fun to have someone to argue operational definitions with). Andy Beck and I found a deep and mutual interest in the phases of group development[1] and discovered that we were impressively congruent in our approach and equally impressively incongruent in our conception of roles. Don Brown became a fast friend, unfailingly supportive. We were on the other end of the phone to each other when either of us hit a glitch in our thinking, and when the phone was not enough we

1   Anita and I brought SAVI to her research project (Simon and Agazarian 2000).

used an aeroplane (he lived in California and I was in Philadelphia!). Jay Fidler is today the person with whom I still have the deepest affection and relationship. It is Jay who, at our final meeting of the GST committee, urged all of us to find ways of making GST real – to apply it in a way that made a difference to our practice. To this day, Jay and I get together over this, although now Jay wants us to apply it to larger societies as groups as well as to small. Finally, it was George Vassiliou who gave me such a good example of 'thinking systems' that I use it whenever I can.

I went to visit George at his Institute of Anthropos in Athens. We were talking about applying general systems theory to group psychotherapy. To illustrate a point, George threw a piece of his hamburger into the goldfish pond. One goldfish swam off with it, but it was too big to swallow all at once, and the other goldfish darted around, nibbling off bits of the meat. 'Look,' said George, 'that poor little fellow is having his dinner stolen from him by the other fish, and if he is not careful, he will have nothing left to eat but the last small bite. On the other hand,' said George, 'you might think, here is a whole shoal of fish with a large meal falling into its midst. Too big a serving for any single fish, one fish holds it, while others nibble away at it and the rest dart after the bits that drift away into the water. Thus all the fish are fed'.

I met with the GST committee twice a year for ten years. I was both challenged and frustrated. With what seemed to me to be a powerhouse of brains around the table, we were still not successfully making the bridge between theory and practice. Time went on. Helen Durkin retired. Don Brown took the chair and soon after, he died (another light went out). At our final meeting, as we separated from each other, Jay again urged us to find ways of applying systems thinking to group psychotherapy. I left with Jay's words in my head – a charter, not unlike the one that Dave had left me with when he suggested that I develop a definition of group. Just as with Dave's challenge, I would work for many years before I managed, to my satisfaction, to develop a theory about systems which could be related directly to practice.

Applying 'Systems' to the Life Space

In the interim, I was increasingly applying systems theory to my work and theorizing. I had started years earlier with SAVI, using the systems concepts of input and output in relation to communication, and in formulating the theory of the invisible group:

It is important to understand the stimulus response nature of the input-output relationship between the individual and group systems. The individual system output serves as a group system input. Similarly, the group system output serves as an individual system input. Clarifying this concept, and learning what can be further understood with this particular interdependence between group and individual system levels is a current theoretical focus for me. (Agazarian 1986a, p.108)

Though I wrote in *The Visible and Invisible Group* (Agazarian and Peters 1981) about applying general systems theory to groups and to the life space, in 1981 I was only beginning to work with the systems constructs and quite a way from understanding all of the implications this had. It would turn out that continuing to apply systems thinking to Lewin's life space (and applying the life space to the systems levels of individual and group-as-a-whole) deepened my understandings. In an unpublished paper (Agazarian 1987b) that I presented at the Lewin symposium in 1987, I began working using systems theory to define the life space:

The dynamics of the systems life space

In order to define the group as a discrete and separate dynamic system from the individual, the concepts of group and individual are defined as hierarchically and isomorphically related systems. What makes a general systems definition of the life space particularly important is that it can then be used to describe the life space of any other system in the hierarchy.

General systems life space equation: Definitions

In translating field theory into systems theory terms, where the living system described can be as small as a cell or as large as society, Lewin's life space has been reformulated to apply to living systems in general. The advantage of this for formulating group-as-a-whole theory is that the life space serves as an operational definition of the behavioral path of all living systems of a defined hierarchy and can be applied isomorphically to either of the two system levels of group that we have defined: the individual and the group-as-a-whole.

Lewin's life space equation 'behavior is a function of the Person in interaction with the Environment' [$b = f(P,E)$] has been reformulated to read: 'System behavior is a function of the System in interaction with the Environment' [$Sb = f(S,E)$]. In group-as-a-whole theory the definition of

System (S) is the particular system being described. When applying the general system life space definition to two particular systems in the hierarchy of systems, the individual and group systems, S can represent either the Individual System (IS) or the Group System (GS) and System behavior (Sb) can be coded as Individual System Behavior (Ib) or as Group System Behavior (Gb). Thus the general living systems life space equation [Sb = f (S,E)] is identified at the level of Individual Systems as Ib = f (IS,E) and at the level of the Group Systems as Gb = f (GS,E).[2]

Definition of System (S) 'Perception'

The nature of perception in living systems is determined by the perceptual style that is developed through past problem solving experience and modified by the present requirements of maintaining the system's equilibrium while the system is interacting with the information in its current environment. The nature of the information input and output between the system and its environment is determined by the nature of the system's boundary permeability. Boundary permeability is a function of the compatibility between the type of information and the current integrational ability of the system. Systems are relatively permeable to compatible information and relatively impermeable to incompatible information.

Compatible information is information that is 'similar enough' to information already organized in the system to require minimum reintegration. Incompatible information is information that is 'different enough' from the existing system's integration to require reintegration that threatens system disequilibration.

The system boundary permeability is thus linked to system equilibrium, and functions either as closed to information that is 'different' (this governs system selective perception) or partially permeable in that the system takes in the information but encodes it separately.

Separately encoded information is 'split-off' and contained within the system as a separate system component. It is not until the system develops the necessary integration potential that the information that has

---

2   It would be important to note here that it is the principles that define the life space that are similar (isomorphic), not the expectation that the behavior itself will be similar. For example, the life space map of an individual may predict a flight into the past while the lifespace of the group-as-a-whole may predict reality testing in the present.

been encoded, split off and stored can be decoded, integrated and made available to the system. Thus information that cannot be integrated at one point in time may come to be integrated at some future point. This system ability to encode and encapsulate non-integratable differences functions to maintain system equilibrium within tolerable limits, determines the informational resources available for current goal directed problem solving and also preserves the potential for maturation of the system's problem solving mechanisms.

The above explanation does more than simply define perception in terms of information inputs and outputs between the system and its environment. It also reflects the dynamics of maturation itself in that system maturation can be said to be a function of the rate of discrimination of similarities and differences, (both the similarities in the apparently different and the differences in the apparently similar) and the integration of those discriminations. Thus, the nature of the communication between the system and the environment governs the maturation potential of the system.

Definition of behavior

Behavior is defined as the vehicle for the input/output communications of the system: the transactions between the system and the environment. System behavior infers both the internal organization of the system and the system perception of the environment. In group-as-a-whole theory, behavior is observed in terms of its role function. As we have explained above, the word role connotes the visible external behavior of the living system in its context, defined in terms of its task and maintenance functions.

Task behaviors

Living systems can be characterized as goal directed. Thus all system behavior can be defined as problem solving behavior in that it can be characterized as moving towards or away from 'solving' the problems that lie along its path to goal. This role behavior is called 'task' behavior to distinguish its function from maintenance behavior, and can be analyzed in terms of the tasks in the system's perceived environment, or the tasks that are defined by the observer as existing objectively in the real environment.

Maintenance behaviors

The maintenance role function for every living system is to maintain a functioning equilibrium while informational transactions are processed. Informational transactions occur within the system (intrasystem), and between the system and its environment (intersystem). Both informational similarities and differences must be integrated into the existing organization of the system. Thus system maintenance requires both a normative role function to maintain the functioning equilibrium of the system; and an integrating role function, to re-equilibrate the system. Thus, system maintenance behavior expresses both the normative roles that process (or contain) the information that is congruent with the organizational norms of the system; and deviant roles that process (or contain) the information that is incongruent with the organizational norms of the system.

A statistical illustration would be to conceptualize the normative maintenance role as expressing the 68 per cent of a system's organizational dynamics that are contained within plus and minus the first standard deviation. The integrative deviant role is conceptualized as expressing the system dynamics past the first standard deviation, and the formalized deviant role as expressing the split-off component, within the system, that contains the information that is 'too different' to be integrated: information that falls past the second standard deviation of organizational dynamics. (Agazarian 1987b, pp.3–4)

Understanding the group levels as isomorphic information-processing systems was an important step for me and laid a key foundation for the theory of living human systems. I was also recognizing the implications of a 'systems life space' for the developmental phases in a therapy group though not yet thinking this through: as I wrote in 'Application of Lewin's Life Space Concept to the Individual and Group-as-a-whole' (Agazarian 1986a):

The second part conceptualizes the development of a psychotherapy group goal specific in Lewin's framework of the life space, with each developmental phase represented as region with a subgoal, and [I] show how by applying a force field to what is happening in a group you have some way of knowing 1) what phase of development the group is in, defined by the behavioral field of force, and 2) which restraining forces you might want to weaken if you want the group to re-equilibrate. (Agazarian 1986a, p.102)

I was applying systems theory to my understanding of role. In the 1988 Foulkes lecture (Agazarian 1988c), I wrote:

> System behavior is the outer expression of inner system dynamics. Therefore system behavior implies the status of the system's dynamic equilibrium and the systems' primary and secondary goals. Primary goals are related to internal system survival: system maintenance and maturation. System maintenance requires making order out of chaos: structuring the systems boundaries of inside and outside, space and time, reality and irreality. Maturation depends upon how successfully the system maintenance role behavior has related to these goals.
>
> Secondary goals are related to external survival in the environment in which the system exists, and can be generated from within or without. Successful achievement of environmental goals depends upon how successfully the system task role behavior is related to these goals, and how congruent the systems secondary, external goals are with the systems primary, internal goals.
>
> Therefore all system role behavior is characterized as moving towards or away from 'solving' the discrimination problems that lie along the path to its goal. Thus all role behavior can be analyzed in terms of its vector and salience characteristics in relation to both its primary and secondary goals. When system primary goals and secondary goals are incongruent, the system's behavioral vector will be directed towards the primary goals, and it is only to the extent that the primary and secondary goals lie in the same direction that the system can take a path towards the secondary goals.
>
> Role behavior, therefore, contains the potential for both defensive and problem-solving communications. Defensive, when the implicit goal of the system is to maintain internal equilibrium by keeping certain non-integrated information separately contained (maintaining the split), problem solving when the goal of the system is to mediate with the environment (discriminate and integrate the input/output comm- unications between the system and the environment) and move along the path to its explicit goal. (Agazarian 1988c, pp.363–364)

These articles are a good example of what happens when one lives in the world of theory. It is difficult to imagine, for those who do not share this kind of experience, how completely satisfying it was to find that Lewin's work translated so easily into systems thinking. I was not, at this time, directly relating theory to practice, even though there is no doubt that what I was thinking influenced my practice indirectly. For example, just as developing the SAVI system had enabled me to be able to understand the relationship between the communication patterns of the group and its members, so envisioning a system life space brought new meaning to my understanding of the relationship between the individual, the group and the role.

I do not believe that applying theory to practice in any systematic and disciplined way was in my mind. I was satisfied thinking about group dynamics and teaching others to think about group dynamics. I was still more a mixture of a researcher and a philosopher. The idea of developing a new system of therapy – and worse, an organization that would grow up around it – was the last thing on my mind.

As I discuss in greater detail in Chapter 6, it was the implications of the impact that health maintenance organizations would have on therapy that terrified me into refocusing my energy. It was as if I had been catapulted from my involvement in theory as a recreational activity into theory as a potential blueprint for developing a practice that might respond to the 'on again, off again' character of this new therapeutic world.

I was not to know then that putting my theory into practice would require skills that I not only did not possess but had no intention of learning. I question whether I would ever have been able to translate my ideas into practice had I not encountered Dr Habib Davanloo and his Short-Term Dynamic Psychotherapy. My work with him was the intervening variable that revolutionized my ability to put my theory into practice in that, through training with him, I changed (with great difficulty) from active listening to active intervention.

Short-Term Dynamic Psychotherapy

I had already 'chased' all the new approaches to therapy that I encountered over the thirty years of practice that it had taken me to reach this point. I had read Wolpe when his book first came out. I had met most of the initiators in the humanistic movement in the early days of the American Association for Humanistic Psychology. I had taken workshops with Bill Shutz, Jack Gibb, Fritz Perls, Virginia Satir and Sid Jourard. I was privileged to be on Abe Maslow's mailing list as he developed his thinking. I also had immersed myself for three weeks in a workshop in transactional analysis and studied Beck's cognitive therapy with David Burns.

It was in my continuing 'chase' that I encountered Davanloo's (1987) Short-Term Dynamic Psychotherapy (STDP) and my whole orientation to group psychotherapy was turned upside down. It was one thing to manipulate happily my own and other people's ideas, almost like a hobby, and it was quite another to manipulate people's behavior and to confront what it meant to put my ideas actively into practice in the real world of people, when the practice led in a direction opposite to everything in which I had been trained and believed.

I had heard that there was someone who was using videotape with patients and I was trying to locate the source and see whether or not this might be a technique that would be useful in therapy. By then Anita Simon and I had been joined in our office practice by Claudia Byram and the three of us had been giving workshops on SAVI and having a great deal of fun doing so. We went off to our first Davanloo weekend workshop together, rather as if it were a vacation. We had no idea of what we were in for.

The largest part of the STDP workshop was watching videotape. For approximately five hours a day we watched Dr Davanloo work with his patients in what he called his 'break through' initial interview. For me, he broke every rule in my unwritten book of what not to do in therapy. It had never occurred to me to question my central belief that one did not lead the patient, one 'followed' for as long as it took, listening with the 'third ear' all the way. Dr Davanloo, it seemed to me, did not listen to his patients at all, nor did he follow, rather they followed him. (He called it 'challenge and pressure' on the defenses to access the super-ego pathology that he claimed was the underlying issue in therapy.)

Dr Davanloo manifestly got results in four hours that I doubted I could have achieved with some of his patients, even after several years of patiently 'following'. He put them 'in a box'. He interrupted them continually. He was on their defenses like a terrier after a rat. When they cried, he challenged them with the 'weepy' defense. When they retreated into silence he confronted them with the 'helpless, passive, crippled defense'. When finally the patient 'broke through' into 'murderous rage' and accessed 'the charnel house' of the unconscious, Dr Davanloo was satisfied that the super-ego pathology had been reached. The patient then had a moment of 'free ego' (we could see it and had to believe it). A therapeutic relationship then existed between Dr Davanloo and the patient and they could then turn to understanding the patient's history and how it had influenced his present character defenses. We were appalled, astounded and envious.

We defended ourselves by interpreting Dr Davanloo's success as the patient identifying with the aggressor. We decided that his methods were dependency inducing, that he was acting out his sadism and that he was aggressive, intrusive and bullying. When we watched the five-year follow-up results and saw how the patients' lives had changed, we had to eat our words. Reluctantly, we abandoned our position of righteous indignation and decided we had better get trained to do what he could do, even though it turned our therapeutic style upside down.

We went back for several weekends and a five-day workshop. Dick Peters, our good friend and colleague, joined us and the four of us (Anita, Claudia, Dick and I) formally went into training. We went to New York once a month for two years to train with Michael Alpert, a colleague of Dr Davanloo. We became moderately good at understanding the STDP rationale and in producing some of the STDP style of intervention. We got together as a study group and watched videotapes of our own attempts at 'challenge and pressure'. We worked with our reaction formations against our own sadism that was aroused by our versions of 'bullying' and then we worked with our sadism.

What made the transition possible for me was SAVI. It was very clear to me that Dr Davanloo's mode of active intervention obtained the kind of therapeutic results that I wanted to be able to get. At the same time, although I was certainly able to produce the intervention style that characterized STDP practioners, I did not want the kind of relating that such a way of working entailed if there was another way. Throughout attending the workshops, I had used SAVI to code the interactions between Dr Davanloo and the patient. Davanloo's communication pattern coded heavily in 'yes-but's', sarcasm, commands, name-calling. In the SAVI system, these are avoidant communications that introduce 'noise' into the system. However, Dr Davanloo's patients' patterns became steadily less vague, with fewer 'yes-but's', less intellectualizations, less self-defense and more direct personal disclosure. I could see that the overall noise in the patients' SAVI communication patterns decreased and their 'approach' communications increased. With the patterns clear, it became a matter of finding alternate paths to goal. I asked myself, how could the therapist communication patterns shift (become less 'noisy') and still achieve the same results?

Once again I had asked a question the complexity of which was to take several years to answer. I first needed to develop the Systems-Centered Therapy (SCT) 'fork in the road' technique of requiring patients to choose which side of a conflict they wanted to explore (not explain). This did indeed successfully put them in a box, in that they had 'no choice' but to choose. However, it was also a free choice in that, although they had no freedom to explain, they did have the freedom to choose whether to explore their tendency to explain (the defense) or to explore what their experience would be if they did not explain (what they were defending against). Once the concept was clear, the strategies of communication were also clear and it became possible to work in an empathic connection with the person and at the same time box them in so that they could learn for themselves how to reduce their defenses.

There are two contributions that STDP made to my life for which I am forever in its debt. The first resulted in my altering permanently the style of intervention that I used in my practice. Had I not made this transition, I would not have been able to establish the methods of Systems-Centered Practice which are dependent upon deliberately weakening the specific forces that resist therapeutic change. Active listening had led me to understand how and why groups did the predictable and maladaptive things they do as they struggle with the underlying dynamic forces in their development. Active intervention was the tool I needed to stop the trouble before it started: to block most of the noise in communication before it entered the group, to introduce functional subgrouping before stereotype subgrouping had elected identified patients and scapegoats, to keep members at the fork in the road between the defense and what was being defended against before maladaptive patterns are established.

The second was the significant work that Davanloo had begun in being specific in defining and recognizing the defenses that must be modified. My interest in defenses as a phenomenon reached back to when I was teaching at the mental health clinic and at Hahneman University. At the clinic, I was teaching Anna Freud's mechanisms of defense (1937). Although Anna Freud had clearly 'observed' the defenses that she wrote about, my teaching colleagues were not as interested as me in being able to recognize the nonverbal behaviors that signaled the defense. (Behind the couch, one does not have such a good view of nonverbal behavior.) In the Hahnemann class we used videotape and did our best to locate the relationship between the facial expressions and gestures and the defense. All of this built upon a deep involvement in the early years with ethology, and particularly with Tinbergen's illustrations of 'intention movements' in animals and birds which I was convinced applied just as well to people. I had subsequently followed much of Birdwhistle's (1955) and Scheflen's (1963) early work, particularly the studies of the nonverbal interactions between therapists and their patients.

Dr Davanloo's emphasis on keeping 'a close eye' on the patient and his use of nonverbal cues to determine whether or not it was appropriate to put pressure on a patient were the kind of real world data that I respected and responded to. Dr Davanloo also had an idea of the hierarchy by which defenses could be modified – starting with the effect of anxiety on cognition and then moving towards motoric restraint to emotion.

Leigh McCullough came next into our STDP lives (1992). She was involved in a research project at the University of Pennsylvania investigating the efficacy of 15 sessions of STDP on anxiety and depression. She invited the four of us to do the therapy. We were delighted. It meant that we would meet with her every week and review our work for two factors: how reliably our therapeutic style reflected STDP and how reliable we were with each other. Leigh was writing the manual for the project at the time and we also used our time with her to think through the rationale behind the practice. I was in my element. Leigh and I took turns using the board in our office to diagram our solutions – sometimes building on each other and at other times diverging. It was useful and exciting to discover where I was not in sync with STDP. What came out of those sessions for me was the first coherent pass at the systems-centered hierarchy of defense modification – and which bears much resemblance to the hierarchy that we use today (see Chapter 6). I do not know whether for Leigh some of the groundwork for the extraordinary achievement of her 1997 book was also laid at that time, but I hope so (Valliant 1997).

The Shame Group

During all of this time I had been working with two groups for many years who were used to my 'Tavistock/group-as-a-whole' leadership. The Philadelphia training group had come to New York with me in 1985 to work as a demonstration group for the Eastern Group Psychotherapy Society (EGPS) conference. Though I continued to understand the dynamics of groups from my psychodynamic, group dynamic and systems frameworks without too much conflict, my group leadership behavior was on the edge of a transformation. I was not fully aware of the gulf that was developing until my group and I reacted so strongly to a psychoanalytically framed question. My training group and I were on stage demonstrating for the members of EGPS when we were confronted by a question from the audience that contained words like 'exhibitionism' and 'narcissism' and 'polymorphous perverse' – a language that had a connotative impact quite different from its denotative intention:

> Can you speak to the role of shame in this group, especially around the pleasures of this perverse exhibitionism that is built in [to the situation], and the anxiety around what kind of exhibitionistic pleasures might be being experienced.

It was my very good friend Anne Alonso who made the comment (she was much interested in the dynamics of shame at the time) and later we made a videotape of ourselves watching the group together and commenting on the process from our psychoanalytic and group-as-a-whole orientations (Agazarian and Alonso 1993).

The group and I were traumatized. We then had probably our most interesting group session ever. For the first half of the group after Anne's question, the group behaved 'as if' nothing had happened. One member then pointed out the 'as if' quality in which we were working and the group began to address their reactions to the question. The group first turned the aggression back on itself, then projected it onto the audience. With the aggression freed, the group then began to explore what part of their reactions were useful to their own work and what part were not. By the end we had not only managed to survive, to discriminate and integrate the experience, right on the EGPS stage, but to end with a feeling of triumph:

Y: Well, maybe there's a difference between the experience, of feeling exposed, and the label...which is the one that is used by the people who are watching us when we are feeling exposed.

Group silence.

K: ...I think that ties in with the analogy I was feeling about the dress rehearsal...part of it for me is the ambivalence – is this, is this the dress rehearsal or is this the real thing? How real are we going to be here? Er, how far are we going to go? How exposed am I going to be? How exposed are we going to be? A tremendous amount of ambivalence about that. There's a part of me that doesn't want to sit here and play dress rehearsal, that feels like a waste of two good group sessions to me.

Y: Yeah, I wonder if the 'dress rehearsal atmosphere' is a defense from letting the audience's comments be toxic to us? The way we will do that is to detoxify them by getting the parts of the message that's meaningful and useful to us, and spitting out the other half just the way one spits out the shell of a nut.

F: Yeah it feels like it I mean I, you know, I really physically want to, kind of want to push...

Y: What? ...what do you want to push back and what do you want to keep?

F: I want to push back the audience, the comments...

A: I want to push back what I've done to some of my patients when I've done this...

Y: You're 'identifying with the aggressor' – a defense!

A: I'm enraged, I'm enraged!

M: Me too!

Sh: Me too!

S: I want to push back the labels, I want to push back not being understood, or not being heard...push back the projections...

A: Not being understood – it's so painful to not feel understood and...

Y: ...what was the label that left you feeling misunderstood?

A: ...that's really a hard question...'wish for exhibitionism...'

M: ...yes, 'exhibitionism' and 'perverse'...

A: ...'perverse'...

M: ...that's the one that got me...

F: Oh, I forgot about that one.

S: I did too, that's right...

Y: What are the labels that hurt, and what part of those labels do we need to work with so that we can take it...back? And what part do we not want to work with so we can get rid of it...

T: I was thinking, yeah, exhibition, I guess that is part of what I was doing, so I'll have to take it back

F: I had some of the exhibitionism too, and what I am having a difficulty with, what I want to keep in the group is the pleasure, right before that, the pleasure of being envied by so many people in the audience, of being in this group, and getting to be here, and getting to do this, is fun [*laughs*] it is fun,

A: Yeah, it's fun, it's not as bad as I thought it would be.

And at the very end the group has reintegrated the differences and feels triumph and mastery.

S: ...this is my group,

M: Right!

S: ...and I'm proud.

F: That's right, that's true, that's part of the pleasure I'm feeling.

Sh: We've done it, we did it, we did it!

S: We did it!

Sh: We made it!

Y: We've crossed a time boundary.

(Agazarian and Alonso 1993)

Understanding the Anguish of Self-Centeredness

Anne Alonso was another of the people in my life who influenced my career and became one of my closest friends.[3] It was Anne who invited me to my first professional presentation as a guest lecturer in group psychotherapy at Harvard Medical School (discussed in Chapter 3). It was also Anne who invited me to be the discussant at the American Group Psychotherapy Association's 1989 Slavson Memorial Lecture given by Sampson and Weiss.

Little did I know that this was to be my trial by fire. I engaged in the challenge with great enthusiasm, looking forward to generalizing to group dynamics the hypotheses that Sampson and Weiss (1986) were testing in relationship to individual psychoanalysis. I summarized their approach in the first few paragraphs of my paper (Agazarian 1989a):

> A person exercises unconscious control over repressions as a function of unconscious appraisals of danger and safety, and it follows that: a patient's appraisal of 'danger' stems from pathogenic, unconscious beliefs about 1) himself, 2) his interpersonal world and 3) himself in relation to his interpersonal world.
>
> Thus maladaptive behavior is governed by the patient's judgment about danger/safety – and both Dr Sampson and Dr Weiss give examples of how, when the psychoanalytic process makes it 'safe enough' for the patient to make the unconscious belief conscious, a therapeutic change takes place.
>
> Dr Weiss says that pathogenic beliefs are unconscious, archaic 'representations' of reality. This implies that these 'pathogenic beliefs' maintain the characteristics of the level of cognitive development that existed at the time of the original repression. As their source is usually in the early phases of development, they reflect archaic and primitive mental processes: discrimination by splitting into primary differences – good (similar) and bad (different); incomplete separation-individuation; egocentric primal guilt; and the retaliatory impulses of talon law.
>
> These beliefs are primarily related to judgments, either about reality (how things are) or morality (how things should be) and thus influence perceptions of reality (Agazarian 1989a, p.1).

I had intended to then lay the background with my 'systems' thinking:

3   She was also the friend I turned to, to help me master some of the later losses in my life, when my two remaining brothers and my sister died within three years of each other.

It is my privilege today to apply the implications of Dr Weiss's hypothesis to group psychotherapy. I have done this by using general systems theory to bridge individual and group dynamics and applied the principle of isomorphy, which requires that what is said about the dynamics of any one system in a hierarchy can also be said about all other systems in the same hierarchy.

In this sense, then, pathogenic beliefs can be likened to a cognitive map that influences how a system perceives its environment and explains how it responds to it. By observing behavior, one can infer the map, and by inferring the map, one can infer the implicit goals of the behavior. Thus behavior that looks explicitly self-defeating can be understood as 'safely' self-preserving in the light of the implicit goal inferred by the map of the pathogenic belief. Hence, the implicit goals are primary determinants of behavior for both individual and group systems.

As we apply Dr Weiss's hypothesis to group psychotherapy, it is important to differentiate between individual system dynamics and the system dynamics of the group-as-a-whole. Individual and group systems exist in a hierarchy of living systems and share a common maturation process: discriminating and integrating similarities and differences. This process characterizes the development of simple and complex systems, from individual cells to psychological and group social processes. But whereas, from the individual perspective, groups are made up of individual members, from the perspective of the group-as-a-whole, groups are made up of subgroups. Thus subgroups are the raw material of group development and contain the group potential, and are the basic container for similarities and differences. Through subgroup interaction, groups develop through predictable phases towards maturation. At each moment of group life, the group-as-a-whole system integrates all subgroup discriminations that are within its integration ability.

Whenever the group or individual system is confronted with differences that are too different, too disequilibrating to integrate and too overwhelming to project, then the difference is split off and isolated within a 'containing' subsystem. It is thus that the system meets its primary goal of maintaining a viable equilibrium. The secondary goals that exist in relation to reality are literally secondary to these primary goals.

Splitting in this sense is in the service of the maturation process of the system remaining in a viable equilibrium while it interacts with its environment and develops secondary goals. I differ here from Dr Weiss and Sampson who attribute the perception of danger and safety to the patient's concern about the consequences in the environment of acting on impulses: from the perspective of group-as-a-whole theory, this is not a simple matter of ego-id and super-ego mediation with reality but rather a system equilibrating mechanism that both protects the integrating mechanism by creating subsystems to contain the 'too different' while the system matures sufficiently to integrate it as sufficiently similar.

For the purpose of maturation theory,[4] the definition of maturation is 'maturation of any system is a function of the rate by which the process of discrimination and integration occurs.' The process of maturation in both groups and individuals can be described in this way. In groups, maturation starts by the splitting and containing separately, conflicting perceptions: containing similarities in subgroups that are perceived to be 'like me and good,' and containing differences in subgroups that are perceived 'not like me and bad.' Once contained, the group can continue the maturation process that enables it to integrate at a later time that which was too different to integrate at the time the conflicted perception occurred (Agazarian 1989a, pp.2–3).

I then turn to Sampson and Weiss's argument:

From the system perspective, the 'pathogenic belief' is an integrational principle, like a faulty map, which induces the system to behave in ways that are primarily related to a need to keep the system in equilibrium at the expense of reality.

In society's groups, in this stage of social development, we still tend to explain the dynamics of all living systems anthropomorphically and egocentrically – and we tend, in psychology, and even in the field of group psychotherapy, to relate all human phenomena to individual experience.

The thinking that characterized the pathogenic belief both reflects the nature of the cognitive development that exists at the time it is set, and determines its virulence.

Egocentric individualism develops in the phase of separation-individuation. This is accompanied by the primal fantasies of retaliation – Talion Law – and the dichotomizing Aristotelian logic that underlies our Western language structure and reinforces the good–bad split.

---

4   Maturation theory was one of the transitional labels along the way: the theory of the invisible group and the group-as-a-whole was briefly renamed integration theory, maturation theory and finally a theory of living human systems.

Drs Sampson and Weiss point out that pathogenic beliefs are the source of inhibitions, symptoms and anxiety.

If the unconscious belief persists in individuals and groups that man is the center of the world, then the price would be narcissistic pain at exposure, shame at separation and survivor guilt. Thus man's individual pain comes from taking things personally (Agazarian 1989a, p.4).

So far all is going well – I have formulated the idea that one of the sources of anguish that characterizes so much of the work of therapy is generated by taking things personally – an idea that will be fundamental to my later work of 'contextualizing': developing individual awareness of various context and the 'membership' roles that are appropriate to it.

I then move on to pointing out, with some satisfaction, that in the group-as-a-whole approach there is less incentive to take things personally in that the therapist treats patients as members as well as individuals:

And perhaps this is where there is the greatest difference in between individual therapy and group-as-a-whole therapy. In individual therapy (and in individually focused group therapy) man is the central focus of the therapist's attention, the patient is treated 'as if' he is the center of the world. (Agazarian 1989a, p.4)

Believe it or not, at this point I entered into a nightmare experience. It suddenly became obvious to me that not only was the analysand in psychoanalysis encouraged to experience him or herself as the center of the world, thus exacerbating the narcissistic pain at exposure, egocentric survivor guilt and shame at separation, but worse, was forced into a mutual denial, preconscious to both the analyst as well as the analysand, that the analyst was really the center of the world!

It seems incredible to me now – but at the time I felt so disloyal and devastated that I was tempted to leave my 'findings' out of my paper. Understanding now that it was my own survivor guilt and shame at separation from psychoanalysis was no help then. What did help, as it always has whenever life has felt too tough, was my brother Jack. If he could survive months of torture and solitary confinement as a political prisoner in a concentration camp in the belief that the world was worth dying for, I could at least stand behind my own beliefs, in a world that was worth living for. And so I finished my paper as follows:

And perhaps this is where there is the greatest difference between psychoanalysis and group-as-a-whole therapy. In psychoanalysis and other forms of individual therapy (and in individually focused group therapy) man is the central focus of the therapist's attention, the patient is treated 'as if' he is the center of the world and thus unconsciously encouraged to take things personally. In group-as-a-whole therapy, relief from the narcissistic pain, shame and survivor guilt that results from this egocentric focus comes when it is safe enough for each group member to experience his role in the subgroup and the group-as-a-whole, and to see his individual self mirrored in structure and function in a hierarchy of living systems.

When applied to the world of theory, it would explain why psychoanalysis looks first to intrapsychic dynamics, and only later to interpersonal, object-related dynamics. It would explain why group dynamics are more usually explained in terms of individual dynamics and why it appears to be so difficult for us, as group therapists, to perceive the isomorphy between, for example, the system dynamics of individuals and the dynamics of groups. Parenthetically, it is also remarkable how tenaciously group members fight against acknowledging the impact of group-as-a-whole dynamics upon their experience and upon their behavior, or in resisting acknowledging their subgroup memberships. It is almost as if they take flight from their subgroup membership and into isolation; choose to suffer alone than to share existential reality. Yet, when a group works past the phase of disenchantment, and experiences in reality that they have membership, there is great relief. When group members learn not to take their group roles personally, when they understand that their behavior is motivated by, not only their own primary and secondary goals, but also the group's goals, much of the guilt appears to resolve, and both the group and the members seem to defend less against primal experience and the promise of its creative potential (Agazarian 1989a, p.6).

There is often a wry irony to life. After all my Sturm und Drang, I sat at the podium next to Anne Alonso and watched first Sampson and then Weiss taking their time, with fewer and fewer minutes available for my discussion. As the minutes passed, I cut more and more passages out of my paper, with Anne sitting next to me, carefully keeping a straight face. When my turn came, there were five of the thirty minutes left for my paper. I bit the bullet and gave the two most important parts of it – my appreciation of the contribution made by Sampson and Weiss and the meaning that I felt it had for us in that group could reduce survivor guilt by reducing egocentric focus. I still expected the sky to fall in. What actually happened was that two people from what was left of the audience came and told me that they appreciated my point very much.

Systems Group Therapy

That same year I was asked to be guest editor for a special edition on the group-as-a-whole for *Group* (1989) and was very excited. I asked Dorothy Whitaker and Pat de Maré for articles and they agreed. When I was first formulating my systems theory and seeking some sense of whether what I was theorizing made sense, I had talked to Dorothy Whitaker who invited me to stay with her on the edge of the Yorkshire moors. And she listened, really listened, to my theory. She was emphatically encouraging. I left her hospitality feeling validated and when I was in need of confidence in less rewarding exchanges I would remember Dorothy's support.

Pat de Maré sent me an article that he prized very highly but had not been able to get published and I was proud to be able to give him the opportunity. Writing my own lead article, however, was the worst experience of writing that I had ever had. My asthma and COPD were being badly managed and I was anoxic a great deal of the time. (I was to discover later that my 'peak flow' was under 150 and that 200 warrants a trip to the emergency room.)[5] All I did know was that as I tried to write this all-important article I was unable to find its flow, could not keep its gestalt in my head and could not even remember what I had covered and what I had not. Even when I read it, I would lose the 'fit' of one passage before I got to the next. It came out as a complex, dense article with an appendix which was almost a second article in itself. The good news and the bad news: as I was my own editor, there was no one but me to reject it or ask me to revise it, a blissful (if not very functional) state which I often wish I could repeat.

---

5   Soon after this I was referred to Dr Sheryl Talbot – who I believe saved my life. She taught me the discipline of keeping myself as well as possible and she continues as a very important person to me, not only because of being a good doctor, but also by her presence.

In the article, I built on von Bertalanffy's (1969) work on systems and presented the individual and group as two isomorphic systems in a 'hierarchy of living human systems'. I argued that the basic unit of all human systems (like individuals and groups) is the subgroup rather than the individual member and that the structure, function and dynamics are equivalent in the individual, subgroup and group-as-a-whole systems (isomorphy). The group-as-a-whole therapist listens to how members voice subgroup and group-as-a-whole issues and the group members' therapy occurs as a side-effect of the group-as-a-whole. (Group maturation demands maturation on the part of its members.) Thus the primary task of the group-as-a-whole therapist is to promote the development of healthy systems. I included my systems hypotheses on 'group-as-a-whole':

> An important set of system hypotheses follow. It is assumed that the basic components of systems are subsystems – that, at each level, the system exists in the environment of the system above and serves as the environment for the system below and that there is a potential for communication at all levels. Thus a major focus for the systems group therapist is the communications between the systems.

> Some of the assumptions basic to this framework are:

> 1. The basic components of systems are subsystems. At each level, the system exists in the environment of the system above and serves as the environment for the system below.

> 2. Communication is an input/output informational exchange within and between systems.

> 3. Communication is the process by which systems discriminate and integrate information.

> 4. System maturation is a function of a communication process that results in discriminating and integrating the similarities and differences within and between systems and subsystems.

> 5. System boundaries are open to information, closed to noise.

> 6. Increases and reductions in ambiguities, contradictions and redundancies in information increase or reduce the noise that is inherent in the communication process itself.

> 7. Altering the ambiguity, contradiction, redundancy balance in the communication process alters the ratio of information to noise; the

boundary permeability among systems; the potential for the transfer of information between systems; and the maturational potential of the system itself and its hierarchy.

8. The system's ability to receive complex inputs and to tolerate the noise that the integration of differences entails is dependent upon the development of the integrational ability of the system.

9. The development of the ability to integrate information is dependent upon the development of the system's ability to evolve from simple to complex organizations.

10. Successful therapeutic consultations decrease the contradictions, ambiguities and redundancies in the information across the boundaries within and between systems.

11. To the extent that the boundaries between systems at all levels of the relevant hierarchy are permeable to information, then system maturation is potentiated. Maturation is a function of the ability to discriminate similarities and differences across all boundaries of the system hierarchy, and to integrate these discriminations in the direction of simple to complex.

12. By changing the structure of boundaries the potential for transferring information is changed. Boundary permeability determines what information the system is open to, and what it is closed to. The existing organization of information determines when information is too different to be integrated and must therefore either be defended against before it enters the system or must be split off and contained separately when it does.

By observing the 'communication output of the system', the system group therapist infers the internal organization of the system and judges the approach/avoidance relationship to its primary and secondary goals. Primary goals are related to integrating discriminations within the system. Secondary goals are related to the system task of discriminating itself from its environment. Ambiguities, contradictions and redundancies increase the difficulty inherent in the maturational process of integration and discrimination, and as such are problems that the system must solve in achieving its primary and secondary goals.

The system group therapist 'consults' to the boundaries in the sense that he influences the 'noise' in the transactions between the subsystems, within the individual, and within the group-as-a-whole, and thus influences both the system's internal integration and its relationship to its environment, and this potentiates the system's developmental adaptation from simple to complex (Agazarian 1989b, pp.134–135).

I continued in the article by defining the systems therapist's job as one of consulting to boundaries and relating boundaries to system goals (which necessitates identifying implicit and explicit goals):

> The systems therapist consults to the boundaries and addresses the two major sources of noise in a communication: noise inherent to the communication process (ambiguity, contradiction, redundancy) or noise that comes from too much difference between the new information and the existing integration of information in a system; for instance, differences that are too different are scapegoated. Consultations focus on reducing the noise inherent in the process of communication which increases the likelihood of information transfer which is the goal of communication, or influencing the discrimination/integration process in the system.

I then address some of the differences and similarities between traditional therapists and systems therapists:

> Similarities, differences and complementarity between systems group therapists and traditional group therapists
>
> I.   Traditionally group therapists work with people, systems group therapists work with subgroups.
>
> A.   From the traditional group therapy perspective, groups are made up of individual members.
>
> B.   From the group-as-a-whole systems perspective, groups are made up of subgroups.
>
> II. Traditionally group therapists interpret to people, systems group therapists intervene at system boundaries.
>
> A.   From the traditional group therapy perspective. therapists interpret to influence the internal dynamics and external behavior of the person through insight.
>
> B.   Systems group therapists intervene to influence system communications: between subgroups and in the group-as-a-whole.
>
> III. Both traditionally and in systems group practice, therapists monitor the way the group works, but:

A. Traditional group therapists influence the way the group works by influencing the way the individuals work in it; monitoring group work by monitoring the interactions between the individual and other group members.

B. Systems group therapists influence the way the group works by influencing the way the subgroups work in it; monitoring group function by monitoring the interactions between subgroups. Attention is drawn to the boundaries between subgroups. When the group-as-a-whole process becomes ambiguous or redundant, attention is drawn to unacknowledged differences between subgroups; when the process becomes contradictory, attention is drawn to unacknowledged similarities. Subgroup communication on similarities and differences undoes stereotyping and potentiates maturation.

IV. Both traditionally and in systems group practice, therapists use communication as the major therapeutic tool, but:

A. The major therapeutic technique of traditional group therapy is communicating insight to the person.

B. The major therapeutic technique of the systems group therapist is influencing the structure and function of the communication behavior itself across the boundaries of the subgroups.

V. Both traditionally and in systems group practice, therapists take responsibility for making decisions about the structure and function of the group; however,

A. From the traditional group therapy perspective, the therapist takes the responsibility for selecting the members, defining the goals, setting the fees, deciding when and where and for how long the group will meet, deciding whether and when to bring in new members and making all the rules for the group.

B. The systems group therapist selects the members and defines the goals and initially sets the fee. But as the group develops, he delegates responsibility for group management decisions to the group. For example, the group develops rules as guidelines that lead to the group goals.

VI. Both traditionally and in systems group practice, therapists aim to modify the dynamics of the person's inner experience and outer behavior; however,

A.   From the traditional group therapy perspective, the therapist does this by interpretations to the individual person's psychodynamics and the manifestations of those dynamics in the individuals' interpersonal behavior, whereas,

B.   The systems group therapist does this by interventions that influence the permeability of the boundaries between the subgroups.

VII.   Both traditionally and in systems group therapy, the therapist has the same treatment goal: therapy of the individual; however,

A.   From the traditional therapy perspective the therapist focuses on the dynamic maturation of the individual as the most direct path to the goal of therapy for the individual members.

B.   The systems group therapist focuses on the dynamic maturation of the group-as-a-whole as the major path to the treatment of the individual members.

VIII.   Both traditionally and in systems group practice, the therapists are concerned with phases of development and look to the developmental history, environmental influences and maturational experience to understand vicissitudes in development and their impact on dynamics; however,

A.   From the traditional group therapy perspective the therapist looks to the past: to the developmental history that the individual member brings with him into the group. The source of data is outside the group. The past developmental issues are the material of current therapy.

B.   The systems therapist looks to the present; the current developmental issues for the group-as-a-whole and its subgroups occur as the group matures. Developmental history arises from the vicissitudes that occur in the phases of group development and are the material of current group-as-a-whole problem solving. The systems group therapist has the opportunity of monitoring how the group develops in the here-and-now. Thus the phases in group-as-a-whole development, and its phase specific maturational challenges, provide the stimulus and the context in which individual members' developmental issues are revisited. (Agazarian 1989b, pp.149–151)

By this 1989 article, I have moved from my group-as-a-whole orientation to my systems orientation, and I was by now understanding the subgroup as the basic unit in the group. Drawing the hierarchy of member, subgroup and group-as-a-whole as three concentric circles enabled me to identify at a theoretical level that the subgroup was the most effective point in which to intervene, as what became obvious when you look is that the subgroup shares its boundaries with both the member and the group. What is more, what I had already understood and observed about group role as a voice for the group also applied to subgroups (isomorphy again.) I seemed to have had some early understanding of this by 1986:

> Parenthetically, the same 'containment' dynamic exists when a subgroup rather than a single group member performs a group role, as, for example, when disagreement in a group is contained in a silent subgroup who do not give voice to their disagreement, or when differences in group feeling are isolated by a split, as when the group functions at a level of intellectualized flight, with all feeling in the group denied and unavailable. (Agazarian 1986a, p.110)

I had redefined Lewin's life space equation, from behavior as a function of a person in interaction with the environment to behavior as a function of the system in interaction with its environment with behavior then defined as a system output.

I was also close to understanding the functional equivalence of energy and information, building on the work of Miller (1978) who worked with the idea of information and energy flowing among open systems. It took many years for the equivalence between energy/information to become intuitively obvious. For those who are in a muddle as I was, there are some analogies that might help. Energy is on a continuum with mass: for example, ice is mass, which can transform into water which can transform into steam, which is energy enough to drive a train. Thus, energy can be frozen, as it is when nothing new happens in a group, or it can be freed, either to vent into the atmosphere as it does when a group discharges its energy in frustration, or it can be directed towards a goal. Living human systems are energy organizing and information organizing. They have the potential to use the process of discriminating and integrating to organize the information in chaos. Information can be organized in many ways. A blueprint, for example, is an example of organizing information that can lead to building bridges, houses, cars, aeroplanes – all of which potentiate survival and development of living human systems. When energy/information are understood as equivalent, reducing the noise in communication at the system boundary reduces entropy and thereby increases the availability of energy that can be vectored toward system goals.

With many of the basic theoretical pieces in place, I was taking the steps of implementing my systems theory in practice. The following year I began the workshops in which I discovered the dynamics that emerged in the group as I applied systems theory and my innovations in methods, using functional subgrouping and beginning to develop the methods and techniques of what was soon to become systems-centered therapy.

CHAPTER 6

Systems-Centered Practice

Ever since my initial experience of designing workshops at Temple University, designing and doing workshops had always been one of the things that I enjoyed very much. In the 1970s, Anita, Claudia and I had designed the SAVI workshops and had good results, both in getting attendance and getting remunerated. We had even briefly teamed up with a large consultant organization, and adding SAVI communication training to their designs was a challenge and a triumph.

By the 1980s, I found myself in demand for presentations and had the opportunity of designing different kinds of workshops for the different organizations, some for staff development and others for training in group psychotherapy. I was becoming known as a group-as-a-whole therapist, which was an orientation that had fewer representatives than the interpersonal or individual patient orientations.

In addition, I was invited to do presentations for the various group psychotherapy associations, not only in the USA, but also abroad — Amsterdam, Calgary, Copenhagen, Heidelberg, Holland, London, Mexico, Montreal, Stockholm, Tokyo, Vancouver. I found it particularly challenging and rewarding to be training members whose English (if it existed) was a second language and discovered how relatively easy it was to recognize the group dynamics of nonverbal behavior.

Best of all, each year the American Group Psychotherapy Association gave me the priceless opportunity to work for two days in its annual institutes, trying out with its members the differences in my own orientation that I had developed in the intervening year.

The SCT Workshops

Since the late 1980s, my ongoing training groups had worked with me through many of the variations in my techniques as I fumbled my way towards developing a leadership style that was specifically systems-centered. Yet it was to be in the systems-centered workshops that I started in the fall of 1990 where the methods would coalesce. About forty people signed up for my first workshop, all of whom came from the training groups that I had been working with over the years. The 'Friday Philadelphia Group' was the oldest group of some ten years. It met weekly and was the veteran of the 'shame' experience on the EGPS stage (discussed in Chapter 5). Having survived that together, the training group and I were fairly well equipped to survive the innovations that I started experimenting with in this first systems-centered workshop.

There were three other groups represented, one from Philadelphia and two from New York, one that had started after I did the demonstration in 1985 and another that started earlier, both of which met once a month on Saturdays. The New York groups were more traditionally group-as-a-whole and psychodynamic than the Philadelphia groups, who had lived with me through many of the subtle changes of leadership reflecting my changes in orientation. In 1990, however, there was nothing subtle about the changes I introduced, nor the group's reactions to them.

We met for this first system-centered workshop in Newark, a compromise between New York and Philadelphia and a reflection of my concern that New Yorkers would not come to Philadelphia anyway. The workshop design seemed like a good one. I alternated large group work with work in small groups. In the small groups, the members had an opportunity to review the large group experience and organize their reactions in force fields. At the end of the day, the whole group came together again and summarized the day in a large group force field. The workshop began with everyone together as a large group where the first task was to choose one of two roles: participant or observer. To get the members to divide themselves into these two groupings, I arranged the chairs in a large spiral – with the instruction that those who wished to be observers sit from the outside in and those who wished to participate sit from the inside out. Where the two groupings met would be the boundary between observers and participants – the 'ins' could then pull their chairs into a circle and the 'outs' could ring the outside like a fishbowl (Figure 6.1).

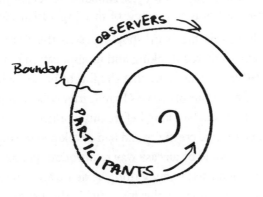

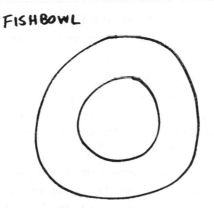

Figure 6.1 Spiral and fishbowl

I also arranged breakout tables for the times that the group would divide into small groups to review the work and generate force fields of the driving and restraining forces, with a purple folder on each table for whoever volunteered for leadership in the small group sessions. (The 'purple folder' became a symbol of status!) In the purple folders were the 'Guidelines to Leadership' paper, as well as my first attempt to introduce my version of systems, as an illustrated guide to a way of thinking and a way of practicing:

The purpose of developing new concepts – new ways of thinking and seeing – is so that we can do things that we couldn't do in the world before we saw it through new eyes. Thinking 'systems-centered' instead of 'patient-centered' is an example of this. (Agazarian 1990a, p.1).

Around the walls in this first workshop I pasted the illustrations for 'A flip-chart of systems-centered thinking and its application to the practice of group therapy (1990b). I was lucky that the fourth person who had joined Anita, Claudia and me at our office was Fran Carter, who was part artist and part licensed social worker. Not long before this workshop, Fran and I had a sudden burst of unexpected creativity and had developed the flip chart in one afternoon. I hoped it would be an easy way to introduce people to the theory which often manifested itself in my writing as dense and somewhat hard to read. Some of these pictures of the force field (the Lewinian tool I had adapted) are included in Figure 6.2.

I was also trying for a light touch with the workshop papers. The excerpt below comes from an unpublished workshop paper 'Systems-centered thinking applied to human systems in general and to systems-centered therapy in particular' (Agazarian 1990a):

> In our role of therapists doing therapy – systems-centered thinking 'should' help us understand the world of psychology differently so that we can do things therapeutically that we couldn't do before – in individual therapy, or group therapy, or family therapy, or any one of the many specialized therapies.
>
> Certainly applying systems-centered thinking to group therapy did help me see and do things differently as a group therapist. I came to see subgroups rather than individuals as the basic unit of the group-as-a-whole, and to focus on 'system roles' rather than group member-roles as the most powerful and economical way to influence therapeutic changes for both the individual and the group.
>
> When I then took this systems-centered thinking about group back into individual therapy (and I can hardly believe how long it took me to recognize the complementarity between groups and individuals as systems!), I worked in new ways that wasted less of my own and my patients' time. My next step was to formalize systems-centered thinking into a coherent theory of human behavior, which I present in this paper.
>
> Systems-centered thinking orients our understanding to the dynamics of systems so that we do not require of ourselves and of others changes that

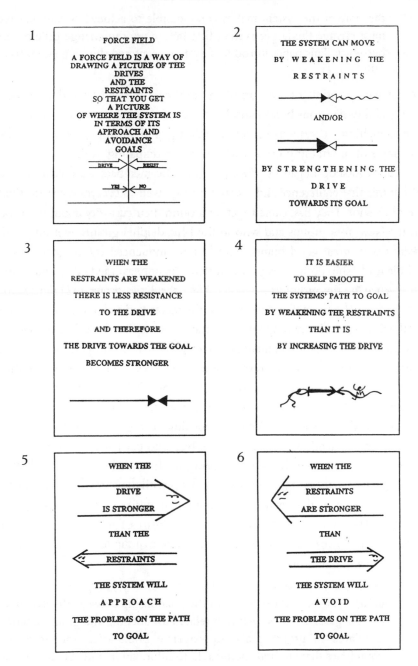

Figure 6.2 Force field

the state of the system makes it impossible to achieve. Sometimes we must change the larger system first before we can change others – or ourselves. This paper introduces Systems-centered thinking (Agazarian 1990a, p.1).

My final preparation for the workshop was the food. I had catered to the best of my ability generous breaks and lunches, reflecting my own excitement at the launching of systems-centered training and in appreciation for the members of my training groups who were participating in the launch.

The workshop began on Friday night. The members were also excited about this first conference and wanted it to go well so everyone was on their best behavior. They first came together around their curiosity about who was in the New York groups and who in the Philadelphia groups, working their rivalry with great good humor. Still heavily influenced by my group-as-a-whole leadership norms, I kept my distance, mainly avoided eye contact, and intervened to the group-as-a-whole. After the large group experience, the group divided into small groups around the tables to develop their force fields of the driving and restraining forces for their process. The force fields conveyed a sense of the group's excitement and hard work, and at this point the driving forces were at least as strong as the restraining forces (see Figure 6.3). We then convened again as a large group to do a group force field on the walls that I had covered in brown paper. The workshop design seemed to go very well.

This was no longer true the next morning. The group that had used the spiral so competently to separate themselves into participants and observers seemed to have lost the skills overnight. It ended up with a lumpy configuration in the middle for the participants with the observers often almost in the circle rather than maintaining their boundaries outside. I was almost amused. The group had struck right to the heart of my emphasis on the relationship between structure and the ability of a group to contain its energy so that it can do its work:

> What makes the difference to the work of any group system are not group dynamics but the clarity of the relationship between the dynamics and the goals. Group structure is related to function, and group function is related to group goals. Appropriate boundaries, therefore, are boundaries that are both permeable to information and able to contain the information so that it can be organized into a driving force in relationship to the group goals. (Agazarian 1992c, p.8)

In spite of the strange structure that the group had created, it did the work I was hoping it would do, which was to explore in subgroups the experience of the group process as it unfolded. In this sense, my own goals were being met in that I was anxious to test out my ideas about subgrouping in both large groups and small. I was testing whether or not working within a subgroup would in fact enable both the group and members to contain dynamics that would otherwise be acted out, and whether the very process of learning how to subgroup was also a developmental step. (Functional subgrouping is discussed at length in the next section of this chapter.)

Driving forces	→	←	Restraining forces
Staying in the here & now experience	→	←	Avoiding the present by focusing on observers
Focusing on members in the group and not observers outside	→		
Speaking the unspoken	→	←	Silence
Open acknowledgment of feelings of exposure, shame, intimidation	→	←	Slow to get to feelings
		←	Feeling intimidated, exposed, shamed
		←	Avoiding feelings
Joining a subgroup			
Identifying the subgroups, both the affective and demographic			
			Not answering questions
			Superficial subgroups
			Discussing the past and the known
			Envy
Built on work with each other	→	←	Interrupting

Figure 6.3 Force field from the first meeting of the first systems-centered workshop

The very process of learning to subgroup requires members to relate to others as well as to themselves. Members learn that there is an important difference between encouraging another member's work, paying lip service to subgroup work, and joining the subgroup with heart as well as words. When the members have difficulty working, rather than being encouraged to struggle through their resistances (as in patient-centered therapy), they are encouraged to turn to their subgroup and make space for a fellow member who has more immediate available salience for (or less resistance to) the next step. In this way, the member who starts to work 'rests' without guilt when he can go no further, while others in his subgroup continue to work. Resonating with the subgroup work, the 'resting' member takes his own next step when he is ready (Agazarian 1994, p.38).

By mid-morning the group had once again established its geographical structure. As nearly all the members by then were working as participants, it was less difficult to form a large circle with clear boundaries in which everybody could see everybody else (keeping in eye contact with subgroup members helps maintain a subgroup, whether it is working or waiting to work.) The major restraining (and driving) forces contained in the lumpy structure had been charted in the force fields that were taking up more and more wall space in the room.

Lunch was served in the same room as the large group – and the hotel staff converted the break-out tables into a dining room to serve lunch. Directly after lunch the group reconvened. I had been particularly careful to ask the staff of the hotel to clear only during the breaks and not intrude into our working time. My heart sank when, after about fifteen minutes of our group work, the staff came in to clear the tables. This precipitated the fiercest authority issue I had experienced up to that time in my group leader life. A veteran of the authority issue, both in my teaching at Temple and in my own training groups, as well as in my own writing (Agazarian and Peters 1981), I was not expecting ever again to be really frightened when the authority issue erupted. I was, however, and although I did not believe the part of myself that expected to be killed and eaten, my disbelief did not alleviate my internal conviction:

Working through the vicissitudes of the transition in the barometric event is dependent upon the leader being able to maintain the role boundaries in the group, and to maintain subgroups as containers for the work... What the group-as-a-whole has to become ready to contain are the regressive, primitive, and often very bloody and violent fantasies of the destruction of the leader. 'These many individuals eventually banded themselves together, killed (the father) and cut him in pieces ... They then formed the totemistic community of brothers, all with equal rights and united by the totem prohibitions which were to preserve and to expiate the memory of the murder' (quoted by Bennis and Shepard 1956, from Freud 1922).

Sometimes the leader is seen as some animal, murdered and thrown into the middle of the group, and savaged. Sometimes the members experience themselves as violent and bloody animals feeding on the carcass, with blood dripping from their faces. Other times the leader is thrown onto a fire, a pyre, danced around, roasted and eaten. Sometimes a duality is experienced: the impulse to rend and tear at flesh in savage hunger, and at the same time, to swallow and digest and be satisfied and full inside. Often, the work is followed by a rush of gratitude and love that the leader can contain so much hate. And afterwards, in the relief, there can be a profound feeling of group communion (Agazarian 1994, pp.59–60).

Those of us who were at that meeting still remember what a 'good, classic' authority issue it was, and what excellent learning occurred about the group response towards the leader when a boundary is violated – how quickly a group becomes afraid that the leader who cannot maintain the boundary between the group and the outside world will be unable to protect the group from the world or from itself.

This first weekend achieved more than I could have hoped. Most of the dynamics of the early phases of flight and fight had been explored in subgroups rather than acted out. After we had all successfully contained the impulses to immolate the leader, the group explored both their primitive impulses and the transference aspects that go hand-in-hand with it. What was particularly rewarding was the ability of this large group to reach, experience and survive the authority issue (the erupting of primitive aspects of the negative transference), all in one weekend.

I sent out a follow-up letter to all participants, starting the process of integrating the work the group had done with the theory. In this 28 pages I included the theory paper everyone had received before the workshop and discussed what had happened to illustrate the theory. Below I have excerpted the illustrations I gave for hierarchy and goals. About the concept of hierarchy, I wrote:

> All human systems exist in a hierarchy, where each system exists as a subsystem in the environment of the system above it in the hierarchy and serves as the environment for the subsystem below it in the hierarchy. A subgroup exists as the environment for the members who are its subsystem and exists as a subsystem in the environment of the group-as-a-whole for which the subgroups are its subsystem components. For example, our systems-centered workshop was the system environment for our large group discussion and our small discussion groups. The large group that was boundaried by the spiral was the environment for our experiential and observer subgroups. In each of the systems we are identifying there were ever-changing subgroups that shifted in time with the shifts in system dynamics.

How you define your hierarchy depends upon your purpose

Depending upon the purpose for which any one of us is reviewing the weekend, we can think about the hotel organization as the environment for our workshop and our workshop as the environment of all the different size groups and subgroups that appeared and disappeared over the weekend.

We can think about the large discussion group and the small discussion groups and the roles of participant and observer in terms of hierarchy. We can think about any one or all of the shifting subgroups in any one or all of the workshop groups. Each individual one of us can think of ourselves as a system with different internal subgroups that appeared and disappeared (sometimes to our individual astonishments).

We can also bring into focus the dynamics of the many overlapping memberships that were created during our shifts from group to group over the weekend, not to mention the overlapping membership that we brought in with us from other hierarchies that belonged to our outside lives! What we choose to bring into focus depends upon the purpose or goal of our thinking (Agazarian 1990c, p.3).

About goals I wrote:

> Goal behavior determines the state of the system's survival and development in relationship to itself and its environment. Internal goals are primary goals and external goals are secondary goals. There were two very interesting contrasting examples of goal-oriented behavior in relationship to the environment.
>
> The first occasion when 'catering' did not remove the clutter was handled by the system – clutter was 'extruded' across the geographical boundary of the 'Essex Room' and the system maintained its time boundary and oriented itself to its work goal.
>
> The second occasion when 'catering' did not remove the clutter, the system did not maintain either a geographical boundary or a psychological boundary. The environment had 'entered' a 'permeable' boundary, the information that entered the system was the equivalent of 'noise' that could not be integrated. The system regressed under stress. (It is VERY interesting to note that the regression was to a classic 'fight' phase which could have been expected to follow the first 'fight' phase in the group on Friday night!)
>
> Chaos resulted with contending and fragmented subgrouping around a primary goal of 'structure' and a work goal of 'feeling.' Even when the geographical boundary was restored, there continued to be subgroup chaos.
>
> It was not until time boundaries were redrawn and the system was oriented to one of the two competing subgroup goals that the system was able to 'survive and develop' in relationship to its secondary goals. It is startling to observe how fast the group was able to work again once the time boundaries were set and the goal was made explicit and brought into focus (Agazarian 1990c, p.5).

This first workshop was by no means the last weekend to exceed my expectations as I began offering the weekend workshop every six months. As the workshops continued, they developed a pattern and a rhythm. The large group work dynamics were well contained in subgrouping. The force fields were used as a tool in diagnosing group defenses in one session that the group would then modify in the next session. Typically, however, the workshops began on Friday night in chaos – almost as if all that was to be contained throughout the weekend erupted in the first session. There was noisy rivalry 'showing off SCT' jargon among the 'old' members, and bewilderment and protest among the 'new'. It is with some astonishment that

I see that in our workshops now, even the initial session is contained in subgrouping. Perhaps I have just gotten better at orienting and training the group; perhaps the 'old' members are no longer filled with the same internal chaos and can therefore contribute to containing the group instead of terrifying it. Whatever the reason, systems-centered workshops are now high on work and learning and low on acting out on the first night.

In the first three or four weekend workshops, members explored dynamics that I had not even guessed existed. For example, as members acquired greater facility in experiencing the connection between their emotions and their 'intention movements', we were all surprised to discover their movements led them into animal as well as human experience. Suspicion and wariness would transform into the wild animal alertness of scanning the jungle. We learned that the experience itself was not as important as the discoveries, understandings and learnings that came from the experience. Thus 'in the jungle', members learned the difference between paranoia and appropriate alertness or wariness. In 'pulling down their kill', members learned that primary aggression is not rage and is better named 'the life force'. Complementary subgroups experienced the relationship between the natural predator and the natural prey – and in this experience an acceptance of a larger order in the universe. There were moments of unexpected humor, as when a member called for the subgroup to raise their 'paws'.

The establishment of functional subgrouping as the SCT method for conflict resolution was one of the most (if not the most) important innovation that resulted from the first five years of pioneering in the bi-annual workshops. I was no longer in doubt about whether or not functional subgrouping could be easily implemented in a group – it could. What is more, I had seen with my own eyes the difference that introducing functional subgroup made to what happened in the groups.[1] The dynamics within each phase of group development were manifested differently when explored in subgroups. For example, when the identified patient and scapegoat dynamics

---

1   Each individual's work is contained, supported and explored (not explained) within a
     similar subgroup, so that members discover first the differences in the apparent
     similarities in their subgroup and then the similarities in the apparent differences in the
     other subgroups.

were explored in subgroups, rather than acted out, the subgroups learned about the underlying dynamics.[2]

What seemed to be happening and is continuing to happen is that in subgroup explorations members are learning how to accept the unknown and to explore the 'unconscious', not as a chaotic and terrifying region, but as a source of knowledge. In the process, we separated two different sources for learning. One is learning comprehensively by which we organize what we come to know in ways that we can talk about and test in the real world. Now in SCT we call this 'turning the researcher on' and engaging the 'observing self-system'.[3] The other source we came to know as the knowledge that is in apprehension, which exists at the edge of the unknown and is accessed through centering into the self without defending against the unknown. We came to recognize this apprehensive knowledge as existential and we are continuing to explore to see how far it goes:

> Comprehension requires being able to discriminate and integrate the information about the world that one lives in and at the same time remain open to the apprehensive knowledge that little of what is possible in one's creative vision can be translated into reality. Defending against the existential pain of this realization results in impairment of the ability to make life potentiating decisions and to implement them. (Agazarian 1997, p.112)

Functional Subgrouping

The idea of functional subgrouping had been developing ever since I had started 'listening' to the voice of the group-as-a-whole and its subgroups. In a 1993 presentation at AGPA, 'Introduction to a Theory of Living Human Systems[4] and the Practice of Systems-centered Psychotherapy', I wrote:

---

2   Another major outcome was the start of developing the hierarchy of defense modification, which synchronized the weakening of specific defenses with the development of an increasing ability to function effectively, which will be discussed later in this chapter.

3   The function of the observing self-system to recognize differences, explore them and integrate them.

4   The theory of living human systems has been presented in other work as systems-centered theory, and has been renamed with the intention of communicating its general application as well as its particular application to systems-centered psychotherapy.

Functional subgrouping does not come naturally in a group. Members have to be able to see a subgroup before they can learn how to join a subgroup. Some subgroups can be seen easily if you look. Others are less obvious and have to be 'believed' before they are seen: for example, accepting that fighting members belong to the same subgroup and are one of two group subgroups balancing the group's fight and flight response. Subgroups come and go. They do not always appear as obviously balanced dichotomies in the group. Subgroups contain the group splits – and emerge with energy when the splits are strong. When strong, dichotomized subgroups emerge spontaneously, the therapist need do little more than draw the group's attention to their presence, and encourage the group to use them functionally.

It is through the work in these functional subgroups that familiar reciprocal role relationships are explored in subgroups rather than acted out by the group-as-a-whole. For example: in the first phase of development, when the compliant and defiant tensions are acted out in a group, the group elects an identified patient or scapegoat to contain the pain and rage aroused by disappointments in the therapist. A good alternative is to explore both sides of the conflict in subgroups. Functional subgrouping is also able to contain the authority issue. When the murderous rage at the therapist is explored and experienced in supportive subgrouping, both the group-as-a-whole and the therapist are less easily induced to act out by its underlying virulence.

Functional subgrouping encourages the members in the group to 'take sides' in the conflict, and to do their individual insight work in a supportive context. By encouraging a conscious splitting into subgroups, defensive splitting is discouraged within individuals. Through membership in a subgroup, individuals are supported in their work of exploring one single side of their version of the conflict instead of denying, projecting or acting out in the struggle to contain both at once.

All stereotypic responses move towards the known, whereas the purpose of the SCT approach in group psychotherapy is to explore the unknown, whether the 'unknown' is to perceive similarities in the apparently different or the differences in the apparently similar. Stereotype role relationships, stereotype responses, stereotype behaviors are easily identified: they are those behaviors which, if any of us are asked to role play, we can all perform without a second thought, and what we do is then instantly recognizable by anybody watching.

Subgroups occur spontaneously in a group and play a fundamental 'role' in group survival and development. How functionally the group subgroups is the key to whether or not the group will reach its goals. All subgroups come together around similarities and separate on differences. Subgroups play all the essential roles in groups. Stereotype subgroups keep the group stable. They come together around stereotype similarities like race, gender or status and are easily seen. Unlike stereotype subgroups, functional subgroups are not so easily seen. Functional subgroups emerge, disappear and re-emerge as different issues in the group become relevant to the group goals. They split the task and maintenance functions between them. They keep the group viable by splitting and containing differences in the group while the group develops sufficient maturity to integrate them. The interplay between stereotype and functional subgroups determines how the group masters each developmental phase, and what overall problem solving styles it has for reaching its goal (Agazarian 1993b, pp 22–23)

In earlier work I had observed that members tend to come together around similarities and separate around differences. I had also noted that the group tends to set up one of its members in a role which, from a systems perspective, encapsulates and separates the group from its differences. Thus the roles of scapegoat and identified patient, which occur so frequently in groups, are an efficient way of isolating differences that the group is not able to integrate (Agazarian and Peters 1981). It was, however, a new idea to me that the forming of subgroups could be deliberately influenced and that influencing them might have a significant impact on the work of the group. With this understanding I was about to embark on the task of changing stereotype subgrouping into functional subgrouping.

As I was interested in how the process of discriminating and integrating differences could be deliberately encouraged in a group, I started experimenting by explicitly encouraging members to choose to work with their similarities rather than with their differences. I had not realized how much all of us tend to manage our interactions with 'yes – but' communications! The 'yes' as a token joining, and the 'but' a way of avoiding dialogue by reinstating a monologue (maintaining the difference and rejecting the similarity). The techniques that evolved lent themselves to an easy-to-remember verse:

Asking 'why are you saying that?'
or 'tell me more about that!'
is a little like giving another member's boat a push out to sea.

Saying 'I'm in your subgroup'
is like an encouraging wave from the shore.

Working as a member in your subgroup
is more than pushing another member's boat out to sea
or waving encouragingly from the shore.

Working in a subgroup is getting into the boat and rowing too!

I did not yet know it, but deliberately introducing functional subgrouping would turn out to be one of the most significant innovations in applying the theory in practice. It was also relatively easy to introduce into a group, in fact easier than I had imagined. It was simply a matter of asking members to join on similarities and to hold their differences until after the similarities had been explored.

Integrating Subgrouping into Therapy

However well subgrouping was working in the training groups, I was still concerned about how well it would work for patients. This change in therapeutic technique seemed a very high risk. In all the ways I had practiced group psychotherapy (leader oriented, patient oriented, group-as-a-whole oriented), however much I had drawn patients' attention to the group, my observations led me to believe that their major transferential relationships were with me, not each other. My data was that group members worked with 'one eye' on each other and the other eye on me.

I was particularly concerned that the constant re-vectoring of work energy away from me and back into the subgroup might be too painful for some group members (if not all). I was, however, somewhat reassured by Anna Freud's concentration camp babies, who survived the concentration camp as a group-as-a-whole and whose norms of looking after each other persisted, even when they were transferred into care in England. In fact, they started their care in England by acting out their negative transference on the staff as a group (Freud 1996).

My other source of strength came from Pat de Maré's work in the large group, where he suggests that one of the advantages of the large group over the small group was that the large group was less likely to evoke family transference and more likely to evoke societal transference (de Maré, Piper and Thompson 1991). I summarized Pat's emphasis in my review of their book:

> It will be of great significance to every group therapist who has wondered how large a therapy group can be that the authors of Koinonia propose a 'median' group (of twenty to forty) as the ideal 'container' for hatred and paranoia. The 'median group', they argue, is the ideal arena for social resolution through 'Koinonic' dialogue which requires the transcendence of individualized narcissism and the development of impersonal and interdependent friendship/citizenship. Thus 'Koinonic dialogue' carries a potential highly relevant to all group work – and particularly relevant to therapy. (Agazarian 1992b, p.443)

I was convinced that many of the current methods of group psychotherapy evoked family transference within structures that could not contain them. Built into the roles of doctor and patient is the 'one-up/one-down' relationship that so easily provokes childhood transference. For many years, I had been interested in finding ways of working with groups that laid more emphasis on building the kind of group society that in itself contributed to containing and exploring the underlying dynamics, rather than increasing the pressure to act out. Pat de Maré had relied on the variable of group size to do this. I had been looking for variables that were independent of the size of the group.

My first step with my patients was to turn the group members' eyes away from me and toward the members of their subgroup. In the process of developing SCT, I was to learn that this 'triangulation by eye contact' (keeping one eye on the leader and the other on other members) occurred predominantly in the early phases of group development, most strongly in the first subphase of flight, less in the subphase of fight, and still less in the difficult subphase of resistance to change where the major group-as-a-whole focus on me was as the object of group disappointment. What is more, I discovered that when the group shifts into the second phase of intimacy, eye contact with me as the leader is hardly more relevant than eye contact with any other member.

This finding led to a useful intervention that SCT leaders use as we promote functional subgrouping in a beginning group, that legitimizes and makes explicit the conflict between looking towards the therapist or looking towards the subgroup:

> Do you notice that you have one eye on me and one eye on your subgroup? Almost everybody does at this stage of group development [normalizing the behavior]. This puts you at a fork in the road. You can explore the conflict between being pulled towards your relationship with me, your therapist, or you can explore your relationship to the subgroup you are working in.

When this triangulation is legitimized as a group issue, then the group-as-a-whole can subgroup around the two sides of the conflict of being drawn in two directions at once. Managing responses to eye contact in this way is an example of accessing the underlying, transferential issues around dependency at a level that the group is able to work with, and then using functional subgrouping to do the work.

To my delight, my patient groups had relatively little trouble making the transition to subgrouping. Using subgrouping to explore the experience in the changes helped. I was also increasingly able to find ways of introducing the changes in small enough bits so they were relatively easily integrated.

I introduced functional subgrouping by consistently asking, 'Anyone else?', 'Anyone else in that boat?' The patients were already used to joining each other around a common theme, but mostly with questions that encouraged the other member to talk, or look-alike anecdotes that joined more on the theme than on the emotional resonance. The second step entailed encouraging members to join with resonance. I introduced the idea of the balance scale – suggesting that members join each other by putting in their contribution with the same depth of feeling that the other members had. The patients liked the idea and seemed to enjoy 'resonating'. Not infrequently, of course, one or another member would react with a depth of emotion that other members could not reach. This was the challenge. In my more traditional group work I would empathize with the depth of a member's emotion, but I would not join. The guidelines for subgrouping, however, require that a member is never left alone. Therefore I tentatively began to join, not only with empathy (communicating my understanding of how it must feel), but also with attunement (communicating my own resonance with their inner experience). This was not always easy to do: when members felt deeply, their distress was often not what I wanted to resonate with. However, learning how to communicate resonance led to communicating my human understanding: 'Remembering your mother brings up the pain – I think we all feel the pain when we recall memories that are still raw – I know, for example, that I have not quite worked through the death of my brother.' My therapy group members not only liked subgrouping, they began complaining when the group did not have a strong subgrouping session. They also told me and Claudia (my co-therapist) that we had finally found a way of doing therapy that was better than all our previous attempts.

Practically, I had now consolidated functional subgrouping as one of the basic processes in developing a SCT group. I now knew that deliberately encouraging the process of discriminating and integrating differences in functional subgrouping could provide an alternative to scapegoating. In other words, subgrouping provided a way to explore differences with containment rather than acting out the impulse to attack differences. Subgrouping was also providing a way to implement the principle of maturation I had first worked with in my analysis of 'The case of Renee' in 1962 (see Chapter 1), that maturation occurs through the discrimination and integration of differences. As members explore their experience in the climate of similarity of a subgroup, they become aware of differences with each other as well as similarities. Thus, in the process of recognizing and integrating differences within the subgroup, human similarities (that were previously denied) become apparent between the different subgroups. As similarities between the apparently different subgroups are recognized, integration takes place in the group-as-a-whole. I was now identifying this principle of discrimination and integration as the basic dynamic of change in systems-centered therapy: systems survive, develop and transform by discriminating and integrating differences, differences in the apparently similar and similarities in the apparently different.

From the beginning of my group work, I had observed group dynamics in the context of the phases of group development as a way of framing the different kinds of work that groups did at different times (Bennis and Shepard 1956). It was a revelation to recognize that the different themes around which subgroups came together were directly related to the different issues that the group had to resolve in order to move from one phase to another in development. I was also able to contrast norms that were established in the groups with functional subgrouping with the norms that were established by stereotype subgrouping. It became clear that without intervention each phase and subphase of group development were characterized by specific kinds of stereotypic subgrouping and defensive communications generic to each phase. By substituting functional subgrouping for stereotype subgrouping, groups moved into and out of each phase with much less of the acting out that I had come to take for granted as characteristic of most (if not all) groups. Learning that groups rarely created identified patients or scapegoats when members explored their impulses in functional subgroups led to establishing the norm of exploring all dynamics in subgroups.

I was also developing the SCT hypothesis that frustration and the management of frustration determines the nature of system development and transformation. With this hypothesis, the issue then becomes developing greater tolerance of a process which is natural (frustration) rather than finding a more acceptable rationalization or a more acceptable discharge. I was again helped in my understanding by Pat de Maré's (De Maré et al. 1991) work with large groups in his reconceptualization of hatred as the natural human response to frustration in communication rather than a superego pathology.[5] De Maré pointed out that when hatred is metabolized, as it can be in the structure of the large group, it transforms into creativity. From my own group work, I now knew that functional subgrouping could provide a structure in which hatred could be metabolized and transformed into creativity. Pat's reframing of hatred into energy was transformational in my own thinking and resulted in the understanding of emotions as a source of energy/information rather than a source of destructive or constructive action. In my review, I emphasized how important was Pat's reframing of hatred into creativity (Agazarian 1992b):

> *Koinonia* is not necessarily an easy book to read but an important one. It is important, not for its scholarship and references, which are impressive, nor for the 'Koinonic' experience awaiting the readers – but for a single,

5   Reading and reviewing (Agazarian 1992b) Patrick de Maré's book, *Koinonia: From Hate Through Dialogue to Culture in the Large Group*, was a challenging and important learning experience for me.

significant reframing of the understanding of the dynamics of aggression which may permanently change the practice of group. 'It has become... clear to us that hate, arising out of the frustrating situation of the larger group,...provides the incentive for dialogue and becomes transformed, through dialogue, into the impersonal fellowship of Koinonia...' (p.4).

The primary problem of large groups centers around primal hate... (p.114) The authors reinterpret the experience of hate in groups from a destructive affect into a natural, inevitable response to frustration – an energy that carries high potential for both destructive and constructive transformation. 'Hate...which in Greek also means grief...then constitutes the basis for psychic energy, which is transformed and expressed in the form of thinking dialogue and learning as distinct from an instinctual process...' (p.141).

The common psychodynamic understanding of hatred is closely linked to Freud's concept of the death instinct and the destructive superego. In *Koinonia* the authors reframe both: the energy of the superego is said to be derived from the Id, but we emphasize again that this energy is not direct and biological, but as the frustrated energy of hate, (not superego guilt! p.122) which can become transformed into mental energy'.(p.125) 'Hate, then, is not the adversary of Eros but the inevitable irreversible outcome of the frustration of Eros: if there is any adversary to Eros, it is...ananke...external necessity. We have to cope with ananke and thereby we evolve dialogue, mind and culture (p.62). The 'structuring of hate through dialogue constitutes transformation' (p.108). Thus the authors transform Freudian pessimism into optimism by contrasting the... 'passive renunciation of instinctual gratification, on which civilization is built (Freud) and the active frustration of hate to which the evolution of culture owes its origins' (de Maré, Piper and Thompson, p.61).

...The implications of reframing hatred as potential creative energy in the service of the ego rather than as a destructive, guilty, death-focused, super-ego force and that therapy could (nay, should!) take place in groups of twenty to forty! This is a particularly challenging reframing in this era of psychotherapy where we are at the threshold of paying attention to which of the dynamic aspects of which we write are issues generic to treating human ills, and which are iatrogenic, regressive, or defensive constellations elicited by our treatment context and methods. For example, if we were to focus less on transference in small groups and more on the socializing requirements underlying the development of Koinonia, would we in truth be looking to a new future rather than to the expected repetitions of the past? Can one envisage groups of the future (whether groups of one, two, three or many) saying: 'I am in hate with you, don't take it personally, let us use the energy to develop Koinonia!' (Agazarian 1992b, pp.443–445).

As I continued working, I began developing the SCT method of defense modification, which reduces the restraining forces or defenses to natural human experiences which could then be explored in subgroups. I discovered that reducing defenses also ameliorated the symptoms that most people came to therapy to resolve. Over the next five or six years, the systems-centered techniques for weakening defenses developed as my experience of the groups (and the group's experience of subgrouping) developed. What has now evolved is a method of systems-centered practice: a method of training individuals to become systems-centered members and a method of developing a systems-centered group. I described this process in my (1997) book, Systems-Centered Therapy for Groups:

> The people who enter a systems-centered group learn specific techniques in order to become systems-centered members. However, membership alone does not make a systems-centered group. Systems-centered group is formed through developing subgroups. Subgrouping…is the intervening variable that brings into being the systems-centered group. Members develop the subgroups, and the subgroups develop the group-as-a-whole.
>
> In forming the systems-centered group, therapists use a sequenced and replicable series of methods and techniques to modify the defenses that restrain the driving forces that are directed toward the goals of therapy. SCT goals are operationalized in terms of vectoring, or directing energy toward system goals – through the methods and techniques of functional subgrouping, boundarying, and defense modification, in the context of the phases of group development (Agazarian 1997, pp.17–18).

Systems-Centered Methods

As a theoretician, I developed the SCT methods by working to apply the theory to practice. When theorizing, in the process of making a connection between the idea and the real world I (like many other theoreticians) rely on a transitional step of illustrating ideas (or doodling). My doodles are usually arrows and circles. The definition of hierarchy (discussed in Chapter 7) was easy to illustrate by three concentric circles, the center one for member, the outside one for the group-as-a-whole and the middle one for the subgroup (Figure 6.4).

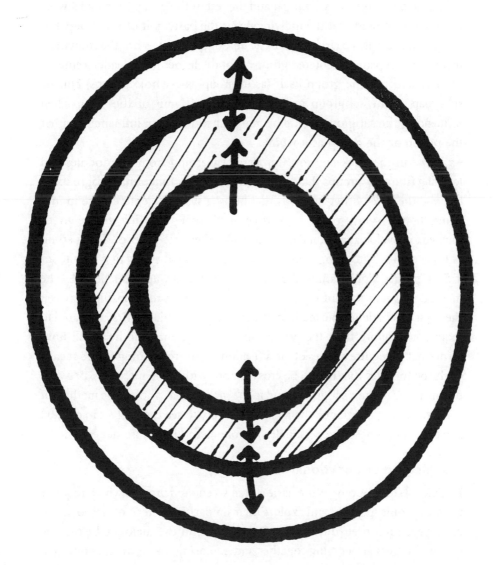

Figure 6.4 Hierarchy and the subgroup

Mulling over this drawing, the implication suddenly hit me. If the subgroup existed in the environment of the group-as-a-whole, and if the subgroup was the environment for its members, then the subgroup, which shared its boundaries with both of the other two, was the central system of the three.

The implication was startling. I and the rest of the group field had always taken it for granted that the individual was the basic unit of the group. But looking at these three circles, the basic unit of groups was not the individual member (as in patient-centered groups); not the leader (as in leader-centered groups); and not the group itself (as in group-as-a-whole groups) but the subgroup. If the subgroup was indeed the basic unit of the group, then influencing the subgroup would be more functional than influencing either the person or the group-as-a-whole.

It was in the back and forth process of learning from my doodles and learning from my groups that I developed not only functional subgrouping but also the three other methods that bring a systems-centered group into being: boundarying, vectoring and contextualizing. At first, the methods seemed to develop as a natural transition from theory to practice. The method of functional subgrouping, which is introduced from the very first minutes of a SCT group, significantly altered the way the groups functioned. The method of vectoring influenced the traditional role relationship between therapist and patient. The method of boundarying, which at first appeared to require little more than the 'vectoring' of energy into the here-and-now, turned out to require a series of modifications of the restraining forces at each of the boundaries that had to be crossed both within the members, between the members in their subgroups and in the group-as-a-whole. The method of contextualizing developed the members' ability to see themselves in context and to not take oneself so personally. All four methods are interdependent.

The Method of Functional Subgrouping

Functional subgrouping is the basic systems-centered process which requires people to come together and explore their similarities instead of stereotyping or scapegoating their differences. For example, in the dialogue below, the group members are coming together and exploring, rather than acting out, the difficult impulse to scapegoat the leader:

A: I am beginning to feel a little irritated.

B: Me, too, I feel irritated and have sort of an agitation.

C: Yeah, it's like a frustration and irritation for me.

A: Every time the leader says something, I get a surge of irritation.

C: Mmm. I'm beginning to feel angry.

B: Me too, it's a real energy, I'm hot.

A: Yeah, hot – full of heat! It feels powerful, sort of exciting.

A: I want to push her out of the way.

B: Me too, I have the impulse to just give her a shove.

C: Yeah, I felt good when you said that.

A: I felt relief.

D: I'm getting excited and energized.

Functional subgrouping puts into practice the dynamic that living human systems survive, develop and transform through the discrimination and integration of differences. In subgrouping, rather than stereotyping, rejecting and scapegoating differences in self or other, conflicts around difference are taken out of the person and contained in the group. Within each subgroup, as the similarities among members are explored, so differences become apparent and accepted. As each subgroup in the group-as-a-whole recognize differences in what was apparently similar within their subgroups, so they start to recognize similarities in what was apparently different between the subgroups. There is then an integration in the group-as-a-whole (Figure 6.5).

In the practice of SCT, the process of discriminating and integrating differences is assumed to be both the necessary and sufficient condition for living human systems to survive, develop (from simpler to more complex) and transform into differentiated entities that work – not only independently, but also interdependently. Thus, by subgrouping functionally, the process of separation, individuation and differentiation is supported within the member, within the subgroups and within the group-as-a-whole.

The method of functional subgrouping is also the SCT conflict resolution technique. By subgrouping functionally, conflicts are contained in the group-as-a-whole in different subgroups, rather than acted out between

Differences create conflict

STEREOTYPE SUBGROUPS
**manage conflict
by coming together around similarities
and splitting off differences.**

Differences create conflict

FUNCTIONAL SUBGROUPS
**manage conflict
by coming together around similarities
and containing and exploring differences**

Figure 6.5 Stereotype and functional subgroups

members or contained in stereotyped subgroups. For instance, in a group
where some members are wanting the leader to take charge and others to
take charge themselves, rather than trying to convince the 'different'
members that one's own position is better, members are encouraged to
explore with those in their own subgroup. This then creates an environment
in the group-as-a-whole where both sides of the conflict are contained and
then explored in the group-as-a-whole in the two different subgroups, one
exploring wanting to depend and the other exploring autonomy. Thus, in an

SCT group, functional subgrouping competes with the predictable impulse to establish a group hierarchy based on stereotype and status rather than on resources.

The major challenge for the SCT therapist in introducing functional subgrouping is to maintain a therapeutic relationship with the patient and at the same time establish the norms for therapeutic work. Dynamically, the therapist revectors the patient's dependency energy away from himself or herself into the functional subgroup so that the explicit source of attunement and containment is the subgroup and not the therapist. Intervening at a subgroup level rather than an individual level reduces the risk of pairing between therapist and member or of setting a member up in a role, and influences both the individual member through their immediate environment and the group-as-a-whole in its ability to integrate differences.

The Method of Boundarying

Boundarying determines the structure of the real group in real space and time (the group room itself and the starting and stopping time). A second kind of boundarying teaches members to recognize 'mental' time and space boundaries: members learn to identify thoughts that take flight away from the here-and-now experience and into the past or future (changing this can be as simple as changing tense from 'I was' to 'I am' or 'I will'). Members also learn about the inevitable 'turbulence' of crossing a boundary and that taking this for granted helps one stay focused on the goal (Agazarian 1999).

The method of boundarying is also aimed at influencing the boundary permeability to information by reducing the noise in the communication process. The more noise that enters the group, the more difficult it will be for the group to enter into clear communication and the more difficult it will be for the members to do their work. SCT aims to filter out the noise before it crosses the boundary into the group, and to reduce noise as soon as it arises in the group rather than allowing noisy communication which inevitably arouses more noisy communication and defensiveness. Noisy commun- ications are defensive communications, most of which are quite familiar: social chatter, vagueness, telling stories, 'yes-but's.'

Influencing group dynamics so that groups develop SCT norms rather than waiting for the norms to emerge was a revolutionary idea for me with implications much beyond what I understood at the time. Deciding to change accepted communication norms from the first few minutes of a group required me to change the way that I had always led groups, from active listening to active intervention. (My training in STDP helped me to do this.) In a surprisingly short time, I was able to interrupt defensive communications as soon as I heard them. For example, 'because' almost always continues into an explanation and 'yes-but' almost always pre-empts the other person's point of view. Interrupting as an intervention posed the challenge of intervening in such a way as to pique sufficiently the members' curiosity so that the interruptions were experienced not only as frustrating but also useful for learning.

The Method of Vectoring

Vectoring interventions make work goals explicit so that the energy of the group-as-a-whole, the subgroups and the members can be redirected towards the work of the group. Learning how to vector energy increases one's ability to make choices and to direct energy away from the fantasies and fears about the past, present and future into the reality of here-and-now. Vectoring energy outside oneself makes it possible to join a subgroup.

In SCT, the choice of a less familiar word (like vector) from the more familiar everyday term (like direction) is made whenever the new word helps in understanding something differently. For example, the advantage of 'vector' is that it implies not only a direction, but also an energetic force that is related to a goal. It is through vectoring that SCT weakens the restraining forces and releases the inherent driving forces towards system transformation. Vectoring teaches members how to deliberately withdraw energy from distractions and refocus it on the here-and-now (a good example is drawing energy away from storytelling about the past so that the energy can be used to discover the present). Through vectoring, one learns to deliberately direct energy towards the aspects of oneself that one wants to learn more about and away from the defenses and symptoms that interfere with curiosity.

The 'fork in the road' is one of the first vectoring techniques introduced into a new systems-centered group. Typically, the first fork in the road that a systems-centered patient chooses is between explaining or exploring (Figure 6.6). The systems-centered therapist encourages the patient to explore the hypothesis that explaining or 'talking about' the problem avoids the problem:

If you explain, you will lead yourself to what you know already. There is an alternative fork in the road, and that is to explore the experience that you are having right now that you are attempting to explain! Test it out, and see whether it is true that explaining takes you to your thoughts whereas exploring leads you to your experience and what you don't yet know.

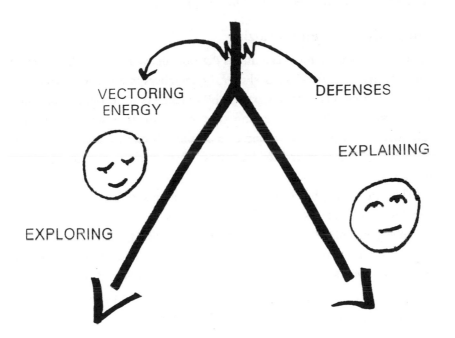

Figure 6.6 DEFENSE MODIFICATION: The fork in the road between exploring experience and defending against experience

The fork in the road immediately orients the group to many of the SCT values. First and foremost, it presents the paradox of choice. On the one hand, the patient is free to choose whichever side of the conflict he or she wants to explore first. On the other hand, the patient has no choice about whether or not to choose. All ambivalence is reframed as a conflict which can then be framed as a fork in the road between two conflicting directions and the patient can decide which side of the conflict to explore first. As the fork in the road requires patients to 'observe' their defensive constellations in order to explore the significance and cost and to explore their own unknown to discover what conflict, sensation, emotion or impulse they are defending against, it is extremely important to frame the vectoring intervention in a way that arouses curiosity rather than resistance. The more a vectoring intervention makes common sense, the more likely it is to arouse co-operation rather than defiance or compliance.

The Method of Contextualizing

In SCT contextualizing interventions develop an awareness of the different contexts that exist simultaneously for the members in a group. Learning to see things from different contexts enables members to recognize that their communications have a meaning, not only for themselves and their subgroup, but also for the group-as-a-whole. Through understanding the context of their experience, members learn not to take things 'just' personally.

The relief when this happens in a group is almost palpable. A very angry member visibly relaxes once she realizes others are angry too. As she finds her subgroup and then as the group continues working, she is able to see her 'angry' subgroup as well as the subgroup that is excited and to understand both responses as normal human responses to a change in structure:

Pam:	I don't think you understand how mad I am!
Leader:	Is anyone else in that subgroup?
Jim:	I'm not as angry as Pam but I am angry.
Leader:	Jim, that's more of a wave!
John:	I can join – I'm hot with anger all through.
Alice:	Me too – I've been angry ever since Dr X said she was going to raise our fees.
Pam:	Boy, it feels good to know I'm not alone.

The idea that all members are a voice both for themselves and also for the group is very often new to people. Recognizing the dual role frequently comes as a great relief: to understand that one cannot take full responsibility for the effect of what one says on the group, because the same statement can get one response one time and quite a different response another time. How the group reacts has more to do with the group than it does with the individual. (This also implies that one can take full responsibility for the effect on the group of what one withholds from it.) Information, equivalent to energy, is the group resource for work.

Contextualizing is the most demanding of the SCT methods and the most difficult for members to acquire. In training groups, members report that learning to contextualize has been significant to their own personal growth as well as giving them the professional skill to decide which system level intervention is appropriate to the context of the group. For patients, being able to learn to contextualize – to see the same event from different perspectives – greatly reduces personal pain and suffering and seems to correlate with a good prognosis. For example, one of the SCT criteria for successful therapy is for patients to be able to experience their past both personally and existentially, recognizing that the personally painful role they played in their family was also one of a constellation of roles that kept the family stable.

Systems-Centered Therapy: How it Works

From the very beginning of the group, the systems-centered therapist is intervening actively to establish the SCT norms and build a systems-centered group by encouraging members to subgroup around similarities instead of introducing differences.

A primary focus is on developing a functional rather than stereotypic role relationship between the therapist and patient. The therapist attempts to avoid the 'one-up' position from the beginning: paying attention to both the verbal and nonverbal communication about this, the therapist stays in consistent, authentic eye contact with the patient and communicates that it is the patient who knows himself or herself and the therapist who knows the techniques of therapy. This clarification alone helps to avoid the Sisyphus syndrome: the endless labor where the therapist pushes the patient up the hill with all his therapeutic strength, only to find that when there is a pause in the labor the patient has 'rolled back down to the bottom again'.

SCT therapists insist that patients 'discover their own reality' by testing their interpretations about reality against their direct experience. The patient is asked, 'Which side of the fork do you want to explore first – the defense or the experience you are defending against?' Exploring either side leads to the discovery of the self that is based on one's actual experience – which in turn leads to self-validation of the true self. Revising one's cognitive maps in the light of reality modifies the unexamined explanations which previously defined reality.

The importance of discovering reality before it is interpreted leads to another major aspect: systems-centered therapists do not interpret the patient's dynamics to the patient. Rather than pathologizing, systems-centered therapists legitimize, normalize, universalize, de-pathologize and humanize. Whenever patients pathologize themselves, the experience that they are pathologizing is reframed in terms of existential human experience. For example, when someone at the beginning of a new group is criticizing himself for being hesitant or going slowly, a systems-centered therapist might respond:

> In a new situation, people tend to react in one of two ways, to leap before they look or to look before they leap.

Or alternatively:

> It is important to scan a new situation – think of a cat, scanning a new territory for information before venturing out, and managing its flight/fight impulse as it does it.

When patients are anxious at the beginning of a group, rather than their anxiety being analyzed or interpreted they are reminded that everyone is anxious at the edge of the unknown and asked to see what happens if they become curious as well. Thus, the response of anxiety (and the worrying that anxiety generates) is changed into a practical test of reality based on a fact of human experience. Becoming curious about what is going to happen next, instead of making negative predictions, changes anxiety into excitement, arousal and anticipation. (In exploring, members often discover that the difference between anticipatory anxiety or anticipatory excitement lies in the connotations of the words one uses to interpret the experience.)

Introducing the defense modification is another major element in applying SCT. The systems-centered hierarchy of defense modification defines a systematic program that teaches patients to first recognize and then undo their defenses in a pre-established hierarchy in the context of the phases of group development. The hierarchy of defense modification identifies the sequence so that the modification of each defense builds upon the modification that preceded it and lays the groundwork for the modification that comes next. This requires that the SCT therapist is able to identify which defenses the patients have the skills and the readiness to undo and which they have not. The discriminatory technique of the fork-in-the-road is useful in this task as it gives the patient the option to choose to explore the consequences of the defense on the one hand, or to explore, experience and learn more about the impulse that is being defended against on the other. Concurrently, the patient gains experience of containing the impulse rather than acting it out.

Defense Modification in the Context of Phases of Development

The sequence outlined by Bennis and Shepard (1956) is the framework on which I have built my observations and work with the phases of group development (Agazarian 1994, 1997, 1999; Agazarian and Peters 1981) ever since my first T-group experience in the group dynamics department in 1961. The theory of group development predicts three discrete phases: authority, intimacy and work (see Chapter 3). An important transformational crisis marks the transition from authority (phase one) to intimacy (phase two). Bennis and Shepard called this the 'barometric event'. I have called it the authority issue and recognize it as a fulcrum event marked by an eruption of the negative transference (Agazarian 1994, 1997, 1999; Agazarian and Peters 1981).

As I developed SCT, I synchronized the hierarchy of defense modification with the developmental phases – and each phase then became the context in which the specific defenses were modified. This revolutionized defense analysis for me. As I watched the groups work and modified the defenses in the sequence I had worked out, I could see that using the sequence led to a common sense progression for group members and phase development in the group-as-a-whole (see Table 6.1, pp.208–209). Undoing cognitive distortions restores the person's relationship with their cognitive common sense. This paves the way for restoring one's relationship with one's emotional self which was constricted within the 'straightjacket of tension'. Restoring the relationship with the emotional self paves the way for exploring the impulses, experiences and conflicts that, when defended against, generate the symptoms of anxiety, depression and irritability. Working with the cognitive defenses, the defenses against emotion and the defenses against impulse comprise the first modules in the defense modification. As these defenses are undone, the group progresses in its development from flight toward the beginning of the fight subphase.

Phase one (authority) contains two subphases. The first is a more passive phase of flight in which the group often offers up an identified patient to the leader for a magical cure. The second is the more active subphase of fight where the group progresses from passive stereotyping to active scapegoating, first of each other and then of the leader. The techniques outlined earlier are introduced into the SCT group from the very beginning of the first phase. It is also in this phase that the members learn to modify their defensive anxiety-provoking thoughts, tension, depression and irritability. In these two subphases, subgrouping provides the supportive climate in which a considerable amount of individual defense modification is done. Towards the end of phase one, the defenses of maladaptive role pairing and scapegoating of authority are worked. This work occurs mainly in subgroups, with different subgroups exploring different sides of the conflict, first the 'one-up, one-down' role pairing, and later the sadism and masochism in scapegoating. After the group members have recognized that their struggle is with their own authority rather than with the leader as the external authority, the group energy is freed and turned towards issues of intimacy.

Work on the defenses in relationship to authority is motivated to reduce pain. Work with the defenses against intimacy is motivated by the wish to find the self. It is extremely important that the intimacy phase be worked in subgroups so that the two subphases of enchantment and disenchantment are not acted out. In SCT groups, these two subphases are worked concurrently in subgroups, unlike T-groups where it is expected that groups progress from the euphoria of belonging to the despair of not belonging. The dynamic issues in the phase of intimacy are those of separation and individuation. The enchanted subgroup explores and modifies the defenses against separation and learns to recognize differences in the comfortable similarities that generate feelings of unquestioning well-being. Concurrently, the disenchanted subgroup explores and modifies the defenses against individuation and learns to recognize similarities in the alienating difference that gives them their secure isolation. Both sets of defenses are the work of the intimacy phase and defend against the original failures in bonding, attachment, attunement and containment. By working the two defenses in concurrent subgroups, the group-as-a-whole learns to contain and integrate both sides of the 'good/bad' split.

The final phase in group development work is the phase of inter-dependent work, love and play. The ongoing work requires the continuing modification of defenses against comprehensive and apprehensive know-ledge. The goal is to establish an ongoing, non-defensive relationship between comprehension and apprehension: comprehensive knowledge that comes from reality-oriented thinking and imagination and apprehensive knowledge that comes from intuition and existential insight. This is achieved by an ongoing communication which develops greater and greater capacity to tolerate the chaos of primary experience, organize it and communicate it comprehensively. In systems-centered therapy, the boundary between app-rehension and comprehension is called the boundary of common sense. Common sense is the basic transaction across the comprehensive and apprehensive boundary. Common sense is intuitively logical. It combines the intuition of apprehension and the rationality of comprehension. When the common sense boundary is permeable, all is right with the world (Table 6.1).

Table 6.1 displays the relationship between the phases of group development, the characteristic issues that arise in each phase, the defensive restraining forces that SCT modifies in a systematic sequence that is synchronized with each phase and the symptoms that are reduced in the process.

Working with groups in the second and third phase of group development for prolonged periods of time was new to me. Much of my experience heretofore had been working with groups in the first phase (which is where most groups in our society live). As the SCT groups continued to discover the underlying dynamics of the different phases, it became apparent that what they were discovering were the same dynamics that I had recognized in psychoanalysis, though with less resistance and without as much regression. Thus, whereas the first two subphases of work had similarities with cognitive therapy, behavioral modification and gestalt, all the later subphases of the authority issue had more similarities with psychodynamic therapies and the intimacy phase most similarities with psychoanalysis. This was a great relief to me. In 'Systems-centered therapy applied to short-term and individual psychotherapy' (Agazarian 1996b) I say:

SCT MODIFICATIONS OF RESTRAINING FORCES TO GROUP DEVELOPMENT

Phase specific conflicts	When the restraining forces below are reduced	these symptoms are modified
PHASE ONE OF GROUP DEVELOPMENT: AUTHORITY		
FLIGHT SUBPHASE impulse to contain dependency in the identified patient	**SOCIAL DEFENSES** stereotypic social communication.	Inauthenticity.
	THE TRIAD OF SYMPTOMATIC DEFENSES 1. anxiety provoking thoughts, ruminations and worrying that divert attention from reality testing. 2. Tension generating stress related psychosomatic defenses, which avoid the experience of emotion.	Anxiety.
TRANSITIONAL SUBPHASE BETWEEN FLIGHT AND FIGHT defenses against differences	3. Defending against the retaliatory impulse by constricting it in depression or discharging it in hostile acting out.	Masochistic Depression Sadistic & Hostile acting out
FIGHT SUBPHASE. impulse to discharge hostility against differences by Scapegoating self & other	**ROLE-LOCK DEFENSES** Creating one up / one-down role relationships like identified patient and helper; Scapegoat and scapegoater; defiant and compliant.	Reciprocal maladaptive role pairing
TRANSITIONAL SUBPHASE BETWEEN AUTHORITY AND INTIMACY Impulse to target authority and act out the negative transference	**RESISTANCE TO CHANGE DEFENSES** 1. Externalizing conflicts onto those in authority: defensive stubbornness and suspicion from the righteous and complaining position.	Role-suction into interdependent roles of victim and exploiter
	2. Disowning authority: defensive stubbornness and suspicion of self that blames personal incompetence.	Crisis of Hatred Resistance to Reality

PHASE TWO OF GROUP DEVELOPMENT: INTIMACY		
ENCHANTMENT AND HOPE SUBPHASE impulses to idealize the group and create a cult	**DEFENSES AGAINST SEPARATION** Enchantment, idealization, blind trust of others, and love addiction as defenses against differences.	Idealization, exploitability and cultism. Dependency at the expense of interdependence and exploitability.
DISENCHANTMENT AND DESPAIR SUBPHASE impulses to alienate self in Existential despair	**DEFENSES AGAINST INDIVIDUATION** Disenchantment and blind mistrust of self, others and groups. Alienation, contempt and despair as a defense against similarities.	Despair and resignation. Independence at the expense of functional dependency and interdependence.
PHASE THREE OF GROUP DEVELOPMENT: INTERDEPENDENT LOVE, WORK AND PLAY		
ONGOING PHASES OF WORK IN THE EXPERIENCED GROUP Directing energy towards Interdependent work	**DEFENSES AGAINST KNOWLEDGE** Defenses against inner reality and comprehensive and apprehensive knowledge. **DEFENSES AGAINST COMMON SENSE** Defenses against outer reality and reality testing.	Impairment of decision making and implementation abilities; loss of common sense and humor. Self-centeredness at the expense of both self and the environment.

Table 6.1 Hierarchy of defense modification in the phases of system development

It is a common experience, I believe, among people who develop something that they think is new, to discover they have invented several wheels all over again. This was my experience. Having developed the hierarchy of defense modification, I took another look and was struck by how familiar much of what I was doing was. For example: the first module of defense modification (the triad of symptomatic defenses) seemed to incorporate, in the following order: cognitive therapy, gestalt therapy, behavioral modification, and mindfulness meditation! These three defense modifications address most of the problems that bring people into therapy: anxiety, psychosomatic symptoms, depressions and acting out by abusing either themselves or others. Moving on to the second module (role locks), there was a resemblance to the understanding in transactional analysis of the 'one up–one down' role relationship. Module three (resistance to change) was certainly a cousin to the Tavistock approach and module four (approach and avoidance in intimacy) looks very like object relations therapy.

It initially came as a shock to discover that so many of the methods and techniques that resulted were significantly different from the familiar and effective techniques of psychodynamic therapy. However, as time has passed, quite surprising similarities have appeared from what was so apparently different. For example, a theory of living human systems was first built in the abstract and then applied to real people whereas the psychodynamic approach grew first from clinical experience with people and only later organized into a theory. In practice, it seems that the relationship between the therapist and patient in SCT is at least as interpersonal as in psychodynamic therapy. Again, although there are more differences than there are similarities between systems-centered and most psychodynamic methods and techniques, the criteria by which they are judged as successful or not are almost identical (Agazarian 1996b, p.30).

It is also useful to compare SCT with the interpersonal approaches to group therapy, the most widely known of which is Yalom's (1995) (see Chapter 2). Distinctly different from the interpersonal approaches, SCT emphasizes the development of intrapersonal integrity in the beginning phases of group and interpersonal experience is not addressed until after the members have acquired specific skills (like subgrouping, and accessing the intrapersonal source of the impulse to question or interpret each other). SCT assumes that is not possible to have an authentic relationship with others until one has developed an authentic relationship with the self.

Understanding the phases of development has always been a great advantage in understanding 'where' a group is and 'what' I could expect it to do. In the development of SCT, it became increasingly clear to me that these phases were the context which determined what work could and could not be done. I began introducing this understanding into my therapy groups so that members would not expect changes in themselves that the phase of development did not support. The example that follows is from a group where one member's depression did not seem to lift, even though she felt better when she had identified the event that triggered her retaliatory impulse. I made a 'contextualizing' intervention with her, based on my understanding that depression is modified in the first phase of development as a defense against anger, and despair is modified in the second phase of development as a defense against personal reality.

> I said to her: You notice that your depressed feelings have gone now that you know that you bypassed your wish to fight back – and you notice that you still have a 'subgroup' inside you that feels very sad. We don't know yet whether your sadness is some sad thoughts, or some grief that we have not discovered yet, or whether you are actually feeling some hopelessness and despair. It is hard to work with despair in the group right now, because mostly we are discovering how to allow ourselves to experience our anger without acting it either out or in. However, we are taking a step towards the work that comes next, when we see how we go into despair when we don't know how to bear our reality. I believe that we have a subgroup brewing around that? Can you hang in for now, and reinforce the work you are doing around depression, and get ready for whatever your work is that is still to come.

Systems-Centered Practice

The SCT 'treatment plan' is based on the assumption that all systems have a specific and identifiable set of developmental phases and subphases, with defenses as restraining forces to the progression from one subphase to the next. The hierarchy of defense modification is based on the assumption that weakening the restraining forces that are relevant to the developmental issues in each phase is easier than strengthening the driving forces. Thus, a valid connection is restored between reality and the intrapersonal self before developing valid interpersonal connections.

I had been prepared to work only with defense modification, with the hope that by reducing the defenses, people would regain a functional relationship with themselves and with the world. However, as the groups worked, it became clear that a functional relationship did not come from simple defense modification, but rather from making the unconscious, conscious, apprehensively. Apprehending the unconscious leads to understanding its existential meaning for human beings, rather than framing the unconscious so it can be explained. Understanding this led to stating the goal for systems-centered therapy: to make the boundary appropriately permeable between apprehensive and comprehensive knowledge. Thus the ongoing work of the third phase of development is to develop our emotional intelligence; free our common sense; open to our instinctive, intuitive sense; and find the words to make this intuitive knowing, comprehensible to ourselves and to others.

Our work with subgrouping helped me formulate a discrimination about the process of insight. Though at one level insight is always a here-and-now, 'in the moment' experience (the unconscious has no sense of time), a recollection from the unconscious is already coded according to the existing comprehensive organizing principles of the person having the insight. In contrast, subgrouping contains experience before it is organized comprehensively so that it can be explored before it is coded. It is an apprehensive journey into the chaos of the unknown with the subgroup containing the chaos and delaying comprehension. When insight comes, it is apprehended first and comprehended second.

From the systems-centered perspective, the boundaries of treatment are defined by the context. For therapists who do not frame group dynamics within the context of phases of group development, there are only two contexts available: the individual as a context and the group as a context. What is not available to group therapists who see only individuals in the group is the existence of the person in the context of the subgroup and also in the context of the group-as-a-whole. Without context, there is no clear understanding that the influence of the psychological environment will have just as much impact as the physical environment.

Human systems are made, not born. In the systems-centered approach to the phases of development in group psychotherapy, the group is not left to develop 'naturally' while the therapist 'contains' the process and judiciously interprets it to make it conscious to the group, as is the case when the approach is primarily psychodynamic. Rather, group forces are deliberately exploited; certain group behaviors deliberately encouraged and others discouraged; all dynamics, however primitive, are legitimized so that they can be explored and understood. For example, predictable occurrences, like the creation of identified patients and scapegoating, are no longer predetermined in a systems-centered group. When subgroups, rather than individuals, contain different sides of predictable group 'splits' and when the group-as-a-whole is required to 'contain' the conflict consciously as a working task, it is no longer necessary to delegate difference to a scapegoat, an identified patient or a deviant pair. Deliberately splitting basic group conflicts into two containing subgroups, which come together around similarities and within which members recognize their differences, leads to differentiation within the system at all levels of the hierarchy.

The phase context also influences the leader's function and tasks. The work in the authority phase is with frustration that is potential energy for problem solving which (when not defended against) is experienced as a powerful feeling of arousal and energy. The leader, during the authority phase, maintains the structure so that frustration can be discriminated from tension and the rage, aroused by exceeding one's frustration tolerance, can be explored. Authority issues and their defenses are easily precipitated by any leader who violates the containing structure even in the most minimal ways. The work in the intimacy phase is to open to yearning and wanting that is potential energy for relating to oneself and others, which (when not defended against) is a full feeling of being oneself. The leaders, during the intimacy phase, maintain containment through attunement so that yearning/wanting is discriminated from negative or positive predictions about getting satisfaction. Any disruption (or failure) of the leader's attunement activates the early attunement failures and precipitates defenses against separation/individuation.

The importance of working in context influences when work is done. For example, feelings about parents are not worked with in the phase of authority before externalization has been undone; all authority is seen as good or bad and the past viewed from the lens of a victim. In an SCT group, work with the past is not done until the second phase (after externalization is undone) in which the work is focused on the conflicts in the self. In the intimacy phase of development the relationship between childhood, the childhood context and the role the child plays in the family system can be resolved. Similarly, it is important not to confuse depression (a first phase, flight subphase defense against the retaliatory impulse) with despair (a second phase defense against realities that seem unbearable).

What the Patient Learns

Systems-centered therapists work with the understanding that the context of the work defines what can and cannot be done. The stages in the hierarchy of defense modification are interdependent with the phases of the development of the therapeutic process, both in group and individual therapy. (This is similar to the interdependence between the phases of human development and the readiness for mastering developmental tasks.) Therefore the goals of each therapy session are determined by the developmental context of the session and the ability of the patient to reduce the defensiveness that is aroused in the context of that phase.

For example, the first major therapeutic learning at the beginning of therapy is recognizing that anxiety has three sources: fear of thoughts, fear of sensations or feelings or fear of the unknown. The first phase of every therapy is predictably one in which there is an initial flight from both the work and the relationship into intellectualization. Flight diverts energy away from the present and into the past or future in psychological space and time. The first step in systems-centered therapy, therefore, is to pay attention to the process, not the content of the communication. *What* is communicated is less important than *how* it is communicated. The *how* of the communication will reveal the specific flight defenses the patient is using. Systems-centered therapists manage the initial stage of flight by refocusing communication into the here-and-now reality and away from negative predictions about the future or expectations of the repetition of the bad experiences of the past. The cognitive defenses (the cognitive maps) are the first addressed in the subphase of flight. Undoing the anxiety that is generated by thoughts requires bringing into reality the negative predictions or mind readings that are going on mentally. Reality testing lowers anxiety whether the worst fears are confirmed or not.

Recognizing that feelings as well as anxiety can be generated by thoughts introduces another fundamental SCT learning – that there are two separate and different sources of feelings: feelings that are generated by thoughts and feelings that are generated by experience.[6] The first is related to information that comes through cognition; the second is related to information that comes through what is experienced via the senses.

Reducing the fear of one's sensations or feelings requires two things: undoing the negative thoughts one has about having them on the one hand, and making space inside to fill up with oneself on the other. When anxiety comes from being on the edge of the unknown, the patient learns that everyone has apprehension when we do not know what is going to happen next, and that it often lowers the natural apprehension to bring one's curiosity to the fore. Before the end of this first step, members have discovered that the feelings generated by thoughts may feel the same but are not the same as feelings generated by direct experience. There is a dramatic difference between, for example, the experience of anger filtered through the negative predictions about what will happen if one experiences anger fully and the actual experience of anger when it is explored and contained. As these realities are discovered by the patient, rather than interpreted to them, the therapy is less characterized by defensive flight and comes closer to the exploration of defensive fight.

The SCT therapist avoids interpreting others' experience or dynamics. Rather, each person is encouraged to discover his own. Interventions in SCT frame differences in terms of the range of human dynamics, not in terms of pathology. When experience is normalized as 'common' and 'human', there is less defensiveness around the exploration of 'good and bad' experiences like over-dependent and counter-dependent compliance and defiance, sadistic and masochistic fantasies, impulses fuelled by love, hate, rage, passion, jealousy, envy, gratitude and generosity.

SCT approaches the modification of defenses systematically – with an awareness that every intervention in SCT is designed to reach a specific goal.

---

6   Damasio's (1994) research on brain functioning confirmed this discrimination.

In this sense, every SCT intervention is a hypothesis that predicts an outcome. If the expected outcome does not happen, this is feedback for the systems-centered therapist to try another way to reach the goal. To the extent that an intervention moves the person closer to a relationship with his true self, the hypothesis has tested positively. To the extent that the intervention is followed by the person moving away from himself, it has tested negatively.

In the systems-centered approach, patients are not free to import into the therapeutic situation the many ways in which they repeat the mismanagement of their relationships with themselves, others and the world. They are not free to be their defensive selves. The therapist is left with the specific task of continuing to intervene to reduce the restraining forces that are making it difficult for the person to cross the boundary between his false self and his true self. Defense modification systematically weakens the restraining forces that inhibit the drive of the true self.

Looking Back

The different stages of the development of systems-centered practice that I have described in this chapter I find well documented in my Institute submissions for AGPA between 1991 and 1999. Year by year the titles of my Institutes shifted as I discovered different applications of the theory.

For example, in 1991, my Institute was titled 'Systems-centered Interventions in Group-as-a-whole Therapy' and described as follows: 'systems-centered interventions potentiate group-as-a-whole maturation as the therapeutic context in which individuals learn to work and play. Participants' experience will be reviewed through the constructs of Systems-Centered theory: boundaries, subsystems, goals and the importance of monitoring the communication transactions across the boundaries at all levels of the developing system.'

In 1991 I also introduced 'Stages of Group Development – A Systems-centered View: Each stage of group development provides the context in which individual developmental issues are aroused, revisited and re-mastered. Members mature as the group learns to work and love and play. How systems-centered interventions potentiate the group-as-a-whole developmental process will be illustrated through role-playing and clinical vignettes.'

By 1992 I had introduced subgrouping, 'Subgrouping in Systems-centered Group-as-a-whole Therapy: the subgroup, not the individual member, is the basic unit of the group in the systems-centered, group-as-a-whole approach to group psychotherapy. Techniques for facilitating the conscious use of subgroups in the context of group development will be illustrated through alternating periods of participant-observation and reviews of the experiential process.'

In 1993, I was still linking systems to the group-as-a-whole: 'Systems-centered Group-as-a-whole Therapy: alternating experiential and review work will focus on how to develop a systems-centered therapy group with emphasis on promoting subgrouping as the major developmental force and attending to boundaries, roles, goals, containment and restraints in communication at all levels of the developing group system: member, subgroup and the group-as-a-whole.'

In 1993 I also introduced roles: 'systems-centered members learn how to change from stereotype to functional roles; how to import their energy across the boundaries into the here-and-now; how to reduce the resistances to crossing boundaries from the outside into the inside; from the past and future into the present; from fantasy into reality; how to contain the energy in the system and how to focus it in the direction of the goals.'

The year 1994 heralded the first exclusively Systems-centered Institute, and at the same time I introduced defense modification: 'Defense Analysis in Systems-centered Therapy: systematic analysis of the hierarchy of defenses is one of the major tasks in systems-centered groups. Through demonstration, practice and discussion, the social, symptomatic, stereotype role-lock and pervasive defenses will be identified and methods for undoing them will be demonstrated and experienced.'

Finally, in 1998, I introduced Short-term Systems-centered Therapy: 'systems-centered therapy systematically introduces techniques for modifying a hierarchy of defenses and symptoms. Adapted to today's market, SCT enables a treatment plan that starts, stops and starts again at the patient's level of skills for managing, in sequence, their anxiety, tension, somatic symptoms, depression and acting out.'

SCT as a Protocol for Short-Term Therapy

There was a major environmental influence that led me to tailor-making SCT as a protocol for therapy: the introduction of health management organizations into the field of psychotherapy which began in the USA in the late 1980s and early 1990s. Like many other therapists, I did not want to read the 'writing on the wall' and see that in the very near future treatment would be based on the allotment of time that the insurance carriers considered appropriate to reduce the symptoms, not on the problem that patients brought into treatment. On the other hand, I did want to address the impending reality. I applied every bit of learning that I had acquired in the process of discovering SCT and turned my energy away from the righteous indignation and moral outrage that I and others felt towards seeing how I could respond to this new reality. In 'Systems-centered Therapy Applied to Short-term Group and Individual Psychotherapy', which I wrote for the *The SCT Journal* (Agazarian 1996b):

> Based on my experience in the early days of the community mental health movement of the 1960s, when health management is based on costs, much of the delivery of service is by relatively inexperienced, and in some cases, relatively untrained therapists. In today's focus on managed care, we have both the good and the bad of it all over again. We have the potential for developing new ways of delivering the service within the new guidelines that managed care requires – as well as compromises to face the exigencies of the limits of time and money that managed care demands. It would seem important to find ways of doing therapy that are simple enough to be delivered by relatively inexperienced therapists, relevant enough to make a difference in a short time and of sufficient dynamic integrity to interest experienced therapists, both in their roles as clinicians and also in their roles as supervisors and case managers.
>
> When a theory of living human systems was operationalized into systems-centered practice, a blueprint was developed for a systematic sequence of therapeutic steps, each one of which stands alone, each one of which provides the patient with something useful that they did not have before, and each one of which builds upon the one before and lays the foundation of the learning that comes next. Finally when the whole sequence is completed, so is the therapy.

In that SCT is a therapy of an ongoing series of choices based upon what the patient is able to choose, resistance is largely bypassed and each session is a mini therapy in and of itself. If the treatment has to stop, the patient will have gotten as much as possible, given the constellation of his defenses at that time, and when the patient starts again (if they return to SCT), the next experience of therapy is built on whatever gains were made in the therapy before. Because SCT is technique and relationship rather than person-based, it can be continued at another time with another therapist in another place.

Given all of the above, and that 'insurance therapy' tends to be a start and stop and start again process – the major question becomes: 'how can therapy be designed so that the next start can build on the work done before, rather than cycling through the next version of the same again?' I don't by any means claim that the systems-centered approach is the only answer. But it is an answer! It has several things going for it:

SCT's major asset for managed care is that systems-centered therapy can be 'chunked': interrupted and started again where it left off.

SCT de-pathologizes and normalizes, and keeps the work energy in the patient, thus avoiding the development of the kind of therapeutic system that relies upon the therapist to fuel the change.

The therapist does not interpret the patient's dynamics to the patient in SCT. Rather, the therapist takes the responsibility for introducing the patient to active techniques that reduce defenses against direct experience. Using these techniques, the patients discover their own dynamic realities.

SCT provides the patient with a systematic series of techniques for modifying the most common symptoms that bring people into therapy: anxiety, tension, somatic symptoms, depression and abusive acting out.

SCT generates a systematic, sequenced, goal-oriented, step-by-step treatment plan with clear criteria for assessing progress at the end of each therapy session in the context of the goals. As each beginning step takes off from the previous learning step, SCT can be stopped at any time, and begun again at any time from where it left off – whether day by day, week by week, month by month or year by year.

As the SCT methods and techniques for delivering treatment are both structured sequentially and standardized, patients can be transferred to different SCT therapists for continuation of treatment when there is therapist rotation. Inherent to the SCT approach is an interdependent, authentic relationship between the therapist and patient. Thus the 'therapeutic alliance', though different with each therapist, contains significant (and perhaps sufficient) similarities.

In SCT the sequence of treatment steps are the same for all diagnoses. All people, however diagnosed, have the same hierarchy of defenses which can be usefully addressed sequentially through the techniques of defense modification and symptom reduction.

Each new modification technique both builds upon the skills learned in modifying the previous defense and serves as the basis for modifying the next defense in the sequence.

Each session of a systems-centered therapy is a complete therapy for that session, in that it involves patients in discovering the particular therapeutic tenet that applies to their difficulty in the here-and-now of the therapeutic session.

Each SCT session focus is on the cost of the particular defenses and symptoms that occur in that session, the skills to successfully modify them immediately, and the cost of those same defenses in the outside life, together with the relationship between the particular defense and symptom and the presenting problem.

The progress of each patient in the overall treatment process is easily assessed by the outcome criteria. For example: patients either do or don't know: how to undo their anxiety, how to decondition their somatic symptoms, how to undo depression, how to contain the retaliatory impulse instead of acting it out in outrages, tantrums or violence. Patients either can or can't recognize their tendency to lock themselves into one-up, one-down relationships; to enter into stubborn stalemates and resistance to change, or to approach intimacy with the conviction that the 'other' is either too close or too far (Agazarian 1996b, pp.31–32).

Applying the theory led to the methods and techniques described in this chapter. Not surprisingly, these applications led me to understand the theory itself more deeply and to being able more fully to integrate the theoretical constructs into the Theory of Living Human Systems and its Systems-Centered Practice.

CHAPTER 7

A Theory of Living Human Systems and its Systems-Centered Practice

Putting It All Together

I now come to the last chapter of this autobiography of a theory. For me it is like a crescendo from the years of orchestrating my thoughts – and is the solution to the cacophony that so often drowned out whatever small steps in reasoning I had achieved. As such, there may be passages in this chapter which must make intuitive sense if they are to make sense at all. I can but ask the reader to read where you want, skip-read when it feels right and flow with the meaning when it is meaningful.

I have no doubt that for me theory does not come from my comprehensive brain. Rather it comes from some subterranean force that has a rhythm of its own. A rhythm that I sometimes experience with such pressure that it is difficult to contain, and no amount of pacing reduces it. At other times it flows sweetly onto paper and I feel like a cipher rather than an author, and often do not comprehend what I have written until after I read it. So this chapter contains both the reasoned arguments and also the flow that demands apprehension before comprehension.

I have mentioned that liberation from the worst of my underground chaos[1] came through my emergent understanding of the concept of isomorphy. Isomorphy is still like Aladdin's lamp to me, the more I massage it, the more the genie looks over my shoulder and there seem to be no end to

---

1   There are many meanings for the word chaos. The one that seems closest to chaos as I know it is Ralph Abraham's understanding: 'There is another level...which I am calling Chaos, or the Gaian unconscious. This contains not form but the source of form, the energy of form, the form of form, the material that form is made of' (Abraham, McKenna and Sheldrake, 1992).

the dimensions of new understanding that appear and transform the world. I suspect that all theoreticians apply isomorphic thinking intuitively. What is so special about isomorphy nested in systems concepts is that it is part of a coherent framework that makes it possible to translate intuitive understanding into a communication.

Thus the construct of isomorphy is fundamental to my formal systems thinking and gives a frame for the many dimensions of understanding that thinking about a hierarchy of living human systems requires. Understanding isomorphy transformed the way I apprehended the world and made quite clear to me just how separate and discrete theoretical reality is from the reality that we call the real world. As I wrote in 'Systems Theory and Group Psychotherapy' (Agazarian 1991a):

> A System does not exist in the real world like 'people' do. A system is a product of imagination. It exists only when you think it, and disappears when you don't. 'Seeing a system' happens when we learn how to think about the world in systems terms. Thinking 'systems-centered' allows the behavior of human systems to be explained in an organized way that applies to all living systems in a hierarchy.
>
> Systems-centered thinking simplifies thinking about many levels of existence: self and others, small groups, large groups, departments, organizations, societies and cultures. Each is a system that survives. Each matures from simple to complex. Each either approaches or avoids solving the problems inherent in living. Each moves in relationship to goals in the environment. The advantage of thinking 'systems' is that the dynamics of all the different living systems can be thought about in the same way, and the same principles can be used to explain behavior from many perspectives.
>
> To think about oneself from a systems-centered perspective, one thinks of oneself as a system with all the different internal 'voices' as subsystems. Each different internal voice is a voice for oneself and also one's own different 'subsystems' or subgroups, as well as a voice for different subgroups that one is a member of in the group, and a voice for the group-as-a-whole. One belongs, in reality, to many different subgroups at all levels of the system hierarchy all the time!
>
> There are many voices within people which join with many voices in any society and thus are an influence on how a system functions: whether it be a group or an organization or a nation. Thinking this way is

thinking 'systems' into existence at different hierarchical levels simultaneously.

Operational definitions have been developed and applied to group and individual psychotherapy as a series of testable hypotheses. Thus the systems-centered group therapy leader has been re-defined as a researcher. The work of the systems-centered leader is to test systems-centered hypotheses in the group-as-a-whole. Operationally this means that systems-centered hypotheses are the guidelines for systems-centered leadership (Agazarian 1991a, p.4).

In 1992, the International Journal of Group Psychotherapy published a series of articles in celebration of the fiftieth anniversary of the American Group Psychotherapy Association. I was invited to contribute 'A Systems Approach to the Group-as-a-whole' to the section on 'Contemporary Theories of Group Psychotherapy'. This article was a milestone to me as it marked my formal transition from a 'group as a whole' theorist to a 'systems-centered' theorist. In the article, I wrote:

> Group as a system is an abstraction. It is not a place in which people live. It 'appears' when you think it and disappears when you do not! This paper introduces the reader to thinking 'systems-centered,' to thinking about group as a system which exists in a hierarchy of systems, which is itself a hierarchy of systems, self-reflexively isomorphic in structure and function (Agazarian 1992a, p.179).

I then go on to summarize the intellectual journey that had brought me to this point.

> In viewing the group as a system I begin, not with Bion (1959) and von Bertalanffy (1969), who are the true forethinkers of group-as-a-whole and systems theory, but with Korzybski (1948) who wrote passionately of the prison that Aristotelian logic has created for our Western minds. Whatever you say a thing is, it is NOT, says Korzybski, striking at the heart of our either/or splits. The map is not the territory, says Korzybski, forcing us to notice that our theoretical maps simultaneously both represent and misrepresent our reality as well as create it! All our observations are self-reflexive, says Korzybski, an important point for us as therapists who so often talk about the group as if we are not part of it. Finally, only when our use of language reflects both the structural and dynamic aspects of reality, says Korzybski, will we understand that there

is both space and time as well as a relationship between space/time, individual and group as well as the individual/group relationship.

The development or consolidation of a theory is rarely done in isolation. Thus, although I have devoted my theoretical self to developing an organized and integrated set of principles for thinking further about group psychotherapy, it is inconceivable that this conceptual journey was in reality taken in isolation or that there will not be many people who, on reading these pages, do not immediately recognize developments of their own.

I began with every group therapist's Sisyphus: the need to think about individuals in group in a psychodynamic way, and to somehow think about the group itself in a group dynamic way. My first attempted solution (Agazarian and Peters 1981) was to conceptualize individual psychodynamics and group dynamics as two discrete but compatible systems: both of which could be understood and influenced by applying the constructs of Lewin's field theory (1951). In this way I integrated Freudian psychodynamics, Bion and the group-as-a-whole theoreticians (Agazarian 1989b), the heritage of Korzybski and the riches of social science theory and research (Agazarian 1986a; Cartwright and Zander 1960; Coleman and Bexton 1975; Coleman and Geller 1985; Miller 1978). After working with Helen Durkin (1972), and the members of the General Systems Theory committee (Durkin 1981), I was able to apply the principle of isomorphy to the problem and develop operational definitions for the structure and dynamic function of human systems.

There are many in our field who intuitively sense that there is a group-as-a-whole perspective (Horwitz 1977) or who intuitively apply general systems theory principles (Anzieu 1984). For example, individually oriented group therapists 'know' that the group influences the individual and the individual influences the group; they 'know' that interpretations speak differently to the systems of the conscious, pre-conscious and unconscious and serve a similar (isomorphic) function for all. Intuition, however, is different from explanation and definition. Leading a group intuitively creates one kind of group reality, leading a group from theory, another. Systems equifinality sets out many roads to Rome.

Group-as-a-whole thinking differs from more traditional thinking about groups in that it is group-centered, not individual-centered (Agazarian 1989b). Members' behavior is therefore understood in terms of group dynamics rather than in terms of individual dynamics. General systems theory, stemming more from social psychology than individual psychology (Ackoff and Emery 1972), adds the heritage of scientific thinking with a potential for providing a meta theory of human behavior (Klein, Bernard and Singer 1992). Thinking of group as a system of systems in a hierarchy of systems is a meta-shift in thinking from both the individual-centered and group-centered approach (Agazarian 1991a) (Agazarian 1992a, pp.177–179).

The Building Blocks

This chapter presents a Theory of Living Human Systems, the definitions of its concepts and constructs and the operational definitions that implement them in the form of systems-centered therapy.

The theoretical foundations for a theory of Living Human Systems are Lewin's field theory, Howard and Scott's theory of stress, Shannon and Weaver's information theory and Simon and Agazarian's SAVI system for analyzing verbal interaction. The primary building block was Lewin's field theory, which seemed to me to hold out the promise of defining human behavior objectively. I had been deeply impressed by the range of research that Lewin's concepts had generated and hopeful that I could apply his life space construct to groups as well as to individuals (and thus answer my ongoing question about developing a single concept that would apply to both group and individual dynamics). It was not, however, until I approached Lewin's life space from a systems perspective that the ideas fell into place.

A major advantage of defining the life space for both the individual and the group in general system theory terms is that systems theory explicitly states what is implicit in field theory, and that is the principle of isomorphy. The isomorphic principle allows the operational definitions of the structure and function of any one system in a hierarchy to be applied to other systems in the same hierarchy. When system structures and functions are described comparably at different system levels, then what is learned about the dynamics of any one system can contribute to understanding the dynamics of all other systems in the same hierarchy.

Lewin states that behavior is a function of the life space. The life space depicts the person's interaction in his perceived environment. In other words, the life space is the implicit representation or map that is drawn from the system's interaction with the environment.

In defining the individual life space, Lewin also states that all behavior is goal directed, in that there is a motivational tension or driving force that connects the person to his goal. Thus to depict a person's life space is not only to draw the map but also to predict the path that the person will take in the direction of his goal: through the regions that he perceives as having permeable barriers, and around those that are perceived as impermeable. In other words, the map of the person's life space charts predicts and explains why he behaves as he does as he journeys from one end of his day to the other (Agazarian 1987b).

Using a systems framework to translate the above paragraph, it can be argued that the behavioral output of a system is a diagnostic of the system life space. In Lewinian language, we are moving from the level of the person to that of the system: behavior as a function of the person's perception of the environment $[b=f(P,E)]$ is replaced by behavior as a function of the system in interaction with the environment $[b=f(S,E).]$ (Agazarian 1987b). From a systems perspective, the life space does not have to be a function of an explicitly perceived environment but can be understood as a function of the way information enters the system and is organized (Agazarian 1987b). Lewin's 'perception' is thus replaced by the principle of function which determines the kinds of information to which system boundaries are permeable (discrimination) and what organizing principles are operating within the system to integrate the information that has entered the system (integration). This of course necessitates defining principles of function which can be used to infer the life space from the behavioral interactions in the context of the here-and-now environment. (This is addressed later in this chapter as I define the constructs of the theory.) The life space map also serves to indicate the relative simplicity or complexity of the system's organization.

The first and most important application is not only understanding the isomorphy between the life space of the individual and the group-as-a-whole, but the isomorphy between one phase and another in group development. (From this orientation, each phase and subphase is a system, existing in a hierarchy of systems whose structure and function are equivalent.)

The first step is to conceptualize each phase of group development as a life space (Agazarian 1986a). As such, it could be inferred that there was a tension system that related to the heuristic goal of moving towards the next phase. This is compatible with the assumption that all living human systems move towards the goal of survival, development and transformation from simpler to more complex (theory of living human systems). This in turn implies each phase can be conceptualized in terms of three concurrent life spaces, one related to the goal of survival, a second related to the goal of development and a third related to the goal of transformation. The benefit of thinking systems at this point is that each life space can be thought of either separately or together as three hierarchically related regions of one life space. (As always with theory, the way one chooses to look at it will depend upon what one wants to learn.)

An essential companion construct in applying Lewin's life space to the phases of development is his force field model, and important here in its adapted form that we developed for SAVI.

The potential permeability of the boundaries between the regions of a life space can be diagnosed by defining the force field of the driving and restraining forces at the boundary. Operationally, the potential boundary permeability will be increased if the restraining forces are reduced, and decreased if the restraining forces are increased. Functionally, therefore, reducing the restraining forces increases the probability that the system will move in the direction of its goals.

If we now enlist Howard and Scott's theory of stress in which it is postulated that all behavior can be understood as either approaching or avoiding the problem that lies on the path to goal, we can say that each boundary is a 'problem to be solved' on the path to the goal and the problem can be either approached or avoided.

If we enlist Shannon and Weaver's information theory we can say 'noise' is the problem that needs to be solved in communication, and that the more we reduce the 'noise' in the communication, the greater the probability that the system boundaries will be permeable to the information in the communication – given the assumption that systems close their boundaries to noise and open them to clear communication.

If we now recall SAVI, we have a system that defines the kinds of verbal behavior that introduce noise in the system (avoidance behaviors) and the kinds of behavior that resolve noise in the system (approach behaviors) – on the assumption that it is the problem of how to communicate that must be solved before problems of what to communicate can be addressed (Agazarian 1968).

We now have all the ingredients for using the theoretical constructs just discussed to understand how to influence the phases of group development so that the system of the group-as-a-whole has a higher potential for moving in the direction of the goals of survival, development and transformation from simple to complex.

In our earlier work with SAVI, Anita and I had obtained the communication patterns that both characterized and discriminated the different phases of group development. We had used these patterns as maps, that enabled us to diagnose in which phase a group was working. As soon as the phases of development are viewed from the perspective of the life space, it becomes possible to draw the group system life space in terms of a series of regions, each of which corresponds to the sequence of phases that Bennis and Shepard have identified. It also becomes possible to use the SAVI maps to define the expected communication patterns in each region. It then becomes relatively easy to draw the force field that maintains the balance of driving and restraining forces at each boundary (Figure 7.1).

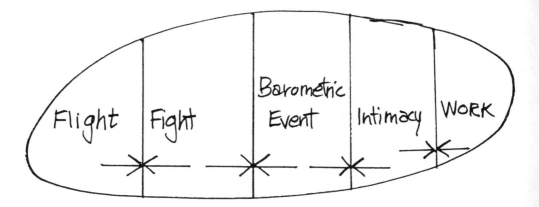

Figure 7.1 Force field that maintains the balance of driving and restraining forces at each boundary

Thus, for example, in the first phase of group development the two initial sub-phases are flight and fight. The SAVI map of the communication in flight is different from the pattern in fight (see Chapter 2). From the perspective of the life space, these would be the two initial regions, defined by their boundaries, and the force field that maintains the boundaries will be a balance of flight and fight behaviors (Figure 7.2).

Force field of driving and restraining forces			
SUBPHASE OF FIGHT	→ ←		SUBPHASE OF FLIGHT
Blame	→	←	Negative predictions
Hostility	→	←	Anxiety
Frustration	→	←	Tension
Retaliatory impulse	→	←	Depression

Figure 7.2 Force field of fight and flight
Source: Agazarian (1999)

Maintaining the status quo within each region relates to the survival goal of the phase or subphase, but at the expense of the goal of development. Development from one region to another depends upon making the boundary between regions permeable by reducing the restraining forces to moving in the direction of the developmental goal.

Bennis and Shepard (1956), in their theory of group development, demonstrated that Bion's dependency, flight/fight and pairing assumptions manifested differently in each phase. They also outlined their subphases so that it was relatively easy to see that one subphase built upon another. In other words, not only was there a relationship between one phase and another, but there was also a developmental complexity. The transition from one region to another is in fact a developmental transformation of the group-as-a-whole system from simpler to more complex.

For example, for the flight subphase to 'survive', the flight behaviors identifiable in the SAVI pattern must remain stable. If, however, the flight behaviors remain stable, the group will not develop into the fight phase. It will remain fixed – or fixated.

The flight subphase, however, just like any other subphase of group development, is not made up of only flight behaviors. It is true that the flight behaviors predominate, which is what gives the subphase its character. Yet, there are also smatterings of all the other behaviors that carry the potential for all the phases in the developing group. This is true of every other subphase. All behaviors (and all group dynamics) exist all the time. Thus, the potential for the entire range of behavior always exists and in fact can be elicited. The issue in the systems-centered approach is to elicit only those behaviors that can be discriminated and integrated into the communication parameters that are typical of the phase. In other words, we are working to identify the clusters of behavior that typify the particular phase and use them as a guide to what kinds of information are likely to be accepted and used and what kinds of information are likely to be rejected.

Incidentally, for research purposes, the transition from one phase to another can be illustrated by using the normal (bell-shaped) curve. In each phase, approximately 68 per cent of the behavior will typify the phase. When the group is preparing to shift from one subphase to another, the curve will be skewed with a pseudopod containing behavior, deviant to the existing phase and within the norm of the next phase. As the group makes the transition into the next subphase, the skew will gradually reverse itself with a pseudopod maintaining the previous cluster of behaviors and the bulk of the curve manifesting the new. When the group has finished entering the subphase, the curve will again be bell-shaped and the process will begin all over again (Figure 7.3).

There are three levels of abstraction here. The first level is the system of the region under scrutiny, which has its own life space and relates primarily to survival and then a particular communication pattern of the subphase remains stable (a normal curve). When the region under scrutiny is taken in context, then the boundary between it and the regions on either side of it mark the difference between lesser and greater complexity (curves that skew either to the right or the left). For example, the fight subphase exists between the flight subphase and the subphase that addresses issues with authority. To cross the boundaries to a system of lesser complexity is to regress from the level of functioning established within the region itself (flight behaviors are simpler and less complex than fight behaviors). To cross the boundaries into the region of greater complexity is to develop (from inter-member fighting

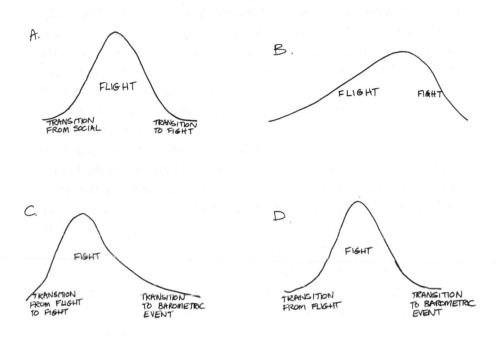

Figure 7.3 The transition from one phase to another

into issues around authority). From this perspective, the developmental goal (coming together around authority issues instead of fighting each other) is of a higher order than surviving the fight and will always remain so unless the survival of the ability to fight is in fact threatened. The third level is the group-as-a-whole system, which is the system life space which contains all the regions. The group-as-a-whole contains the potential for development through all phases and each transition from one phase to another is a transformation at all levels.

To translate this thinking into practice becomes a moderately simple matter of weakening the forces at the boundary between regions so that the inherent drive towards the development moves the group into the next region where it consolidates the communications of the next phase.

For example: crossing the boundary between flight and fight is a simple matter of using less flight behaviors (weakening the restraining force) and more fight behaviors (strengthening the driving forces): weakening the restraining forces simultaneously releases the driving forces (see Figure 7.2).

To put it all together: if it is true that in all living human systems there is an intrinsic drive towards the goals of survival, development and transformation, then systematically weakening the defensive restraining forces at the boundaries of the phases of system development will automatically release the intrinsic drive. In other words, the 'problems' (Howard and Scott 1965) that lie on the path to goal are boundary problems, and reducing 'noise' (Shannon and Weaver 1964) in the communications across those boundaries will increase their permeability to information. As the information crosses the boundary and is discriminated and integrated, the system will develop from simpler to more complex, both in its ability to discriminate differences in the apparently similar and similarities in the apparently different and also in its ability to integrate information (Figure 7.4).

DRIVING	→	←	RESTRAINING
Discriminating differences in the apparently similar	→	←	Ambiguity
Discriminating similarities in the apparently different	→	←	Contradictions
Integrating information in new ways	→	←	Redundancy

Figure 7.4 Force field of driving and restraining forces to system development through discriminating and integrating information

Shannon and Weaver defined 'noise' in the communication as the ambiguities, contradictions and redundancies that reduce the probability that the information contained in the communication will be transferred (as anyone in a conversation knows who has been frustrated by vagueness, disoriented by contradictions or bored by redundancy). Systems-centered practice deliberately reduces the noise in the communication at the boundaries of the system and within the boundaries of the system, in the context of the subphase of development, so that information is integrated in relationship to system goals.

A Theory of Living Human Systems and its Systems-Centered Practice

It has been and continues to be my ambition to define the constructs of the theory well enough so that a clear connection can be drawn from the constructs to the methods that are developed from the constructs and in turn the techniques that put these methods into practice. If systems-centered therapy does indeed serve as a blueprint for treatment that can reliably predict where patients are in their therapy by assessing where they are in the hierarchy of defense modification, and if the sequence of defense modification does correlate reliably with a reduction in the symptoms that is predicted through the modification of each defense, then a theory of living human systems will have been validated and its methods demonstrated to be reliable. In the service of this task, it continues to be my ambition that each systems-centered intervention serves as a testable hypothesis so that the therapist can get immediate feedback as to how reliably the therapeutic system is traveling along the path to the therapeutic goals.

An overall view of a theory of living human systems and its definitions is summarized in Table 7.1. The constructs of the theory of living human systems are defined, the methods that operationalize the constructs are described and the techniques that implement these methods are identified. The methods serve as practical working hypotheses and are intended to serve as guidelines for a systems-centered approach.

The theory chart (Table 7.1) is structured with four columns and four rows. The first row gives the definitions of hierarchy and isomorphy, structure, function and energy. The second row defines the methods developed from the theory and the third row identifies the techniques that translate the methods into practice. The columns define the basic constructs of the theory and trace the steps from theory, through the operational definitions of the constructs, to the techniques that test the theory in reality.

The constructs of A Theory of Living Human Systems are defined as a hierarchy of isomorphic systems that are energy organizing, goal directed and self-correcting. The specific methods that are the operational definitions of the constructs are *contextualizing, boundarying, functional subgrouping* and *vectoring*. These methods define systems-centered practice: for example, the method of subgrouping developed from making an operational definition for the hypothesis that transformation occurs through discrimination and

A THEORY OF LIVING HUMAN SYSTEMS AND ITS SYSTEMS-CENTERED® PRACTICE
Yvonne M. Agazarian

A theory of living human systems defines a hierarchy of isomorphic systems that are energy-organizing, self-correcting and goal-directed.

THEORETICAL DEFINITIONS

HIERARCHY

Every system exists in the environment of the system above and is the environment for the system below.

System-centered hierarchy
The systems-centered hierarchy is defined by the member system, the subgroup system and the group-as-a-whole system

ISOMORPHY

Systems are similar in structure and function and different in different contexts. There is an interdependent relationship between the dynamics of structure, function and energy.

Structure
systems-centered structure define boundaries in space, time and reality that are potentially permeable to information.

Energy
systems-centered energy/information is defined as a force field of vectors approaching or avoiding system goals.

Function
systems-centered systems function to survive, develop and transform by discriminating and integrating information.

SYSTEMS-CENTERED METHODS

contextualizing: developing the systems-centered hierarchy.	Boundarying: organizing energy / information.	Vectoring: directing energy / information.	Subgrouping: correcting energy / information.
Person system: primary personality Observing self-system: discriminates & integrates information. Member system: directs energy into sub-groups. Subgroup system: contains and explores information. Group-as-a-whole system integrates information.	Survival: managing the permeability of system boundaries (in the hierarchy of systems) by reducing noise in the communications within and between systems.	Development: directing information towards the primary goals of survival, development and transformation and/or towards the secondary environmental task goals.	Transformation: containing, discriminating and integrating differences (in similarity) and similarities (in difference) at all three system levels.

SYSTEMS-CENTERED TECHNIQUES

Eliciting the SCT group requires developing an observing self-system and establishing the member, subgroup and group-as-a-whole roles by using boundarying, subgrouping and vectoring interventions tailored to the context of each phase of system development.	Applying the SCT "Hierarchy of Defense Modification" weakens the restraining forces to valid communication and releases the drive towards system goals.	The "fork-in-the-road" techniques frees the energy bound up in defenses and redirects it towards exploring the conflicts or impulses defended against.	The SCT conflict-resolution technique of "Functional Subgrouping" contains, explores and integrates differences instead of stereotyping or scapegoating them.

Table 7.1 The Theory of Living Human Systems (TLHS) and its Systems-Centered® Practice (SCT®). The theory of living human systems defines a hierarchy of isomorphic systems that are energy organizing, self-correcting and goal directed.

Source. Agazarian (1999) Please do not reproduce without permission. The trademark for Systems-centered®-and SCT-® is owned by Yvonne M. Agazarian.

integration of information. Boundarying methods developed from making operational the hypothesis that boundary permeability influences the availability of work energy in a group and that boundarying into the here-and-now across psychological space and time increases the energy that will be available for work. Vectoring methods test the hypothesis that energy can be directed toward system goals. Contextualizing defines the systems-centered group hierarchy (member, subgroup and group-as-a-whole) and introduces roles as related to context and goals which tests the hypothesis that increasing the capacity to take things in context decreases human anguish.

Each of the above four methods is expected to modify a specific dynamic and is made operational by specific techniques that enable a systems-centered therapist to put each method into practice. Thus a *boundarying* technique will be expected to modify communication at the boundaries (by reducing the restraining forces at all system levels). *Functional* techniques manage conflict and foster discrimination and integration through functional subgrouping. *Vectoring* techniques discriminate between the defensive restraining forces and the goal-oriented drive. (The 'fork in the road' technique enables energy to be directed away from the defense and towards the conflict, impulse, or reality that is being defended against). *Contextualizing* techniques draw attention to the larger context of experience so that it is not taken 'just' personally (Agazarian 1999). Each of these different methods tests a different set of hypotheses. Outcomes serve as feedback about whether SCT methods get the predicted results. Thus systems-centered practitioners are researchers as well as change agents (therapists, counselors and organizational consultants). Developing research hypotheses strengthens clinical practice and makes explicit the links between theory and practice as well as developing paths for formal research.

In the section below, the definitions of the basic constructs of the theory are summarized and their connection to the methods and techniques of systems-centered practice is discussed. At the end of each section, some research hypotheses are proposed that are supported informally in practice, but have yet to be formally tested.

Constructs, Methods and Hypotheses

Hierarchy

Systems in a hierarchy move from simple to complex. It is assumed that the basic components of every system are its subsystems and that in the system hierarchy every system exists in the environment of the system above and is the environment for the system below it. In Figure 7.5, this is drawn from two perspectives.

The hierarchy defined for group is the isomorphic system of member, subgroup and the group-as-a-whole. Thus the subgroup exists in the environment of the group-as-a-whole and is the environment for its

EVERY SYSTEM

EXISTS

IN THE ENVIRONMENT

of

THE SYSTEM ABOVE IT

and

IS

THE ENVIRONMENT

for

THE SYSTEM BELOW IT

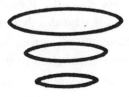

Figure 7.5 Hierarchy

members. In Figure 7.6 it is clear that the middle circle (the subgroup system) shares its boundaries with both the member system and the group-as-a-whole system.

Figure 7.6 SCT group psychotherapy hierarchy

Looking at Figure 7.6, a general hypothesis appears self-evident that the most efficient system to influence is the subgroup rather than either the member or the group-as-a-whole. The idea that the subgroup rather than the individual member is the basic unit of a group was a personal 'eureka' and introduced a 'systems-centered' orientation to the existing leader-centered, member-centered and group-as-a-whole approaches to group psycho-therapy (Agazarian 1992a). This will be discussed in more detail under structure.

ESTABLISHING HIERARCHY IN AN SCT GROUP

In systems-centered therapy, *hierarchy* is operationalized by the method called *contextualizing* by which the observing self-system and role functions of member, subgroup and group-as-a-whole are developed. The function of the observing self-system is to discriminate and integrate information about reality. In the process of developing their observing self-system, people acquire the ability to experience themselves, not only as a person-as-a-whole with membership in many internal subgroups (a functioning self-centered system) but also as members of the group-as-a-whole and its subgroups. Figure 7.7 shows how the observing self-system is the first discrimination required of a systems-centered member, the ability to tell the difference between thinking and feeling: cognitions and emotions. As we discussed in Chapter 6, thoughts can 'time travel' to the past or the future, whereas

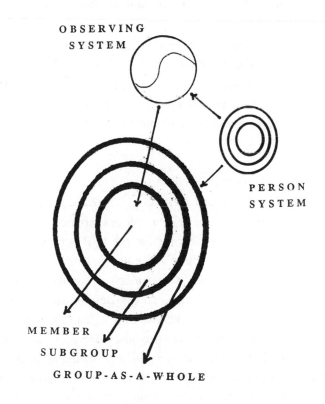

Figure 7.7 Observing self-system

emotions are always experienced in the here-and-now (although emotions can be explained in terms of past or future). Thus the goal for members joining a systems-centered group is to join a subgroup with emotional intelligence, that connects the individual person system with the group system.

Contextualizing involves developing an awareness of the self *in the role that is appropriate to the context* – which has as many emotional meanings as there are contexts in which to understand it.

HIERARCHICAL HYPOTHESES

1. Defining the SCT group psychotherapy hierarchy (member, subgroup and group-as-a-whole) introduces the concept of roles, as they relate to context and goals, which increases the development of the capacity to take things in context rather than out of context and personally.

2. Relating experience to different hierarchical contexts increases the ability to discriminate and integrate multiple levels of experience.

3. The ability to discriminate the goals and role behaviors relevant to the changing contexts decreases the probability that old, maladaptive roles will be acted out (decreases the power of the repetition compulsion).

ESTABLISHING CONTEXT IN AN SCT GROUP

Contextualizing in SCT means increasing the awareness of the different contexts of one's experience. For example, experience in the role of a member of one's personal context (where the goal is personal growth) is different from the experience of one's member role in the subgroup system (where the goal is to resonate with others) or in the context of the group-as-a-whole system (where the goal is to develop an environment that will potentiate therapeutic goals). When a member is in danger of losing the system context and taking his experience 'just personally', a common SCT intervention is to ask 'What role are you in?' Personalizing an event takes it out of context and is one of the major sources of human anguish. Introducing the systems perspective reframes personal pain in the context of shared human experience.

1. *Contextualizing* generates an increasing ability to be objective and to transform personalized human anguish into existential insight.

2. Increasing the ability to discriminate and integrate information from multiple contexts increases the appropriate permeability of the boundary between apprehension and comprehension with the resultant increase in emotional intelligence (Goleman 1995).

Isomorphy

It is assumed that systems in a defined hierarchy are isomorphic: similar in structure and function and different in different contexts. Like looking at the hierarchy of multiple reflection of an image in a double mirror, the structure and function of each system is equivalent to the ones behind it and the ones in front of it. The systems that systems-centered therapy defines for group are the member, subgroup and group-as-a-whole systems, each with an equivalent structure, function and dynamic principles of operation (Figure 7.8).

SYSTEMS

ARE SIMILAR IN

STRUCTURE AND FUNCTION

AND

DIFFERENT

IN DIFFERENT CONTEXTS

Figure 7.8 Isomorphy

ESTABLISHING ISOMORPHY IN AN SCT GROUP

Becoming a systems-centered therapist depends upon learning how to see the group as a hierarchy of living human systems. Thus, in addition to their attunement to the individual people who come into membership in a systems-centered group, the SCT therapist discovers that however different the group, its members and subgroups may appear, when framed as isomorphic systems, they all have in common their structure and the principles by which they function.

Structure and function are interdependent and the SCT therapist works with both from the very beginning. For example, at the start of a group the leader asks the members to move their chairs in relationship to each other so that 'everybody can see everybody'. Establishing 'eye contact' is important to both structure and function of a systems-centered group. Deliberately meeting each other's eyes encourages SCT members to shift their attention (vector their energy) across the boundary and to take up the responsibilities of membership in the group. It is also through eye contact that members take their first step into 'subgrouping'. By maintaining eye contact subgroup members maintain their resonance with each other — both when their subgroup is working actively and when the work of the subgroup is to 'contain their work energy' while a different subgroup works.

ISOMORPHIC HYPOTHESES

1. What is learned about the structure and/or function of any one system applies to all other systems in the defined hierarchy.

2. In a therapy group, influencing the dynamics of any one system influences all.

Structure

The structure of each system is similar in that each is defined by its boundaries in space, time, reality and role. Boundaries in space and time are the structural elements common to all the systems in the hierarchy.

Each living human system has geographical boundaries and time boundaries which bring it into existence and out again. Each system has functional role boundaries which are connected to a goal or purpose. Each system exists in an existential reality which differentiates it from its existential potentiality. The nature of the boundary permeability determines the system's ability to maintain its energy – and the relationship between the system and its goals determines the system's ability to direct its energy. Dynamically, the state of the energy at the boundaries of the system can be analyzed through the use of the force field model.

System boundaries are the structural elements common to all the systems in the hierarchy. Structure is operationally defined by *boundarying* and tested in reality by techniques that modify boundary permeability.

System boundaries open to information and close to noise. Noise is generated whenever information is too discrepant to be integrated. Sometimes noise enters the system through inadequate boundaries. At other times the communication process itself generates noise within the system. When internal noise threatens to overwhelm the system, the system maintains equilibrium by encapsulating the noisy information within a subsystem with impermeable boundaries.

Examples of encapsulated subsystems are non-functional roles, like the identified patient and scapegoat, which are created by the group. It is worth noting, however, that these roles serve as restraining forces in one context and driving forces in another. For example, the identified patient and scapegoat serve as restraining forces to functional group development in that they split off and encapsulate information that is potentially important to later group transformations. However, these same roles serve as driving forces in stabilizing group structure when the differences in the group are too different to be integrated and incipient chaos threatens group survival.

In systems-centered groups, the method used to modify the defensive restraining forces in communication is called *boundarying*. The major boundarying technique is the SCT *hierarchy of defense modification* by which the restraining forces to valid communication are systematically weakened and the drive towards system development released (Agazarian 1997).

ESTABLISHING BOUNDARIES IN AN SCT GROUP

SCT therapists assume that boundarying determines not only how the group reaches its goals, but also whether or not it can reach its goals. SCT therapists use boundarying like a filter: to keep ambiguous, redundant, contradictory and certain other noisy communications out of the group. For example, when the group speculates in vague and obscure and meandering ways, this will flood the group. Thus SCT therapists always draw the group's attention to the 'ambiguity defense' when it occurs and introduce specificity by asking for clarifications like 'who?', 'what?', 'where?', 'how?' and never 'why?' 'Why' questions all too easily encourage members to give an explanation instead of exploring the experience that their ambiguity was defending against. Redundancy, when the group goes on and on saying the same thing over and over again, will stall the group. The SCT therapist will point out to the group that it has already covered this particular ground several times and wonder what the group would be exploring if it did not repeat a familiar pattern. All contradictions in communication irritate the group, even socially acceptable contradictions like a 'yes-but' or 'don't you really think' or 'I wouldn't put it quite like that'. SCT therapists think of these as 'touch-and-go' communications and from the very earliest stages of group will ask how group experience would change if members joined on similarities rather than unwittingly separating on differences.

BOUNDARYING

The method of boundarying is the method which brings system energy across the boundaries into being and into role – by systematically and sequentially reducing defenses and symptoms – thus increasing the permeability of the boundaries to communications which contain the energy that relates to the goals. Boundarying enables members to focus their attention away from their past into the here-and-now and deal with the defenses that prevent them from being who they want to be and saying what they want to say in the group. By boundarying, people learn to recognize how they leave their here-and-now reality and emigrate across the boundaries of space and time. People leave in two ways: in reality by changing locations or ignoring clock time; in psychological reality by turning their thoughts and emotions towards the past or future, or leaving the here-and-now experience and living in the reality created by their thoughts (Figure 7.9).

BOUNDARYING HYPOTHESES

1. Titrating boundary permeability increases available work energy in the group.

	PAST	PRESENT	FUTURE
explain	interpreted reality	misconstructed reality	negatively predicted reality
explore	past experience	reality testing in the here-and-now	plans and goals

Figure 7.9 Vectoring energy across the boundaries of time and experiencing the realities of the present

2. The drive towards survival, development and transformation (inherent to all living human systems) is released when the restraining forces specific to the developmental goals are reduced by the techniques of *boundarying.*

3. Reducing ambiguities, contradictions and redundancies in the communication process increases the probability that the information contained in the communication will be discriminated and integrated.

Function

The basic hypothesis is that system survival, development and transformation is a function of the system's ability to discriminate and integrate differences. System development is determined by its ability to discriminate and integrate information – transformations of matter/energy – (Miller 1978). System transformation is determined by its ability to contain the unknown.

Discrimination is the ability to see differences in the apparently similar and similarities in the apparently different. Integration is the process by which information is organized within the system so that it is available for work. From this, the functional hypothesis is generated that the dynamics of system survival, development and transformation are governed by the processes of discrimination and integration of information.

Systems survive by developing internal organizing principles to manage the information in communications within, between and among the system hierarchy.

Systems develop by developing appropriate boundary permeability to communication transactions within, between and among systems in the hierarchy: opening to information that is similar enough to be integrated and closing to information that is too different.

Systems transform by the process of discriminating and integrating differences and thus changing from simple to complex in both structure and function. Dynamically, system transformation is a function of the process of discriminating and integrating the information contained in the communication transactions that cross the boundaries between, within and among systems in the hierarchy. The process of transformation depends upon system recognition and integration of both similarities and differences: both differences in the apparently similar and similarities in the apparently different. Organizing and integrating new information leads to transformations of living human systems from simpler to ever more complex in relationship to the primary goals of survival, development and transformation and the secondary goals of environmental mastery. How the system functions in relationship to these goals will, however, be different in different contexts.

FUNCTIONAL SUBGROUPING

The SCT technique of functional subgrouping emerged through operationalizing the definition of system function: that all living human systems develop, mature and transform through the process of discriminating differences and integrating them. Integrating differences, however, requires the system to change. Before a system can reorganize itself into a different structure it must first change its existing structure. Differences that are not too different are relatively easy to integrate into an existing structure. Differences that are too different are not.

The method of functional subgrouping puts into practice the dynamic that SCT uses to explain the survival, development and transformation of living human systems: the ability to discriminate and integrate differences instead of stereotyping or scapegoating them. In subgrouping, rather than stereotyping, rejecting and scapegoating differences in self or other, conflicts around difference are taken out of the person and contained in the group. Within each subgroup, as the similarities among members are explored, so differences become apparent and accepted. As each subgroup in the group-as-a-whole recognizes differences in what was apparently similar within their subgroups, so they start to recognize similarities in what was apparently different between the subgroups, and so there is an integration in the group-as-a-whole (Figure 7.10).

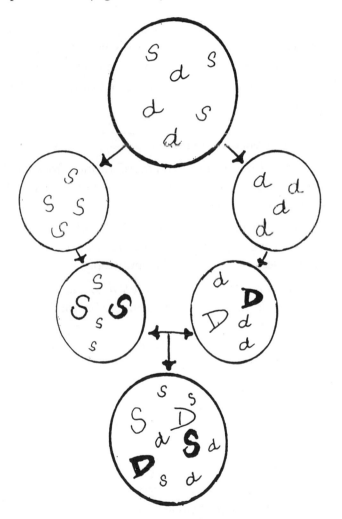

Figure 7.10 Functional subgroups recognize and integrate differences

ESTABLISHING FUNCTIONAL SUBGROUPING IN AN SCT GROUP

SCT leaders deliberately discourage stereotype subgrouping (in which differences are typically institutionalized or scapegoated) and encourage functional subgrouping instead, which requires members to subgroup around similarities before differences are addressed. By subgrouping functionally, members explore and build on their common experience rather than using the defensive kinds of communications, like 'yes-but,' in which members appear to be building on what the last member said but are actually pre-empting the conversation. In an SCT group, when members introduce explicit differences the therapist intervenes and says something like, 'That is an important difference. Could you hold that, and not forget it, and bring it in later after we have finished exploring the issue that we are talking about now?'

FUNCTIONAL SUBGROUPING HYPOTHESES

1. System survival, development and transformation from simple to complex increases as the system's ability to discriminate and integrate information increases.

2. Containing system conflict in *functional subgrouping* reduces the probability that group conflict will be projected and contained in the group roles of scapegoat and identified patient.

3. When a group is dynamically too cohesive to take necessary risks, pointing out the differences in the comfortably similar will induce change in the desired direction.

4. When a group is in conflict over differences, pointing out the similarities in the apparently different will induce change in the desired direction.

5. When a group is fixated, introducing new differences and similarities for the group to integrate will induce change in the desired direction.

Energy

Energy exists as actual or potential, organized or disorganized. Miller (1978) states that system drive-energy can be equated with information. Shannon and Weaver (1956) state an inverse relationship between noise in an informational message (defined in terms of ambiguities, contradictions and redundancies) and the probability that the information it contains will be transferred. Lewin (1951) introduced the model of the force field to diagnose the relationship between the system and a defined goal, and demonstrated that it was more efficient and effective to weaken the restraining forces on the path to the goal than it was to increase the driving forces. Building on this work, I hypothesized that reducing noise (ambiguity, redundancy and contradictions in communication) increases the probability that information will be discriminated and integrated and energy vectored towards system goals. The model of a vector, with a direction, a force (drive) and a point of application (goal), is used to illustrate communication as a field of force related to a goal. Thus the driving and restraining forces that define the system relationship to the goal (both primary and secondary goals) are defined in terms of communication vectors.

The method of *vectoring* is central to the practice of systems-centered therapy, made operational by the 'fork in the road' technique which requires group members to make a series of proactive choices between exploring a defense or exploring what is being defended against. It is assumed that:

1. Exploring the defense weakens the restraining forces

2. *Re-vectoring* the energy to exploring what is being defended against releases the driving forces towards system survival, development and transformation at all system levels: person, member, subgroup and group-as-a-whole.

ESTABLISHING VECTORING IN AN SCT GROUP

Energy is always available and can be directed as a driving or restraining force in relationship to work. It is important to discriminate between the boundaries that are crossed in a flight from work and when boundaries are crossed in search of information that is relevant to work.

VECTORING

The method of vectoring is the method which directs the energy in the hierarchy of systems and connects the system roles to the system goals. Vectoring is the word that describes the process that enables members to deliberately choose to direct their energy towards the aspects of themselves that they want to learn more about and to deliberately direct their energy away from the defenses and symptoms that interfere with their curiosity. Learning how to vector their energy also increases members' ability to direct their energy away from the fantasies and fears about the past, present and future into the reality of here-and-now. Vectoring also makes it possible for members to focus their energy outside themselves so that they can join a subgroup.

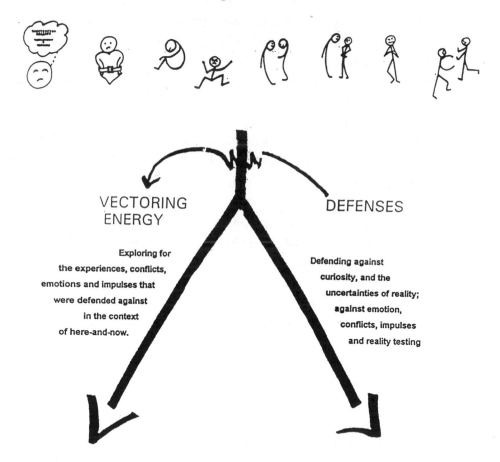

Undoing Defenses

VECTORING
ENERGY

DEFENSES

Exploring for
the experiences, conflicts,
emotions and impulses that
were defended against
in the context
of here-and-now.

Defending against
curiosity, and the
uncertainties of reality;
against emotion,
conflicts, impulses
and reality testing

Figure 7.11 Defense modification: The fork in the road between exploring experience and defending against experience

Functional subgrouping is a method which enables members to work together by joining and exploring similarities rather than separating on differences. It often comes as a surprise when people discover that the way they direct their energy is actually under their control. Both in subgrouping and boundarying, people learn that if they do not give energy to their defenses, symptoms, distractions, negative predictions and mind readings, they not only have plenty of energy available to direct towards testing their reality, but they also do not generate the defenses and symptoms that exhaust their energy. The activity of directing energy deliberately in relationship to the goal of the contextual moment is called vectoring. The final step in systems-centered work is to become continually aware of the context in which one is living – and the fact that it is the context that governs what you can and cannot accomplish in reality at any one time (Figure 7.11).

VECTORING HYPOTHESES

1. The vectorial energy available for work will depend upon the balance of driving and restraining forces in the context of the moment, which in turn will determine the potential for movement along the path towards the group goals.

2. The direction of the group movement on the path to its goal is directly related to whether it approaches or avoids the problems that are inherent to the journey (Howard and Scott 1965).

3. Less work is required to reduce the forces of avoidance rather than to strengthen the forces of approach (Lewin 1951).

4. *Re-vectoring* energy from defenses towards recognizing the underlying impulses, conflicts and emotions that are being defended against increases the probability that defensive symptoms and acting out will be reduced.

Summary and Conclusion

I summarized the constructs of systems-centered therapy in 'A Systems Approach to the Group-as-a-whole' (Agazarian 1992a):

> Systems-centered group therapy is a new discipline based on some different constructs. First and most important to understand is that the *subgroup*, not the individual member, is the basic unit of the

systems-centered group. The subgroup exists in the environment of the group-as-a-whole and is the environment for its members. It follows then that the subgroup is the fulcrum. Subgroups form around similarities and separate around differences. Functional subgroups contain differences in the system while the system develops sufficiently to integrate them.

Dynamics of systems are *isomorphic*, as is system structure and function. Therefore a change at any system level influences a change at all. The structure of a system is defined by its boundaries. The condition of the system's *boundaries* in space, time, reality and role, contain the energy available for work. The system functions to remain in quasi-stationary equilibrium in relationship to its *self-correcting goals* (Bowlby 1969) of survival, development and environmental mastery. For a system's *energy* to be directed in relation to its goals, potential energy must be transformed into active energy (Miller 1978). Active energy will either be contained in a freeze or be directed in flight, fight or work. The behavioral output of the system (individual member, subgroup and the group-as-a-whole) implies the internal and external goal orientation of the system.

The *developmental principle* of all living systems can be formulated as a function of discrimination and integration of information (Agazarian 1989a). Systems-centered therapy takes place by facilitating the process of discriminating, communicating and integrating perceptions of differences in the apparently similar and similarities in the apparently different.

Communication takes place at the boundaries between systems at all levels of the hierarchy: the group, the subgroup and its members. The major focus of intervention is thus, not [system] level, as in the group-as-a-whole, but system boundaries (Agazarian 1989b). All content is potential information. All content is conveyed in communications which occur in time and space. System change occurs when the boundaries of the system become appropriately permeable to communication and a flow of energy is released. Content in the communication indicates which boundary is involved: time–space boundaries, fantasy–reality boundaries, functional role boundaries or subgroup boundaries (Agazarian 1992a, pp.179–180).

If indeed a theory of living human systems is a meta-theory, then systems-centered therapy will be just one of the ways it can be applied. Theory belongs to everyone. On the other hand, systems-centered therapy (SCT) belongs only to those who have been trained to practice it. Originally, I had hoped that it would be the fast lane to the unconscious, that it would do the work in a shorter time than some of the more traditional approaches. Part of my wish came true. There is no longer any question among those who practice it that SCT is a much more direct route to undoing the symptoms of anxiety, tension, depression and the righteous indignation that covers up the fear of one's rage. Therefore, for symptom relief, SCT is certainly efficient and effective in providing symptom relief.

Systems-centered therapy, however, was not designed for symptom relief. It was designed to reduce the restraining forces (defenses and symptoms) so that energy can be redirected to the service of the innate driving force in human beings to survive and to develop and, most important, to forever transform in existential understanding, common sense and humor. As someone once said to me (critically I'm afraid), 'Oh, you're trying to develop a therapy in which people can know themselves!' 'Yes,' said I, convinced that it is not symptom relief, but knowing oneself and being able to be oneself in the existential context as well as in the context of our world, that brings people into therapy.

Since 1990, my training group members have pioneered the discoveries that, by subgrouping functionally, the course of knowing oneself is different from what is traditionally expected. The first major understanding came when we recognized that so much of what had been our preoccupations in therapy were a function of unresolved negative transference – and that working the authority issue in subgroups made it possible to make the transition into experience that authority is inside oneself, not outside it. This alone seemed almost enough, as it revolutionized our working life, as well as freed us from some of our conflicts around control in our intimate connections. We were not to know until we explored the greater depths of the phase of intimacy that, quite simply, separation means being able to tolerate the differences in those that we want to keep close and similar, and that individuation means learning to recognize the similarities between us and others in our alienation. Exploring this conflict in subgroups, we discovered the pervasive transferences that fuel experience in both sides of the split: the merged, symbiotic satisfaction that all is always good, and the alienated, despairing dissatisfaction that everything is always bad. Reaching these depths in subgrouping opened up other dimensions, that under the source of these universal human transferences were other pervasive transferences: the pervasive transference that comes from the family, from our ethnicity and from our phylogeny. Experiencing and understanding these dimensions in the holding environment of containment in a subgroup is a very different experience from working alone.

We discovered that, rather than a signal of pathology, 'falling apart' was necessary, rather like shedding a shell that we had outgrown, and that at the end of the Alice-in-Wonderland descent, we fell into ourselves. In this process we learned that dynamics which have been considered dangerous are only dangerous if they are experienced out of context. And that it is the deep, universal dynamic knowledge of our phylogenetic inheritance that is the 'strange attractor' in the work of groups that subgroup functionally. This is not short-term therapy.

So what has a theory of living human systems and its systems-centered practice contributed to group and individual psychotherapy? It has contributed an understanding that it is not the human dynamics themselves which contribute to the success or failure in therapy, but the development of the context in which they can be addressed and explored rather than acted out. It has contributed the knowledge that unbearable human anguish arises from taking things 'just personally' and that there is no human emotion that is unbearable, only deeply felt as both personal and existentially human, when it is taken in context.

References

Abraham, R., McKenna, T. and Sheldrake, R. (1992) *Trialogues at the Edge of the West.* New Mexico: Bear and Co. Publishing.

Ackoff, R. and Emery, E. (1972) *On Purposeful Systems.* Atherton NY: Aldine.

Agazarian, Y.M. (1962) 'Group dynamics.' Unpublished paper.

Agazarian, Y.M. (1963a) 'Human relations training.' Unpublished paper.

Agazarian, Y.M. (1963b) 'Three-day session in human relations training for forty professional employees of the state office for the blind.' Unpublished paper.

Agazarian, Y.M. (1964) 'Renee: Sechehaye's Renee case.' Unpublished paper.

Agazarian, Y.M. (1965a) Draft manuscript on communication.

Agazarian, Y.M. (1965b) 'Case of Sarah.' Unpublished paper.

Agazarian, Y.M. (1966) 'Preliminary analysis of some of the driving and restraining forces in the process of change.' Unpublished paper.

Agazarian, Y.M. (1968) 'A theory of verbal behavior and information transfer.' Dissertation submitted at Temple University.

Agazarian, Y.M. (1969a) 'A theory of verbal behavior and information transfer.' *Classroom Interaction Newsletter of the Research for Better Schools, Inc., Philadelphia 4*, 2, 22–33.

Agazarian, Y.M. (1969b) 'The agency as a change agent.' In A.H. Goldberg (ed) *Blindness Research: The Expanding Frontiers.* University Park and London: Penn State Press.

Agazarian, Y.M. (1970) 'Report to Devereux.' Unpublished paper.

Agazarian, Y.M. (1971) 'Creative and exploitive relationships.' Unpublished paper.

Agazarian, Y.M. (1972) 'A system for analyzing verbal behavior (SAVI) applied to staff training in milieu treatment.' *Devereux Schools Forum 7*, 1, 1–33.

Agazarian, Y.M. (1982) 'Role as a bridge construct in understanding the relationship between the individual and the group.' In M. Pines and Rafaelson (eds) *The Individual and the Group, Boundaries and Interrelations I.* New York: Plenum Press.

Agazarian, Y.M. (1983a) 'Theory of invisible group applied to individual and group-as-a-whole interpretations.' *Group: The Journal of the Eastern Group Psychotherapy Society 7*, 2, 27–37.

Agazarian, Y.M. (1983b) 'Some advantages of applying multi-dimensional thinking to the teaching, practice and outcomes of group psychotherapy.' *International Journal of Group Psychotherapy 33*, 2, 243–247.

Agazarian, Y.M. (1986a) 'Application of Lewin's life space concept to the individual and group-as-a-whole systems in psychotherapy.' In Stivers and Wheelan (eds) *The Lewin Legacy: Field Theory in Current Practice.* New York: Springer-Verlag.

Agazarian, Y.M. (1986b) 'Towards the formulation of a group-as-a-whole theory. The Lewin legacy: application of modified force field analysis to the diagnosis of implicit group goals.' Unpublished paper delivered at the Second International Kurt Lewin Conference, sponsored by The Society for the Advancement of Field Theory, Downingtown, September.

Agazarian, Y.M. (1987a) 'Bion, the Tavistock method and the group-as-a-whole.' Guest Lecture, Group Psychotherapy, Harvard Medical School, Department of Continuing Education, sponsored by Massachusetts General Hospital, Department of Psychiatry, 3–5 April.

Agazarian, Y.M. (1987b) 'Theory of the invisible group: group-as-a-whole theory framed in terms of field theory and general systems theory.' Unpublished paper presented at the 'The Lewin Legacy', Symposium, at the Ninety-fifth Annual Convention of the American Psychological Association, New York City, August.

Agazarian, Y.M. (1987d) 'Group-as-a-whole theory applied to scapegoating.' Unpublished supplementary paper to the workshop on 'Deviance, Scapegoating and Group Development', Eastern Group Psychotherapy Society Annual Conference, New York, 31 October.

Agazarian, Y.M. (1987e) 'Three reactions to a new member: an interpersonal tale retold from the perspective of the group-as-a-whole.' Unpublished paper presented at Friends Hospital Speaker Series, Philadelphia, December 11, 1987.

Agazarian, Y.M. (1987f) 'The difficult patient, the difficult group.' *Group: The Journal of the Eastern Group Psychotherapy Society 11*, 4, 205–216.

Agazarian, Y.M. (1988a) 'Analysis of a script of a demonstration group from the perspective of the group-as-a-whole.' Friends Hospital Group Psychotherapy Training Series, Spring.

Agazarian, Y.M. (1988b) 'Application of a modified force field analysis to the diagnosis of implicit group goals.' Unpublished paper delivered at the Third International Kurt Lewin Conference, sponsored by the Society for the Advancement of Field Theory, September.

Agazarian, Y.M. (1989a) 'Pathogenic beliefs and implicit goals.' Discussion of 'The Mount Zion Group: The Therapeutic Process and Applicability of the Group's Work to Psychotherapy' presented by Harold Sampson and Joseph Weiss. Slavson Memorial Lecture, American Group Psychotherapy Association, San Francisco, February.

Agazarian, Y.M. (1989b) 'Group-as-a-whole systems theory and practice.' *Group: The Journal of the Eastern Group Psychotherapy Society 13*, 3, 4, 131–154.

Agazarian, Y.M. (1989c) 'Group-as-a-whole theory and practice.' Panel presentation for 'The Group-as-a-whole Perspective: Tool for Understanding' at the Tenth International Congress of Group Psychotherapy, Amsterdam, August.

Agazarian, Y.M. (1989d) 'The invisible group: an integrational theory of group-as-a-whole: Twelfth Annual Foulkes Memorial Lecture.' *Group Analysis: The Journal of the Group Analytic Psychotherapy 22*, 4, 74–96.

Agazarian, Y.M. (1990a) 'Systems-centered thinking applied to human systems in general and to systems-centered therapy in particular.' Paper for Systems-Centered Training Workshop, Newark NJ.

Agazarian, Y.M. (1990b) 'A flip chart of systems-centered thinking and its application to the practice of group therapy.' Unpublished paper for Systems-Centered Training Workshop, Newark NJ.

Agazarian, Y.M. (1990c) Follow-up letter – Systems-Centered Workshop.

Agazarian, Y.M. (1991a) 'Systems theory and group psychotherapy: from there-and-then to here-and-now.' *The International Forum of Group Psychotherapy 1*, 3.

Agazarian, Y.M. (1991b) 'Videotape introduction to group-as-a-whole dynamics, presented by Yvonne M. Agazarian.' (Videotape). Philadelphia: Blue Sky Productions.

Agazarian, Y.M. (1992a) 'A systems approach to the group-as-a-whole.' *International Journal of Group Psychotherapy 42*, 3, 177–203.

Agazarian, Y.M. (1992b) 'Book review of *Koinonia: From Hate, through Dialogue, to Culture in the Large Group* by Patrick de Maré, Robin Piper and Sheila Thompson.' *International Journal of Group Psychotherapy 42*, 3, 443–445.

Agazarian Y.M. (1992c) 'The use of two observation systems to analyze the communication patterns in two videotapes of the interpersonal approach to group psychotherapy.' [Based on I.D. Yallom *Understanding Group Psychotherapy* (videotape). Pacific Grove, CA: Brooks-Cole.] Panel on 'Contrasting views of representative group events' at the Forty-ninth Annual Conference, American Group Psychotherapy Association.

Agazarian, Y.M. (1993) 'Reframing the group-as-a-whole.' In *Changing Group Relations: The Next Twenty-five Years in America*. Proceedings of the Ninth Scientific Meeting of the A.K. Rice Institute, Hugg, T., Carson N. and Lipgar, T. (eds). AKRI. Institute, Florida.

Agazarian, Y.M. (1993b) 'Introduction to a theory of living human systems and the practice of systems-centered psychotherapy.' Special presentation at the thirty-seventh annual meeting of the American Group Psychotherapy Association, San Diego, CA.

Agazarian, Y.M. (1994) 'The phases of development and the systems-centered group.' In M. Pines and V. Schermer (eds) *Ring of Fire: Primitive Object Relations and Affect in Group Psychotherapy*. London: Routledge.

Agazarian, Y.M. (1996a) 'An up-to-date guide to the theory, constructs and hypotheses of a theory of living human systems and its systems-centered practice.' *The SCT Journal 1*, 1, 3–12.

Agazarian, Y.M. (1996b) 'Systems-centered therapy applied to short-term and individual psychotherapy.' *The SCT Journal 1*, 1, 23–34.

Agazarian, Y.M. (1997) *Systems-Centered Therapy for Groups*. New York: Guilford.

Agazarian, Y.M. (1999) 'Phases of development in the systems-centered group.' *Small Group Research 30*, 1, 82–107.

Agazarian, Y.M. and Alonso, A. (1993) 'Discussions around shame in a shamed group.' (Videotape). Philadelphia: Blue Sky Productions.

Agazarian, Y.M. and Carter, F. (1993) 'The large group and systems-centered theory.' *The Journal of the Eastern Group Psychotherapy Society 17*, 4, 210–234.

Agazarian, Y.M. and Janoff, S. (1993) 'Systems theory and small groups.' In I. Kapplan and B. Sadock (eds) *Comprehensive Textbook of Group Psychotherapy* (3rd edn). Maryland: Williams and Wilkins.

Agazarian, Y.M. and Peters, R. (1981) *The Visible and Invisible Group, Two Perspectives on Group Psychotherapy and Group Process*. London: Routledge and Kegan Paul.

Agazarian, Y.M. and Philibossian, B. (1998) 'A theory of living human systems as an approach to leadership of the future with examples of how it works.' In E.

Klein, F. Gabelnick and P. Herr (eds) *The Psychodynamics of Leadership*. Madison CT: Psychosocial Press.

Agazarian, Y.M. and Simon, A. (1989) 'An analysis of excerpts from the Chicago group script of a psychotherapy group by SAVI, a behavioral observation system.' Paper presented to the American Group Psychotherapy Association.

Agazarian, Y.M. and Simon, A. (1996) 'Summarizing SAVI.' Unpublished paper.

Anzieu, D. (1984) *The Group and the Unconscious*. London: Routledge, Keegan and Paul.

Bales, R.F. (1950) *Interaction Process Analysis*. Cambridge MA: Addison-Wesley.

Beck, A.P. (1981) 'The study of group phase development and emergent leadership.' *Group 5*, 4, 48–54.

Bennis, W.G. and Shepard, H.A. (1956) 'A theory of group development.' *Human Relations 9*, 4, 415–437.

Bertalanffy, L. von (1968) *General Systems*. New York: George Braziller.

Bion, W.R. (1959) *Experiences in Groups*. London: Tavistock.

Bion, W. (1985) 'Container and contained.' In A.D. Colman and M.H. Geller (eds) *The Group Relations Reader 2*. Washington DC: A.K. Rice Institute.

Birdwhistell, R.l. (1955) 'Background to kinesics.' *Etc, A Review of General Semantics 13*, 10–18.

Bowlby, J. (1969) 'Instinctive behavior, an alternative model.' In *Attachment and Loss, Vol.1. Attachment*. New York: Basic Books.

Bridger, H.C. (1946) 'The Northfield experiment.' *Bulletin of the Menninger Clinic 10*, 3, 71–76.

Bridger, H. (1990) 'Courses and working conferences as transitional learning institutions.' In E. Trist and H. Murray (eds) *The Social Engagement of Social Science: A Tavistock Anthology. Vol. I: The Socio-psychological Perspective*. Philadelphia, PA: University of Pennsylvania Press.

Cartwright, D. and Zander, A. (eds) (1960) *Group Dynamics, Research and Theory*, 2nd edn. New York: Row, Peterson.

Coleman, A.D. and Bexton, W.H. (eds) (1975) *Group Relations Reader*, vol. 1. Washington DC: A.K. Rice Institute.

Coleman, A.D. and Geller, M.H. (1985) *Group Relations Reader*, vol. 2. Washington DC: A.K. Rice Institute.

Damasio, A. (1994) *Descartes Error*. New York: Gosset/Putnam.

Davanloo, H. (1987) 'Clinical manifestations of superego pathology.' *International Journal of Short-Term Psychotherapy 2*, 225–254.

De Maré, P., Piper, R. and Thompson, S. (1991) *Koinonia: From Hate, through Dialogue, to Culture in the Large Group.* London: Karnac.

Durkin, H. (1972) 'Group therapy and general systems theory.' In C.J. Sager and H.S. Kaplan (eds) *Progress in Group and Family Therapy.* New York: Brunner/Mazel.

Durkin, H. (1981) 'General systems theory and group psychotherapy.' In J.E. Durkin (ed) *Living Groups: Group Psychotherapy and General Systems Theory.* New York: Brunner/Mazel.

Durkin, J.E. (ed) (1981) *Living Groups: Group Psychotherapy and General Systems Theory.* New York: Brunner/Mazel.

Festinger, L. (1957) *A Theory of Cognitive Dissonance.* Evanston IL: Rowe, Peterson.

Flanders, N.A. (1965) 'Teacher influence, pupil attitudes and achievement.' US Department of Health, Education and Welfare, Office of Education. Cooperative Research Monograph no. 12.

Foulkes, S.H. (1965) *Therapeutic Group Analysis.* New York: International Universities Press.

Freud, A. (1937) *The Ego and the Mechanisms of Defense.* London: Hogarth Press.

Freud, A. (1966) *The Writings of Anna Freud: Vol. IV.* New York, NY: International Universities Press.

Freud, S. (1922) *Group Psychology and the Analysis of the Ego* (Trans. and ed. J. Strachey, 1957). London: Hogarth Press and Institute of Psychoanalysis.

Gibb, J.R. (1961) 'Defensive communication.' *Journal of Communication 11,* 141–148.

Goleman, D. (1995) *Emotional Intelligence.* New York: Bantam.

Horwitz, L. (1977) 'A group-centered approach to group psychotherapy.' *International Journal of Group Psychotherapy 27,* 423–439.

Horwitz, L. (1983) 'Projective identification in dyads and groups.' *International Journal of Group Psychotherapy 33,* 259–279.

Howard, A. and Scott, R.A. (1965) 'A proposed framework for the analysis of stress in the human organism.' *Journal of Applied Behavioral Science 10,* 141–160.

Klein, M. (1975a) *Envy and Gratitude and Other Works 1946–1963.* New York: Free Press.

Klein, M. (1975b) *Love, Guilt and Reparation and Other Work 1921–1945.* New York: Free Press.

Klein, R.H., Bernard, H.S. and Singer, D.L. (1992) *Handbook of Contemporary Group Psychotherapy.* New York: International Universities Press.

Korzybski, A. (1948) *Science and Sanity: An Introduction to Non-Aristotelian Systems and General Semantics*, 3rd edn. Lakeville CT: International Non-Aristotelian Library.

Kuhn, A. (1963) *The Study of Society*. Homewood IL: Richard D. Irwin and The Dorsey Press.

Leeper, R. (1943) *Lewin's Topological and Vector Psychology*. Eugene OR: University of Oregon Press.

Lewin, K. (1927) 'Zeigarnik, B., das Behalten von erlediglen und unerlediglen Handlungen.' *Psychologische Forschung 9*, 1–85.

Lewin, K. (1951) *Field Theory in Social Science*. New York: Harper and Row.

Lewin, K., Lippitt R. and White R.K. (1939) 'Patterns of aggressive behavior in experimentally created "social climates".' *Journal of Social Psychology 10*, 271–299.

Lorenz, K.Z. (1935) 'Der Kumpan in der Umvelt des Vogels.' F. Orn. Berl. 83. Eng. trans. in C.H. Schiller (ed) *Instinctive Behaviour*. New York: International Universities Press.

Malan, D., Balfour, F.H., Hood, U.G. and Shooter, A.M. (1976) 'Group psychotherapy: A long-term follow-up study.' *Archives of General Psychiatry 33*, 11, 1303–1315.

Mahler, M.S. (1968) *On Human Symbiosis and the Vicissitudes of Individuation*. New York: International Universities Press.

Miller, J.G. (1978) *Living Systems*. New York: McGraw-Hill.

Raven, B.H. and Rietsema, J. (1957) 'The effects of varied clarity of group goal and group path upon the individual and his relation to his group.' *Human Relations 10*, 19–45.

Sampson, and Weiss, J. (1986) 'Testing hypotheses: the approach of the Mount Zion Psychotherapy Research Group.' In L.S. Greenberg, W.M. Pinsof (eds) *et al. The Psychotherapeutic Process: A Research Handbook*. New York: Guilford Press.

Scheflen, A.E. (1963) 'Communication and regulation in psychotherapy.' *Psychiatry 26*, 2, 126–135.

Schrödinger, E. (1944) *What is Life? The Physical Aspect of the Living Cell and Mind and Matter*. New York: Cambridge University Press.

Sechehaye, M.A. (1951a/1969) *Symbolic Realization: A New Method of Psychotherapy Applied to a Case of Schizophrenia*. New York: International Universities Press.

Sechehaye, M.A. (1951b) *Autobiography of a Schizophrenic Girl*. New York: International Universities Press.

Shannon, C.E. and Weaver, W. (1964) *The Mathematical Theory of Communication.* Urbana IL: University of Illinois Press.

Simon, A. (1993) 'Using SAVI (system for analyzing verbal interaction) for couples' therapy.' *Journal of Family Psychotherapy 4,* 39–62.

Simon, A. (1996) 'SAVI and individual SCT therapy.' *The SCT Journal: Systems-Centered Theory and Practice 1,* 65–71.

Simon, A. and Agazarian, Y. M. (1967) *S.A.V.I., Sequential Analysis of Verbal Interaction.* Philadelphia: Research for Better Schools.

Simon, A. and Agazarian, Y. M. (2000) 'The system for analyzing verbal interaction.' In A. Beck and C. Lewis (eds) *The Process of Group Psychotherapy: Systems for Analyzing Change.* Washington, DC: American Psychological Association.

Simon, A. and Boyer, G.E. (1971) *Mirrors for Behavior.* Philadelphia: Research for Better Schools.

Tinbergen, N. (1963) *The Study of Instinct.* Oxford: Oxford University Press.

Vaillant, L.M. (1997) *Changing Character.* New York: Basic Books.

Vassiliou, G. and Vassiliou, V. (1976) 'Introducing disequilibrium in group therapy.' In L.R. Wolberg and M.L. Aronson (eds) *Group Therapy.* New York: Stratton Intercontinental.

Weiss, J., Sampson, H. and Mount Zion Psychotherapy Research Group (1986) *The Psychoanalytic Process: Theory, Clinical Observation, and Empirical Research.* New York: Guilford Press.

Yalom, I.D. (1995) *The Theory and Practice of Group Psychotherapy,* 4th edn. New York: Basic books.

Subject Index

Page numbers in italics refer to figures

Name Index